I0754364

WASHINGTON CITY—VIEW FROM THE CAPITOL.

THE SIGHTS AND SECRETS

OF THE

NATIONAL CAPITAL:

A Work Descriptive of Washington City

In all its Various Phases

BY

DR. JOHN B. ELLIS.

NEW YORK:
UNITED STATES PUBLISHING COMPANY,
411 Broome Street.
1869.

THE TROW & SMITH
BOOK MANUFACTURING COMPANY,
46, 48, 50 GREENE ST., N. Y.

PREFACE.

The pet child of the Republic, Washington City, is unknown to the majority of the American people. Few have seen it, and there is no work in print describing its varied attractions and sights, or making plain that inner life which daily transpires within it, and in which the whole country is so much interested. It is the centre from which radiate those influences which make our national existence great or feeble, and the entire Republic is affected by its weal or woe. There is a growing desire manifested on all sides to know more of the Capital of the Nation, and it is the object of this volume to gratify this laudable and natural curiosity. It is believed that the picture herein presented is complete, and the author has labored faithfully to make it accurate. The Publishers, on their part, have spared no expense to render the book attractive. As a guarantee of the excellence and fidelity of the engravings of the Public Buildings, it is only necessary to mention that they were prepared in the famous establishment of Messrs. Harper & Bros.

J. B. E.

January 23, 1869.

CONTENTS.

IV.

CONGRESS.

PAGE

V.

THE LOBBY.

VI.

THE RINGS.

VII.

THE PRESIDENT.

VIII.

THE WHITE HOUSE.

IX.

THE JUDICIARY.

X.

THE DEPARTMENT OF STATE.

XI.

THE TREASURY DEPARTMENT.

XII.

THE CURRENCY.

XIII.

COUNTERFEITING.

XIV.

THE WAR DEPARTMENT.

XV.

THE NAVY DEPARTMENT.

XVI.

THE NAVY-YARD.

XVII.

THE DEPARTMENT OF THE INTERIOR.

XVIII.

THE PATENT OFFICE.

XIX.

THE BUREAU OF AGRICULTURE.

XX.

THE POST-OFFICE DEPARTMENT.

XXI.

OFFICIALS.

XXII.

FEMALE CLERKS.

XXIII.

THE SMITHSONIAN INSTITUTION.

PAGE

XXIV.

GAMBLERS.

XXV.

THE NATIONAL OBSERVATORY.

XXVI.

SOCIETY.

XXVII.

THE OLD CAPITOL.

PAGE

XXVIII.

HOTELS AND BOARDING-HOUSES.

XXIX.

THE CONGRESSIONAL CEMETERY.

XXX.

PLACES OF AMUSEMENT.

XXXI.

FORD'S THEATRE.

XXXII.

THE SOCIAL EVIL.

XXXIII.

THE ARSENAL.

XL.

IMPOSTORS.

THE SIGHTS AND SECRETS

OF THE

NATIONAL CAPITAL.

I.

GOING TO WASHINGTON.

At present, there are but two ways of reaching Washington City. Visitors from the North, East, and West enter the Capital of the Nation by means of the Washington Branch of the Baltimore and Ohio Railroad, which they reach either at Baltimore, or at the Relay House, nine miles west of that city; and those from the South arrive by the Potomac River.

BY RAIL.

The traveller by Railroad, after leaving the Relay House, passes through a country naturally rich and full of resources, but sadly neglected by the inhabitants. The land is good, but has not received the careful cultivation which has so benefited those sections of the Union blessed with white labor. The farms, with a few exceptions, have a dilapidated appearance, and the people generally are extremely rustic and "old-timey."

Between the Relay House and Laurel Factory, the road runs along the dividing line of Howard and Anne Arundel Counties, the former being on the right and the latter on the left of the train moving towards Washington. Upon reaching Laurel Factory, the Patuxent River, here a mere creek, is crossed, and the traveller enters Prince George County, the great tobacco-producing section of Maryland. The system of agriculture is better in this county than in those just mentioned, but is still behind that of the white-labor States. The road passes some fine farms, and the traveller catches a distant view of the Maryland Agricultural College, which institution, it is to be hoped, will do much towards improving the farming system of the State. Pine thickets, scrub forests, and swampy lands are in abundance. The stations, with the exception of the Relay, Laurel, and Bladensburg, are mere hamlets, springing up in the midst of lonely pine woods, which give to them an infinitely desolate appearance.

Bladensburg gives warning that the traveller through this lonely region is once more approaching life and civilization. It is a quiet, peaceful little village, situated on the Eastern Branch of the Potomac, in Prince George County, Maryland, and is only a short distance from the boundary-line of the District of Columbia. The country here loses its flat, marshy character, and rises in a succession of hills towards the Potomac. On either side of the road, we see, crowning these eminences, the grim red lines of the earthworks built for the defence of the Capital; each with its lonely, towering flag-staff from which once flapped in defiant pride the starry banner of the Republic, standing out against the blue sky like so many ghostly sentinels keeping solemn watch over the scenes they once guarded so well. A swift plunge of the train into a deep cutting, and we are whirled through this now historic ridge, and in a few minutes are steaming through the suburbs of Washington.

The first glimpses of the Federal City are not pleasant. The train passes through a succession of old fields, over which are widely scattered a few dirty, dingy frame houses. Some of these aspire to the dignity of paint, but the majority are ornamented with whitewash. Very few have yards, and the outhouses are so arranged as to seem entirely independent of the main structure. The fields are full of stagnant pools, and the geese, pigs, and children swarming about them appear to be on a footing of perfect equality. The denizens of this section are both white and black, and both classes seem to be very poor. They have a decided "hard-times" look, and evidently have to struggle desperately with poverty. During the war these fields had a busy appearance, which makes them now seem doubly dilapidated. Then they were covered with long rows of cars, wagons, carts, tents, and shanties, and alive with soldiers and laborers connected with the Quartermaster and Commissary Departments. Then the inhabitants of this section drove a thriving trade in newspapers, cheap books, pies, cakes, apples tobacco, and contraband liquids. The war was a God send to them, and it is not improbable that some of the most enterprising and thrifty will, if they have not already done so, date their rise to fortune from the "start" which this trade gave them.

Passing on, with slackened speed, the train enters the grounds belonging to the railroad company. Looming up on the left is the huge white dome of the Capitol, and to the right the city proper is in full view. A few moments more, and the cars are standing in the station, and the passengers are descending to the platform.

Hurrying through a dirty, cheerless hall, the traveller passes out of the building into New Jersey Avenue. He is greeted by a series of shouts and yells which startle and bewilder him unless he be a man of uncommon nerve. A dense line of omnibuses and hacks is drawn up before the Station, and scores of porters and drivers are crowded around the station entrance, each and all yelling at the top of their lungs the names and merits of their respective hotels. "Metropolitan 'otel, Sir, best 'ouse in the City, Sir." "National, Sir, National. This way, Sir. Only first class 'ouse in Washington." "Willard's. Whose a-goin' to Willard's? Every *gentleman* knows Willard's." "Hack, Sir." "Carriage, Sir. Take you anywhere in the City, Sir, cheap." These, and a hundred other cries, shouted as only Hibernian and African voices can shout them, tell the stranger that he is in the Capital of his country.

BY STEAMBOAT.

Travellers from the South—in short, all who approach the city from Virginia—take a steamer for that purpose either at Acquia Creek, or at Alexandria. The former place is fifty-five miles from Washington, the latter eight miles. The Aquia Creek boat passes nearly all the points on the lower Potomac made famous during the late war, and also affords a view of Mount Vernon and Fort Washington. After passing Mount Vernon, and sweeping around a graceful bend in the stream, the cities of Alexandria and Washington come in sight at the same moment—the one in plain view, and the other surrounded by a faint haze. The boat touches at Alexandria for a moment, and then speeds on.

Washington is now in full view. The gigantic Capitol looms gradually up against the sky, with the sunlight glittering on the glorious embodiment of Freedom which surmounts it. Below the Capitol, and clinging along the river-shore, are the Navy Yard, the Arsenal, and the Penitentiary. To the left the city rises gradually from the river to the high grounds in the rear, and the eye can easily distinguish the stately outlines of the Government buildings. The unfinished monument to Washington attracts but a momentary gaze, and few think of their remissness in allowing it to remain in this condition. Georgetown is seen in the distance, beyond the Long Bridge, and Arlington Heights rise boldly on the left. An excellent view of the city is gained from the deck of the steamer, and it is a pleasure which should not be missed by any one who can afford to enjoy it.

The steamer lands at the foot of Maryland Avenue, from which point the street-cars, omnibuses, and hacks convey passengers to any part of the city.

II.

THE CITY OF WASHINGTON.

THE City of Washington lies on the left bank of the Potomac River, a few miles below the head of tide-water. It is 295 miles from the ocean, 226 miles from New York, 1,200 miles from St. Louis, 432 miles from Boston, 544 miles from Charleston, 497 miles from Cincinnati, 763 miles from Chicago, and 40 miles from Baltimore. It has connections by railroad and steamboat with all parts of the continent, and the telegraphic lines extend from it all over the world. The Potomac is navigable for ships of the largest size as far as Greenleaf's Point, the site of the Arsenal and Penitentiary. The British fleet anchored here in 1814, and the frigate Minnesota was launched at the Navy Yard some years ago, and carried down the stream after being equipped.

The Capitol, which is nearly the centre of the city, is located in 38° 52′ 20″ north latitude, and 77° 0′ 15″ west longitude from Greenwich.

THE DISTRICT OF COLUMBIA.

After the close of the Revolution, Congress continued to meet in the city of Philadelphia. In June, 1783, a band of mutinous soldiers broke into the hall where Congress was in session, and in a grossly insulting manner demanded the "back pay" due them, which amounted to a considerable sum. This insult was felt deeply by the members, and it was agreed by common consent that it would be better for the seat of Government to be removed to a part of the country where the danger of a repetition of the occurrence would not be so imminent. Elbridge Gerry introduced a resolution authorizing the building of a Federal City, on the banks of the Delaware or Potomac, and the erection of buildings suitable for the use of Congress, provided a good location and the proper amount of land could be obtained on either of those rivers. This resolution was carried on the 7th of October, 1783, but was amended by a provision for buildings on both rivers, and was repealed on the 26th of April, 1784. Congress met at Trenton, N. J., in October, 1784, and appointed three commissioners, who were authorized to lay out a district between two and three miles square on the Delaware, for a Federal City. The next January, Congress met in New York, and efforts were made to locate the district on the Potomac, but without success.

In September, 1787, the present Constitution of the United States was adopted, which provides that Congress shall have power "to exercise exclusive legislation, in all cases whatsoever, over such district (not exceeding ten miles square) as may, by cession of particular States, and the acceptance of Congress, become the seat of Government of the United States."

This clause of the Constitution fixed definitely the size of the new district, and was the first real step towards its acquisition. Appreciating the advantage of having the Capital within its limits, the State of Maryland, through its Legislature, on the 23d of December, 1788, offered to Congress "any district (not exceeding ten miles square) which the Congress may fix upon and accept for the seat of Government of the United States." The matter was debated in Congress in 1789.

It was agreed on all sides that the district ought to be located in a section of the country easy of access from all parts of the Union, and ought to be as central as was consistent with the wealth and population of the section chosen. The North and the South,—for the sectional division of the country had been made even at that early day,—each desired to secure the location of the new city within its own limits. The former demanded that the capital should be built on the banks of the Susquehanna, and the latter made a similar demand in favor of the Delaware or Potomac. New York, Philadelphia, Germantown, Havre de Grace, Wright's Ferry, Baltimore, and Conococheague (now Washington City), each had its partisans. The controversy ran very high, and came near resulting in a serious quarrel between the States. On the 5th of September, 1789, the House of Representatives passed a resolution, "That the permanent seat of Government of the United States ought to be at some convenient place on the banks of the Susquehanna, in the State of Pennsylvania." This resolution gave great offence to the Southern members, and even Mr. Madison went so far as to declare that had such an action on the part of Congress been foreseen, Virginia would not have ratified the Constitution. The matter was made worse by the immediate passage of a bill by the House for the purpose of carrying the resolution into effect. The vote stood, thirty-one to nineteen. The Senate amended the bill by inserting Germantown, Pennsylvania, instead of the location on the Susquehanna, which amendment was accepted by the House. The House further amended the Act by providing that the laws of Pennsylvania should continue in force in the new district until Congress should order otherwise. The Senate decided to postpone the consideration of this amendment until the next session, and the matter went over. Germantown was thus actually chosen as the Federal City, and it needed only the consent of the Senate to the last-mentioned amendment to make the transaction complete.

Thus far none of the States but Maryland had taken any official action in this matter. The South was greatly excited over the course of Congress, all of the Northern States were not pleased, and the matter was felt to be a very serious danger to the harmony of the new Confederation. On the 3d of December, 1789, the General Assembly of Virginia passed an Act ceding a district to Congress on the banks of the Potomac. The coöperation of Maryland was asked in inducing Congress to accept the offer, and a sum not exceeding $120,000 was pledged for the erection of public buildings, if Maryland, on her part, would contribute a sum not less than two-fifths of that amount for the same purpose. Maryland at once agreed to the request of Virginia, and pledged herself for the money. Other States now made offers of territory to Congress, but no immediate action upon the subject was taken by that body.

The great question which at that time occupied the attention of the people, was the funding of the public debt. Congress was divided upon the subject. An amendment had been presented to the House, and had been rejected, providing that the General Government should assume the State debts to the amount of twenty-one millions of dollars. This question had become very closely interwoven with that of selecting a Federal district. The Northern members were in favor of the assumption, but did not desire the location of the district in the South, and the Southern members, while divided upon the assumption question, were to a man in favor of having the offers of Maryland and Virginia accepted. Matters were at a dead halt, and the future seemed ominous.

Jefferson was at this time Secretary of State, and Hamilton Secretary of the Treasury. Both were anxious to avert the danger which the vexed questions threatened, and after discussing the matter confidentially, came to the conclusion that a compromise was necessary. Hamilton urged that the South should consent to the assumption of the State debts by the Government, and declared that he felt sure if they would do this, the North would agree to locate the Capital on the Potomac. It was decided that Jefferson should ask the members whose votes would accomplish this, to dine with him the next day, and lay the matter before them. The dinner was given, the plan proposed by Hamilton discussed, and a sufficient number of votes pledged for the assumption bill. Hamilton undertook to win over the Northern members to the Capital scheme, and succeeded. The assumption bill became a law, and Congress, in the following Act, definitely accepted the offer of Maryland and Virginia:

"AN ACT for establishing the temporary and permanent seat of the government of the United States.

"SEC. 1. *Be it enacted, by the Senate and House of Representatives of the United States of America in Congress assembled,* That a district of territory, not exceeding ten miles square, to be located as hereafter directed, on the river Potomac, at some space between the mouths of the Eastern Branch and Conococheague, be, and the same is hereby, accepted for the permanent seat of the government of the United States: *Provided, nevertheless,* That the operation of the laws of the State within such district shall not be affected by this acceptance until the time fixed for the removal of the government thereto, and until Congress shall otherwise by law provide.

"SEC. 2. *And be it further enacted,* That the President of the United States be authorized to appoint, and by supplying vacancies happening from refusals to act, or other causes, to keep in appointment as long as may be necessary, three Commissioners, who, or any two of whom, shall, under the direction of the President, survey, and by proper metes and bounds define and limit a district of territory, under the limitations above mentioned; and the district so defined, limited, and located, shall be deemed the district accepted by this act for the permanent seat of the government of the United States.

"SEC. 3. *And be it enacted*, That the said Commissioners, or any two of them, shall have power to purchase or accept such quantity of land on the eastern side of the said river, within the said district, as the President shall deem proper for the use of the United States: and, according to such plans as the President shall approve, the said Commissioners, or any two of them, shall, prior to the first Monday in December, in the year one thousand eight hundred, provide suitable buildings for the accommodation of Congress, and of the President, and for the public offices of the government of the United States.

"SEC. 4. *And be it enacted*, That, for defraying the expense of such purchases and buildings, the President of the United States be authorized and requested to accept grants of money.

"SEC. 5. *And be it enacted*, That, prior to the first Monday in December next, all officers attached to the seat of government of the United States shall be removed to, and, until the said first Monday in December, in the year one thousand eight hundred, shall remain at the city of Philadelphia, in the State of Pennsylvania, at which place the session of Congress next ensuing the present shall be held.

"SEC. 6. *And be it enacted*, That on the said first Monday in December, in the year one thousand eight hundred, the seat of government of the United States shall, by virtue of this act, be transferred to the district and place aforesaid. And all the offices attached to the seat of government shall accordingly be removed thereto by their respective holders, and shall, after the said day, cease to be exercised elsewhere; and that the necessary expense of such removal shall be defrayed out of the duties on imposts and tonnage, of which a sufficient sum is hereby appropriated.

"Approved, July 16, 1790.

"GEORGE WASHINGTON,
"*President of the United States.*"

On the 19th of December, 1791, the Legislature of Maryland passed the following act ratifying and confirming the cession of the District of Columbia:

"*Be it enacted by the General Assembly of Maryland*, That all that part of the said territory, called Columbia, which lies within the limits of this State, shall be, and the same is hereby acknowledged to be, forever ceded and relinquished to the Congress and Government of the United States, in full and absolute right and exclusive jurisdiction, as well of soil as of persons residing or to reside thereon, pursuant to the tenor and effect of the eighth Section of the first article of the Constitution of Government of the United States: *Provided*, That nothing herein contained shall be so construed to vest in the United States any right of property in the soil, as to affect the rights of individuals therein, otherwise than the same shall or may be transferred by such individuals to the United States: *And provided, also*, That the jurisdiction of the laws of this State over the persons and property of individuals residing within the limits of the cession aforesaid shall not cease or determine until Congress shall by law provide for the government thereof, under their jurisdiction, in manner provided by the article of the Constitution before recited."

On the 3d of March, 1791, Congress adopted an amendment repealing so much of the act already given as required the district to be located *above* the Eastern Branch, and authorizing the President to include as much of the Eastern Branch, and the land below, above the mouth of Hunting Creek, as should be deemed desirable. By this same amendment, the town of Alexandria was made a part of the District; but it was provided that none of the public buildings should be located on the Virginia side of the Potomac. President Washington at once issued the following proclamation, fixing the boundaries of the District:—

"*Whereas*, By a proclamation, bearing date the 14th of January of this present year, and in pursuance of certain acts of the States of Maryland and Virginia, and of the Congress of the United States, therein mentioned, certain lines of experiment were directed to be run in the neighborhood of Georgetown, in Maryland, for the purpose of determining the location of a part of the territory of ten miles square, for the permanent seat of the Government of the United States; and a certain part was directed to be located within the said lines of experiment, on both sides of the Potomac, and above the limits of the Eastern Branch, prescribed by the said Act of Congress.

"And Congress, by an amendatory act, passed on the 3d day of this present month of March, have given further authority to the President of the United States to make any part of the said territory, below the said limit, and above the mouth of Hunting Creek, a part of the said District, so as to include a convenient part of the Eastern Branch of the lands lying on the lower side thereof, and also the town of Alexandria;

"Now, therefore, for the purpose of amending and completing the location of the whole of the said territory of ten miles square, in conformity with the said amendatory act of Congress, I do hereby declare and make known that the whole of the said territory shall be located and included within the four lines following, that is to say,—

"Beginning at Jones' Point, being the upper cape of Hunting Creek, in Virginia, and at an angle in the outset of 45 degrees west of north, and running in a direct line ten miles, for the first line; then beginning again at the same Jones' Point, and running another direct line at a right angle with the first, across the Potomac, ten miles, for the second line; then, from the terminations of the said first and second lines, running two other direct lines, of ten miles each, the one crossing the Eastern Branch aforesaid, and the other the Potomac, and meeting each other in a point.

"And I do accordingly direct the Commissioners named under the authority of the said first-mentioned act of Congress to proceed forthwith to have the said four lines run, and by proper metes and bounds defined and limited, and thereof to make due report under their hands and seals; and the territory so to be located, defined, and limited, shall be the whole territory accepted by the said act of Congress as the District for the permanent seat of the Government of the United States.

"In testimony whereof, I have caused the seal of the United States to be affixed to these presents, and signed the same with my hand. Done at Georgetown aforesaid, the 30th day of March, in the year of our Lord, 1791, and of the Independence of the United States, the fifteenth.

"George Washington."

The District was laid out by three Commissioners, appointed by the President, in accordance with the Act of Congress, in January, 1791. These Commissioners were Thomas Johnson, David Stuart, and Daniel Carroll. On the 15th of April, in the same year, they superintended the laying of the corner-stone of the District, at Jones' Point, near Alexandria. This act was performed with the ceremonies prescribed by the Masonic ritual. The District was named Columbia, in honor of the great discoverer of the continent.

Having thus acquired a Federal District, and having definitely located its boundaries, the next step was to lay off the new city which was to be the Capital of the nation. This task was confided to Major L'Enfant, a distinguished engineer, who was informed by the

Commissioners that the new city would bear the name of "Washington."

THE FEDERAL CITY.

Long before the Revolution, Thomas Lee, the grandson of the founder of the famous Virginian family of that name, declared that the Colonies would one day become independent of the mother country, and that the seat of government, under the new order of affairs, would be located near the falls of the Potomac. Impressed with this belief, he acquired large estates in Virginia near the head of tide-water on that river. Washington, when a poor surveyor, was struck with the advantages of the location for a similar purpose, and when President, expressed himself warmly in favor of its selection. His wishes are said to have had great influence in determining the final action of Congress.

The boundaries of the city are thus described by the Legislature of Maryland:

"The President of the United States directed a city to be laid out, comprehending all the lands beginning on the east side of Rock Creek, at a stone standing in the middle of the road leading from Georgetown to Bladensburgh; thence along the middle of said road, to a stone standing on the east side of the reedy branch of Goose Creek; thence southeasterly, making an angle of sixty-one degrees and twenty minutes with the meridian, to a stone standing in the road leading from Bladensburgh to the Eastern Branch Ferry; then south to a stone eighty poles north of the east and west line, already drawn from the mouth of Goose

Creek to the Eastern Branch; then east, parallel to the said east and west line, to the Eastern Branch; then with the waters of the Eastern Branch, Potomac River, and Rock Creek, to the beginning,—which has since been called the City of Washington."

The land on which the city now stands belonged to Daniel Carroll, Notley Young, David Burns, and Samuel Davidson. These gentlemen deeded the land embraced within the limits specified above, to Thomas Beall and John Mackall Gant, trustees, who conveyed the same to the Commissioners and their successors in office, for the United States, forever. The following are the terms of sale, as mentioned by Washington in a letter to the Secretary of State, dated March 31, 1791:

"The terms entered into by me, on the part of the United States, with the landholders of Georgetown and Carrollsburgh, are, that all the land from Rock Creek, along the river to the Eastern Branch, and so upwards to or above the Ferry, including a breadth of about a mile and a half, the whole containing from three to five thousand acres, is ceded to the public, on condition that, when the whole shall be surveyed and laid off as a city (which Major L'Enfant is now directed to do), the present proprietors shall retain every other lot; and for such part of the land as may be taken for public use, for squares, walks, etc., they shall be allowed at the rate of twenty-five dollars per acre,—the public having the right to reserve such parts of the wood on the land as may be thought necessary to be preserved for ornament. The landholders to have the use and profits of the grounds until the city is laid off into lots, and sale is made of those lots, which, by this agreement, become public property. Nothing is to be allowed for the ground which may be occupied for streets and alleys."

The task of laying off the city was, as we have said, assigned to Major L'Enfant, who began his labors under the supervision of the President. He proved stubborn and hard to manage, however, and Washington removed him, and appointed Mr. Andrew Ellicott in his stead.

Mr. Ellicott at once proceeded to lay off the plan of the city. After drawing a meridional line, by astronomical observation, through the site selected for the Capitol, he designed two sets of streets crossing each other at right angles. Those running north and south he distinguished by means of numbers; those running east and west, by means of letters, taking the Capitol as a starting-point. Avenues were then run boldly across the city, at various distances from each other, connecting the most prominent points. They were named after the States.

Congress directed a series of magnificent improvements to be laid off, but, at the present day, not one of these ornaments has been erected, with the single exception of an equestrian statue of Washington.

The boundaries of the city cover an area four miles and a half in length, from northwest to southeast, and two miles and a half in breadth. When the plan was completed, an act was passed allowing aliens to hold lots in the city; and copies of the plan were sent to

Europe. Extensive investments were made by foreign capitalists, but in a manner which proved unfortunate for them. It was supposed that the best quarter would be the immediate neighborhood of the Capitol, and the principal investments were made there; but the result proved the neighborhood of the President's house the most attractive, and the Capitol Hill lots were found to be poor investments.

The law authorizing the removal of the Government to Washington City required that the public buildings should be completed before the first Monday in December, 1800. This was no slight task, as these edifices had to be erected in what was almost a forest. President Washington exerted himself during his administration to have the work finished by the appointed time, but labored under many disadvantages in his efforts, not the least of which was a lack of funds. The money advanced by Maryland and Virginia was soon exhausted, and though Congress authorized loans for the purpose of completing the work, money was scarce and hard to obtain. Washington made a personal application to the Legislature of Maryland for a loan of $150,000, and that body, on the 22d of December, 1796, granted a loan of $100,000, on condition of the individual responsibility of the Commissioners. The money was procured on these terms, and the work pushed forward with such energy that, on the 15th of June, 1800, the Commissioners reported the buildings ready for the use of the Government. The public offices were at once removed from Philadelphia to Washington City, and, on the third of November of that year, Congress assembled in the Capitol.

The new city thus became the seat of the Govern ment of the Republic, and has grown steadily in population and importance.

THE PRIMITIVE CAPITAL.

The Capital of the country was at this time only a city on paper. It was, in reality, a mere village, and possessed all the inconveniences and annoyances of a new settlement. Those who had opposed its selection ridiculed it unmercifully as "The City of Magnificent Distances," and by no means did it justice. The Hon. John Cotton Smith, of Connecticut, thus describes its appearance, just after the removal of the Government thither:

"Our approach to the city was accompanied with sensations not easily described. One wing of the Capitol only had been erected, which, with the President's house, a mile distant from it, both constructed with white sandstone, were shining objects in dismal contrast with the scene around them. Instead of recognizing the avenues and streets portrayed on the plan of the city, not one was visible, unless we except a road, with two buildings on each side of it, called the New Jersey avenue. The Pennsylvania, leading, as laid down on paper, from the Capitol to the Presidential mansion, was then nearly the whole distance a deep morass, covered with alder bushes, which were cut through the width of the intended avenue during the then ensuing Winter. Between the President's house and Georgetown a block of houses had been erected, which then bore, and may still bear, the name of the *six buildings.* There were also two other blocks, consisting of two or three dwelling-houses, in different directions, and now and then an insulated wooden habitation,—the intervening spaces, and indeed the surface of the city generally, being covered with shrub oak bushes on the higher grounds, and on the marshy soil either trees or some sort of shrubbery. Nor was the desolate aspect of the place a little augmented by a number of unfinished edifices at Greenleaf's Point, and on an eminence a short distance from it, commenced by an individual whose name they bore, but the state of whose funds compelled him to abandon them, not only unfinished, but in a ruinous condition. There appeared to be but two really comfortable habitations in all respects within the bounds of the city, one of which belonged to Dudley Carroll, Esq., and the other to Notley Young, who were the former proprietors of a large proportion of the land appropriated to the city, but who reserved for their own accommodation ground sufficient for gardens and other useful appurtenances. The roads in every direction were muddy and unimproved. A sidewalk was attempted in one instance by a covering formed of the chips of the stones which had been hewn for the Capitol. It extended but a little way, and was of little value; for in dry weather the sharp fragments cut our shoes, and in wet weather covered them with white mortar. In short, it was a 'new settlement.' The houses, with two or three exceptions, had been very recently erected, and the operation greatly hurried in view of the approaching transfer of the national government. A laudable desire was manifested, by what few citizens and residents there were, to render our condition as pleasant as circumstances would permit. One of the blocks of buildings already mentioned was situated on the east side of what was intended for the Capitol square, and, being chiefly occupied by an extensive and well-kept hotel, accommodated a goodly number of the Members. Our little party took lodgings with a Mr. Peacock, in one of the houses on New Jersey avenue, with the addition of Senators Tracy, of Connecticut, and Chipman and Paine, of Vermont; and Representives Thomas, of Maryland, and Dana, Edmond, and Griswold, of Connecticut. Speaker Sedgwick was allowed a room to himself,—the rest of us in pairs. To my excellent friend Davenport and myself was allotted a spacious and decently-furnished apartment, with separate beds, on the lower floor. Our diet was various, but always substantial, and we were attended by active and faithful servants. A large proportion of the Southern Members took lodgings at Georgetown, which, though of a superior order, were three miles distant from the Capitol, and of course rendered the daily employment of hackney coaches indispensable.

"Notwithstanding the unfavorable aspect which Washington presented on our arrival, I cannot sufficiently express my admiration of its local position. From the Capitol you have a distinct view of its fine, undulating surface, situated at the confluence of the

Potomac and its Eastern Branch, the wide expanse of that majestic river to the bend at Mount Vernon, the cities of Alexandria and Georgetown, and the cultivated fields and blue hills of Maryland and Virginia on either side of the river, the whole constituting a prospect of surpassing beauty and grandeur. The city has also the inestimable advantage of delightful water, in many instances flowing from copious springs, and always attainable by digging to a moderate depth; to which may be added the singular fact that such is the due admixture of loam and clay in the soil of a great portion of the city that a house may be built of brick made of the earth dug from the cellar; hence it was not unusual to see the remains of a brick-kiln near the newly-erected dwelling-house or other edifice. In short, when we consider not only these advantages, but what, in a national point of view, is of superior importance, the location on a fine, navigable river, accessible to the whole maritime frontier of the United States, and yet easily rendered defensible against foreign invasion,—and that, by the facilities of internal navigation and railways, it may be approached by the population of the Western States, and indeed of the whole nation, with less inconvenience than any other conceivable situation,—we must acknowledge that its selection by Washington as the permanent seat of the Federal Government affords a striking exhibition of the discernment, wisdom, and forecast which characterized that illustrious man. Under this impression, whenever, during the six years of my connection with Congress, the question of removing the seat of Govern ment to some other place was agitated—and the proposition was frequently made—I stood almost alone as a Northern man in giving my vote in the negative."

The place was incorporated as a city by an Act of Congress dated May 3d, 1802. It grew very slowly at first. It had been expected that the location of the Government at this place would induce settlers to flock there, but those who entertained such expectations simply cherished foolish hopes. The city, as we have said, was partly a forest and partly a swamp. The few dwelling-houses which had been erected were small and inconvenient, and besides this, it was for some time more than probable that the seat of Government would be removed to some other place.

THE CITY BURNED BY THE BRITISH.

In 1814 the city was captured by a British expeditionary corps under General Ross. Having defeated the handful of Americans which opposed him in a feeble manner * at Bladensburgh, Ross marched his troops into the Federal City. The Capitol, the President's House, the Navy Yard, the Departments, and a few private houses were burned by the enemy, the Government having escaped before the arrival of the red-coats. After completing the work of destruction, General Ross embarked his troops and went back to the Chesapeake. The Government returned to Washington as soon as the coast was clear, but it was com

* The marines and sailors of the U. S. Navy fought bravely in this engagement. The bulk of our army—militia—acted with great cowardice.

monly believed that the barbarous action of the British had definitely settled the question of removal in the affirmative.

"When Congress next assembled, the subject of rebuilding these edifices came before that body, and the question as to the removal of the legislature was necessarily discussed. An effort was made for the removal of the seat of government. The national feeling, however, coöperated with other considerations to influence the decision; it was voted not to remove, and the requisite amount was enthusiastically voted to efface the memorials of British triumph. From this time, the corporation of the city seemed to be animated with a new soul, and individuals, relieved from the fear of change, risked all they had in real estate. Landed property rose in value, and hope, energy, and active business took the place of despair, listlessness, and wasting and repining indolence. New streets were opened, dwelling-houses and stores were then erected. The trade came to the city, the boarders left Georgetown, and came to Washington, and a new face was put on every thing in the city. Churches were built, institutions of learning arose, and large, if not ample provision was made for other necessary improvements on the face of nature. This work has been going on ever since the close of the war;* but it must be pleasant to the citizens of Washington to reflect, when all things are taken into consideration, that they are not indebted to the Government, in equity, for one dollar for all their grants and favors; but that

* The second war with England.

in truth, the Government is indebted to the city for more than a million of dollars, putting a fair value on the property now owned within the city, which cost them nothing. Blessings are said to come in clusters, for as soon as the city began to flourish it became healthy. The low grounds were drained, and the fever and ague, once prevalent, is now rarely known among the evils of Washington; and at present the city is decidedly as healthy as any in the United States, or perhaps in the world. The water of Washington is of the best quality, and can be brought to every door in great quantities."

WASHINGTON BEFORE THE WAR.

The rapid growth of the Union naturally produced a similar expansion in the various departments of the Government, and the Capital become more and more important every year. At first it was the habit of the city authorities to depend on the Government for every thing, but it was not long before it became evident to them that they must act for themselves if the city was to grow at all. Impressed with this conviction, they went to work in earnest, and the place grew steadily under their direction. Its present condition is due to the energy and enterprise of its people, and not to the Government.

Previous to the Rebellion, Washington was a quiet, retired place, whose slow steady growth drew upon it but little of the public attention. During the Sessions of Congress it was busy and gay, but in the long recesses it seemed to be asleep. It was then insufferably dull, hot, and dusty. Every body lived in the expectation and hope of the coming of winter and the meeting of Congress, with the throngs of strangers which these events were sure to bring to the city.

As the month of December approached the town began to fill up, hotels and boarding-houses lost their deserted aspect, and their proprietors' grum faces began to be wreathed with smiles. The Departments commenced to show signs of life and activity. Clerks and officials, who had dozed away the summer months, assumed energetic and important airs, and every body in any way connected with the Government seemed to undergo a marvellous transformation. The winter was gay and lively, but when the "Honorable Members" of the two houses took their flight, the old dulness came back and settled over every thing.

THE CITY DURING THE WAR.

Previous to 1861, the mass of the visitors to Washington came from the Northern and Southern States. The West had very few representatives except those who came for office, and did not exercise the same influence in the city as the other sections, either socially or politically. The Government having been Democratic for some time, society was strongly conservative and Southern in its tone and tendencies. It was exclusive and aristocratic, and turned up its nose at any thing and every thing pertaining to the common people.

The inauguration of Abraham Lincoln brought a new class of visitors to the Capital. The hard-handed, rugged men of the West came by hundreds, and the other sections of the country sent their commoners there to meet them. Society was astonished. Caste and privilege pronounced the bold, independent new-comers barbarians, but the horror thus affected accomplished nothing. Power had passed out of the hands of the privileged few, and had reverted to the people, and a new order of affairs had been inaugurated.

The war occurring immediately after Mr. Lincoln's inauguration completed the change in the city. It was no longer simply the Capital of the Nation; it was also a great military post. The plains around it were crowded with camps, sheds, trains, &c., and the Government had filled with its hosts of officials every available building in and about the city. The streets were full of soldiers and civilians, regiments were constantly passing to and fro through the town; the houses were all decorated with flags; and every thing had an appearance of life and bustle. In a few months the population increased from 61,400 to nearly a quarter of a million, which was its average size during the war. The correspondent of the *London Times*, returning to the Capital in July, 1861, after an absence of only three months, thus writes of this sudden and marvellous change:

"It is about forty miles from Baltimore to Washington, and at every quarter of a mile for the whole distance a picket of soldiers guarded the rails. Camps appeared on both sides, larger and more closely packed together; and the rays of the setting sun fell on countless lines of tents as we approached the unfinished dome of the Capitol. On the Virginia side of the river, columns of smoke rising from the forest marked the site of Federal encampments across the stream. The fields around Washington resounded with the words of command and tramp of men, and flashed with wheeling arms. Parks of artillery studded the waste ground, and long trains of white-covered wagons filled up the open spaces in the suburbs of Washington.

"To me, all this was a wonderful sight. As I drove up Pennsylvania Avenue I could scarcely credit that busy thoroughfare — all red, white, and blue with flags, filled with dust from galloping chargers and commissariat carts; the sidewalks thronged with people, of whom a large proportion carried sword or bayonet; shops full of life and activity, — was the same as that through which I had driven the first morning of my arrival. Washington now, indeed, is the Capital of the United States; but it is no longer the scene of beneficent legislation and of peaceful government. It is the representative of armed force engaged in War — menaced whilst in the very act of raising its arm by the enemy it seeks to strike."

All sorts of people came to Washington with the War; and the entire character, as well as the appearance of the city, was changed. Whatever had been the state of its morals previous to the great struggle, there can be no doubt that they were at a very low ebb during the Rebellion. Honesty, both private and official, was thrown aside, and rascality took its place. Female virtue was at a discount. Intrigues and immorality of all kinds became the order of the day, and these crimes were unjustly laid to the charge of the Washingtonians proper. The truth is, that the real inhabitants of the city held themselves aloof from the strangers which inundated the place. They were powerless to resist the tide of excess which so changed the character of their old home, and so protested against the orgies of the new-comers by refusing to take part in them.

At the close of the Rebellion the army was disbanded, and the Government brought back to a peace footing. There was at once an exodus from Washington of those who had lived on the public plunder during the four years of the War. The city had been benefited in many ways by the presence of the army and the vast crowd of civilians during that period. It had grown to a considerable extent, both in size and in its permanent population. New interests had been developed, and its trade had received an impetus which was but the beginning of better days. The increasing demands of the Government brought many skilled workmen and people of almost every avocation known to man, large numbers of whom came to settle there permanently; so that the War left the city far more thriving and prosperous than it had found it.

THE STREETS.

A stranger has considerable difficulty in learning the street plan of Washington. The thoroughfares of the city, however, are laid out upon a simple plan, and with reference to affording quick communication between distant points.

The Capitol is the centre and starting point of the whole system. The streets running east and west are designated by letters. They are divided into two classes or sets—those north of the Capitol, and those south of it. Thus, the first street north of the Capitol is A Street North, and the first street south of it, A Street South; the next is B Street, North or South, and so on. The streets running north and south are numbered. Thus, the street immediately east of the Capitol is First Street East, and that immediately west of it First Street West, and so on. These distinctions of North, South, East, and West are most important, as forgetfulness of them is apt to lead to very great blunders.

The streets are laid off at regular distances from each other, but for convenience, other thoroughfares, not laid down in the original plan, have been cut through some of the blocks. These are called "Half streets," as they occur between and are parallel with the numbered streets. Thus, Four-and-a-half Street is between Fourth and Fifth streets, and runs parallel with them.

The avenues run diagonally across the city, cutting the streets at right angles. New Jersey, Pennsylvania, Maryland, and Delaware avenues intersect at the Capitol, and Pennsylvania, New York, Vermont, and Connecticut avenues intersect at the President's house. Pennsylvania Avenue is the main thoroughfare. It is one hundred and sixty feet wide, and runs the entire length of the city, from the Eastern Branch to Rock Creek,—which latter stream separates Washington from Georgetown. It was originally a swampy thicket. The bushes were cut away to the desired width soon after the city was laid off, but few persons cared to settle in the swamp. Through the exertions of President Jefferson, it was planted with four rows of fine Lombardy poplars,—one on each side and two in the middle,—with the hope of making it equal to the famous *Unter den Linden*, in Berlin. The poplars did not grow as well as was hoped, however, and, when the Avenue was graded and paved by order of Congress, in 1832 and 1833, were removed. The street is now well paved and lighted. It is handsomely built up, and contains some buildings which would do credit to any city. The distance from the Capitol to the President's house is one mile, and the view from either point along the Avenue is very fine.

There are 1170 blocks or squares, bounded by 22 avenues ranging from 130 to 160 feet in width, named, as far as they go, after the different States; and 100 streets, from 70 to 100 feet wide. The circumference of the city is 14 miles. There are 199 miles of streets, and 65 miles of avenues. The paving and grading of the streets has been done almost entirely by the city. The Government claims every privilege accorded to it by the original design, but steadily refuses to carry out the part assigned it by that same plan.

GENERAL REMARKS.

In 1850, the population of Washington was 40,101;

in 1860, 61,400. Its present population is estimated at over 100,000. It is, as we have said, vastly superior to the city of a few years ago. It is being rapidly built up, and the style of the buildings is improving every day. In the neighborhood of the President's House and Lafayette Square, there are many handsome residences. The bricks of which the majority of the houses are built, are made of clay found within the city limits, and are of a bright, cheerful red. The Baltimore style is adopted in the construction, and the houses built within the past ten years will compare favorably with any in the country.

As a general rule, however, there is little to see after one has explored the public buildings and grounds. The city does not offer many attractions to a stranger, and few care to remain after seeing the National property.

III.

THE CAPITOL.

The dome of the Capitol is the first object which greets the eye of the traveller approaching Washington. The building is situated on the western brow of a commanding hill, and overlooks the city and the surrounding country. The site was chosen by Washington, who was greatly impressed with its advantages. The structure faces the east, its exact position having been determined by astronomical observations. It stands in latitude 38° 55′ 48″ north, and longitude 77° 1′ 48″ west from Greenwich.

The design of the old building, which is the centre of the present edifice, was drawn by Dr. William Thornton, and submitted to President Washington, who, in accordance with an Act of Congress for that purpose, accepted it. Work was at once begun.

On the 18th of September 1793, a grand masonic, civic, and military procession was formed in front of the President's House, from which point it marched to the site designed for the Capitol. Upon reaching the grounds, the Grand Sword Bearer, followed by George Washington, President of the United States, marshalled the Masonic fraternity between the double lines of the procession to the Corner-stone. Their arrival at the spot was announced by a salvo of artillery, when

UNITED STATES CAPITOL.

the Grand Marshal handed to the Commissioners of the District a large silver plate bearing the following inscription, which was read aloud:

"This southeast corner-stone of the Capitol of the United States of America, in the city of Washington, was laid on the 18th day of September, 1793, in the thirteenth year of American Independence, in the first year of the second term of the Presidency of George Washington, whose virtues in the civil administration of his country have been so conspicuous and beneficial, as his military valor and prudence have been useful in establishing her liberties, and in the year of Masonry, 5793, by the President of the United States, in concert with the Grand Lodge of Maryland, several lodges under its jurisdiction, and Lodge No. 22 from Alexandria, Virginia.

"Thomas Johnson, David Stuart, and Daniel Carroll, Commissioners; Joseph Clarke, R. W. G. M. P. T.; James Hoban and Stephen Hallet, Architects; Collin Williamson, M. Mason."

The artillery again discharged a volley, and the plate was delivered to the President, who, attended by the Acting Grand Master and three Worshipful Masters of the Masonic Fraternity, deposited the plate on the corner-stone, and poured corn, wine, and oil upon it. A prayer was then offered, the Masonic rites pertaining to such occasions were celebrated, an oration was delivered by the Acting Grand Master, and the ceremonies concluded amidst the thunders of the artillery and the cheers of the multitude. The company then partook of a sumptuous feast which had been prepared close by, and a discharge of artillery at sunset closed the day.

The work was pushed forward as rapidly as possible, and the North wing was ready for the use of Congress in the Summer of 1800. The walls of the South wing were carried up twenty feet, and roofed over for the temporary accommodation of the House of Representatives, the North wing being assigned to the Senate. This building was styled the "oven," and was used by the House from 1802 until 1804, when the roof was removed, and the building completed by Mr. Benjamin H. Latrobe, the Engineer. In the meantime the House sat in the room used for the Library of Congress, which was on the West side of the North wing. In 1808, the South wing being sufficiently advanced to permit the hall to be used, the House returned to its old quarters.

The House wing was finished in 1811, and the hall was regarded as a very beautiful work of art. It was semicircular in form, with a vaulted wooden ceiling, and was handsomely ornamented by various appropriate devices. The Senate wing was not so handsomely finished. It was merely a temporary affair in its internal arrangements, and was intended to be succeeded by a much more elaborate structure. The walls of both wings were constructed of sandstone, procured from an island in Acquia Creek, in Virginia. The central building was not yet begun, and the two halls were connected by a covered wooden passage-way.

On the 28th of August 1814, the British burned the interior of both wings. Fortunately the outer walls remained uninjured. Mr. Latrobe was appointed by Congress to superintend the reconstruction of the building. He remained in charge of the work until December 1817, when he resigned his position, and was succeeded by Charles Bulfinch. On the 24th of March 1818, the foundation of the central building was laid, and the entire edifice was completed in 1825, according to the original plan of Dr. Thornton.

Upon returning to Washington after the destruction of the Capitol by the British, Congress sat in the building used by the Post Office Department. On the 8th of December 1815, an act was passed leasing a building situated on the Eastern side of the Capitol Park. Congress sat in this building for ten years, and from this circumstance it gained the name of the "Old Capitol." It acquired a not very pleasant reputation during the late war as a Government prison.

The Capitol of 1825 was considered a grand affair, and was an object of pride to the whole country; but handsome as it undoubtedly was, did not compare with the present magnificent structure.

THE NEW CAPITOL.

As the Government expanded with the growth of the country, the old building was found to be too small for the requirements of Congress, and on the 30th of September 1850, an act was passed, providing for the extension of the Capitol according to such plan as might be approved by the President. Mr. Fillmore selected, from the numerous designs submitted to him, the plan of Mr. Thomas U. Walter, Architect, and on the 10th of June 1851, appointed him to superintend the work.

The corner-stone of the extension was laid, with appropriate and imposing ceremonies, by the President, on the 4th of July 1851. The following record was deposited in the stone:

"On the morning of the first day of the seventy-sixth year of the Independence of the United States of America, in the City of Washington, being the 4th day of July, 1851, this stone, designed as the corner-stone of the extension of the Capitol, according to a plan approved by the President, in pursuance of an act of Congress, was laid by

"MILLARD FILLMORE,

"PRESIDENT OF THE UNITED STATES,

assisted by the Grand Master of the Masonic Lodges, in the presence of many members of Congress, of officers of the Executive and Judiciary Departments, National, State, and District, of officers of the Army and Navy, the Corporate authorities of this and neighboring cities, many associations, civil and military and masonic, officers of the Smithsonian Institution and National Institute, professors of colleges and teachers of schools of the District, with their students and pupils, and a vast concourse of people from places near and remote, including a few surviving gentlemen who witnessed the laying of the corner-stone of the Capitol by President Washington, on the eighteenth day of September, seventeen hundred and ninety-three.

"If, therefore, it shall be the will of God that this

structure shall fall from its base, that its foundation be upturned, and this deposit brought to the eyes of men, be it then known, that, on this day, the Union of the United States of America stands firm; that their Constitution still exists unimpaired, and with all its original usefulness and glory growing every day stronger and stronger in the affections of the great body of the American people, and attracting more and more the admiration of the world. And all here assembled, whether belonging to public life or to private life, with hearts devoutly thankful to Almighty God for the preservation of the liberty and happiness of the country, unite in sincere and fervent prayers that this deposit, and the walls and arches, the domes and towers, the columns and entablatures now to be erected over it, may endure forever!

"God save the United States of America.

"DANIEL WEBSTER,

"*Secretary of State of the United States.*"

The oration was delivered by Daniel Webster.

The extension consists of two wings, each of which has a front on the east of 142 feet 8 inches, and a depth of 238 feet 10 inches, not including the porticoes and steps. The porticoes front the east, and have each twenty-two monolithic fluted columns. They "extend the entire width of the front, having central projections of 10 feet 4 inches, forming double porticoes in the centre, the width of the gable. There is also a portico of ten columns on the west end of each wing, 105 feet 8 inches wide, projecting 10 feet 6 inches, and like porticoes on the north side of the north wing and south side of the south wing, with a width of 121 feet 4 inches. The centre building is 352 feet 4 inches long and 121 feet 6 inches deep, with a portico 160 feet wide, of twenty-four columns, with a double façade on the east, and a projection of 83 feet on the west, embracing a recessed portico of ten coupled columns. The entire length of the Capitol is 751 feet 4 inches, and the greatest depth, including porticoes and steps, is 324 feet. The ground actually covered by the building, exclusive of the court-yards, is 153,112 square feet, or 652 feet over three and a half acres.

"The material of which the extension is built, is a white marble slightly variegated with blue, and was procured from a quarry in Lee, Massachusetts. The columns are all of white marble obtained from Maryland.

"The principal story of the Capitol rests upon a rustic basement, which supports an ordonnance of pilasters rising to the height of the two stories above. Upon these pilasters rests the entablature and beautiful frieze, and the whole is surmounted by a marble balustrade.

"The main entrances are by the three eastern porticoes, being made easy of access by broad flights of stone steps with massive cheek-blocks, and vaulted carriage-ways beneath to the basement entrances."

The building faces the east, and the rear is in the direction of the principal part of the city. This location was made under the impression that the neighborhood of the Capitol would be first settled up in the growth of the new city, but the designs of the projectors not having been realized, the building now faces the wrong way.

Standing in front of the edifice, and at a distance sufficient to take in the whole view, the effect is indescribably grand. The pure white marble glitters and shines in the sunlight, and the huge structure towers above one like one of the famed palaces of old romance. The broad flights of steps of the wings and central buildings have an air of elegance and lightness which is surprising when their massive character is considered. The pediments of the porticoes will contain magnificent groups of sculpture. The central pediment is decorated with a group sculptured in alto-relievo. The Genius of America, crowned with a star, holds in her right hand a shield bearing the letters U. S. A., surrounded with a glory. The shield rests on an altar inscribed with the date, "July 4, 1776," encircled with a laurel wreath. A spear is behind her within reach, and the eagle crouches at her feet. She is gazing at Hope, who stands upon her left, and is directing her attention to Justice, on her right, who holds in her right hand a scroll inscribed, "Constitution of the United States," and in her left the scales. The group is said to have been designed by John Quincy Adams, and was executed by Signor Persico.

The northern pediment contains Crawford's famous group, representing the progress of civilization in the United States. America stands in the centre of the tympanum, in the full light of the rising sun. On her right hand are War, Commerce, Youth and Education, and Agriculture; on her left the pioneer backwoodsman, the hunter, the Indian and his squaw with an infant in her arms, sitting by a filled grave.

The Southern pediment has not yet been filled. It is said that the design adopted for it is by William R. Barbee, and represents the discovery of the country by Columbus.

The cheek-blocks of the steps to the central portico are ornamented by two fine groups of statuary. The group on the right of the steps represents the discovery of America, and is by Persico. Columbus, landing in the New World, holds aloft in his right hand a globe, symbolic of his discovery. He is clad in armor, which is said to be a faithful copy of a suit worn by him. An Indian maiden crouches beneath his uplifted arm, her face expressive of the surprise and terror of her race at the appearance of the whites.

The group on the left is called "*Civilization*," and is by Greenough. A terror-stricken mother, clasping her babe to her breast, crouches at the feet of a stalwart Indian warrior, whose arms, raised in the act of striking her with his tomahawk, are seized and pinioned by the husband and father, who returns at the fortunate moment, accompanied by his faithful dog, which stands by ready to spring to the aid of his master.

The entire cost of the Capitol and its improvements, when completed, will be over twelve millions of dollars.

THE OLD BUILDING.

The old building is now the centre of the whole edifice. Entering it at the basement, we find ourselves in a large crypt, whose vaulted ceiling is supported by two concentric peristyles, of forty Doric columns. It was the intention of Congress to place the remains of Washington in a mausoleum, in the sub-basement below this crypt, and Mrs. Washington gave her consent to the removal of the body; but when the Capitol was ready to receive the precious trust, the Legislature of Virginia protested against the removal; and John A. Washington, Esq., the proprietor of Mount Vernon, refused to allow the body to be removed, on the ground that it was Washington's wish that his ashes should rest with those of his family. Having failed to make the Capitol the mausoleum of the "Father of His Country," it would be a grand and glorious deed for Congress to secure and place there the ashes of Columbus.

The vaults are massive, and are models of strength and durability, and decidedly one of the most interesting portions of the building.

A narrow passage, on the left of the Western entrance to the crypt, leads to the Guard-room of the Capitol Police, who use the apartment to secure offenders, should their detention become necessary.

Under the old Senate wing are the store-rooms belonging to the Supreme Court, where documents, papers, and books are carefully filed away. The room beneath the Old Senate Chamber and the present Supreme Court-room is of the United States. It is semicircular in form, and is of the same dimensions as the room above, though not so high. It was formerly the chamber of the Supreme Court, and is connected with the room above by a winding stairway of stone. The ceiling consists of massive arches, which rest upon Doric columns. The wall is lined with alcoves, which contain twenty-five thousand volumes. This is the largest and most complete collection of legal works in the United States, and one of the largest in the world. The library was removed to its present location for the convenience of the Court. It is open from nine o'clock A. M., until the adjournment of Congress. When Congress is not in session, the hour of closing is three P. M. The judges of the Supreme Court, members of the Cabinet, and members of the Senate and House alone are allowed to take books from the library; but strangers are permitted to consult any work in the room.

The Court of Claims occupy the rooms under the Library of Congress, in the western end of the building.

Passing into the basement of the old South or House wing, the visitor is saluted with a peculiar odor which a literary man will at once recognize as proceeding from freshly printed matter. The narrow passage-way is obstructed with piles of mail-bags crammed full of books and papers; and blotches of ink and sealing-wax disfigure the walls and stone floor. The gas is kept burning constantly, as the full light of day rarely reaches these apartments, which constitute the

FOLDING ROOMS OF THE HOUSE.

The entire ground floor of this wing, consisting of twenty-two rooms, is devoted to storing, folding, and mailing of the House Documents. The whole department is in charge of a superintendent, whose business it is to receive, register, and store the various publications of the House, as they come in from the Government Printing Office. The speeches of members are also received and prepared for mailing here. The folding is generally done by boys, but men are required for the heavier work. Several tons of mail-matter, from a single copy of "The Globe" newspaper to a thousand-page folio book, are sent off daily by the members to their friends and constituents. Many of these publications are both useful and important, but the majority of them are used merely as waste paper by the persons to whom they are sent. Thousands of books already wrapped and sealed for mailing, are stored away in the vaults. Lists of their titles are affixed to the inner side of the doors of the rooms in which they are kept, so that they can be easily found at any moment.

During the great political contests of the country, publications and newspapers of all kinds are sent off from this room by members; and the expense of this means of electioneering falls on the whole people.

THE ROTUNDA.

Leaving the vaults of the old building, one may either climb the inner stairway at the western entrance, or, passing out into the grounds again, mount the broad stairs, and enter by the main, or eastern door. Let us avail ourselves of the latter means, and pause a moment as we reach the splendid colonnade which is the chief ornament of the portico. It is from this portico that the President of the United States delivers his inaugural address, in the presence of his assembled countrymen, upon the occasion of his accession to power. Only a few months from the time these lines are written, and the grounds below will be thronged with anxious thousands, who will flock thither from all parts of our broad land, to hear our Silent Warrior declare the policy which is to guide him as a statesman.

Passing through the massive doors, we enter the Rotunda.

This immense chamber occupies the central portion of the old building, and lies immediately beneath the dome. The floor is of freestone, and rests upon the arches of the crypt below. A line drawn across it from wall to wall would measure ninety-five and a half feet, and the distance from the floor to the frescoed canopy is one hundred and eighty feet three inches. The room is handsomely panelled and frescoed, and is surrounded by an ordonnance of fluted pilasters thirty feet in height, supporting an entablature and cornice of fourteen feet.

"Above this cornice, a vertical wall will be raised, with a deep recessed panel nine feet in height, to be filled with sculpture, forming a continuous frieze three hundred feet in length, of figures in alto-relievo. The subject to be the History of America. The gradual progress of a continent from the depths of barbarism to the height of civilization; the rude and primitive civilization of some of the ante-Columbian tribes; the contests of the Aztecs with their less civilized predecessors; their own conquest by the Spanish race; the wilder state of the hunter tribes of our own regions; the discovery, settlement, and wars of America; the advance of the white and retreat of the red races; our own revolutionary and other struggles, with an illustration of the higher achievements of our present civilization, will afford a richness and variety of costume, character, and incident, which may worthily employ our best sculptors in its exécution, and which will form for future ages a monument of the present state of the arts in this country."

Above the portion reserved for this frieze, is a series of attached columns, the spaces between which are filled with large, handsome windows, which admit a sufficient light to the rotunda.

Above this colonnade rises the dome, which contracts to a space of sixty-five feet in diameter, and reveals another and a lighter colonnade at a much higher level. The whole is closed in at the base of the lantern, but just below the lantern a large canopy obstructs the view, and is covered with a magnificent fresco, by Brumidi, which we shall have occasion to notice shortly.

The walls of the rotunda, between the pilasters below, contain eight paintings on canvas, set in panels, each painting being eighteen feet long and twelve feet high. Four of these are by Colonel John Trumbull, who was an aide-de-camp to Washington during the Revolution. These are "The Declaration of Independence," "The Surrender of Burgoyne at Saratoga," "The Surrender of Lord Cornwallis at Yorktown," and "The Resignation of Washington as Commander-in-chief of the Army in 1783." These paintings were ordered by the Government at an expense of $8,000 each. They are faithful representations of the scenes and events they depict, and contain accurate portraits of the personages represented. This fact alone renders them amongst the most valuable of the national possessions.

The other four are "The Embarcation of the Pilgrims in the 'Speedwell,' at Delft Haven," by Robert W. Weir; "The Landing of Columbus," by John Vanderlyn; "De Soto Discovering the Mississippi River," by William H. Powell; and "The Baptism of Pocahontas," by John Gadsby Chapman. They were painted by order of Congress, and cost the Government from $10,000 to $20,000 each. They are all faulty — the whole eight —in many respects, but are still great works of art, and merit a careful study. To our mind, "The Departure of the Pilgrims," by Weir, is the best in the rotunda. No finer specimens of manly and female beauty are to be found anywhere, than in the characters of this painting. New England still retains a few women who are blessed with the loveliness which makes Rose Standish so attractive to the gazer, and seems to have been given what is left to us of such men as those whom Weir has chosen for his heroes. This type of masculine beauty is found chiefly in Connecticut.

Panels of arabesque, in bas-relief, ornament the walls above these paintings. Four alternate panels contain heads of Columbus, Sir Walter Raleigh, La Salle, and Cabot. Over the four doors of the rotunda are the following alto-relievos in stone:—"Penn's Treaty with the Indians," by M. Gevelot; "The Landing of the Pilgrims at Plymouth," by Causici; "The Conflict of Daniel Boone with the Indians," by Causici; and "The Rescue of Capt. John Smith by Pocahontas," by Capellano.

A marble statue of Alexander Hamilton stands in the centre of the rotunda, and is an object of much curiosity.

THE DOME.

Leaving the rotunda by the north door, we enter the lobby of the old Senate Chamber. The first door on the left swings ajar, and we open it, mount the stone stairway, and soon find ourselves on an iron platform in a small court between the rotunda and the north wing. An iron stairway, winding around the outer side of the base of the dome, conducts us to a second door. Entering it, we find ourselves at the base of the dome, in a handsome gallery, which encircles the walls of the rotunda, and affords an excellent and picturesque view of the room below. The dome rises from the level of this gallery, and is constructed entirely of iron. It consists of an inner and an outer shell, joined and held together by an infinity of bars and bolts, and between which an iron stairway leads to the lantern. Half way up the dome is a gallery, running around the exterior of the outer shell, from which a fine view of the city and surrounding country may be obtained. Mounting still higher by the stairway, we enter the gallery just beneath the canopy and look down on the floor beneath, nearly two hundred feet distant. The persons moving about below seem like so many pigmies, and their footfalls and voices sound far off. Above us is

BRUMIDI'S ALLEGORICAL PICTURE.

The painted figures which appeared so small from the floor beneath, now seem colossal, and the work which was so soft and delicate as seen from below, looks coarse and rough. The picture is well worth seeing, and the view from the various heights is very fine.

Washington is seated on the rainbow in glory, surrounded by bright-colored clouds. The Goddess of Liberty on his right holds a scroll towards him, and on his left is the winged representation of Fame and Victory. Before the three are thirteen maidens with joined hands, representing the thirteen original States, and forming a semicircle. They hold aloft a bright-colored scarf, on which is inscribed the legend "*E Pluribus Unum.*" They are arranged geographically, and not historically. Beginning on the left of Washington, they occur in the following order: New Hampshire, Massachusetts, Rhode Island, Connecticut, New Jersey, New York, Pennsylvania, Maryland, Delaware, Virginia, North Carolina, South Carolina, and Georgia. The States are distinguished by the coloring, drapery, attitudes, and the leaves and blossoms worn by the maidens. The prevailing hue of the Northern States is here a delicate green, which grows stronger and richer as the South is approached. The staple productions of the States are used as ornaments, and aid in distinguishing them.

This constitutes the central group. Around it are six other distinct and characteristic groups. We shall begin with that on the west, and proceed in describing them from left to right, taking the position of Washington in the central group as our standpoint.

1*st Group*. WAR.—Freedom, with drawn sword and in full armor, has smitten down Tyranny and Oppression, and is driving them away. By her side an eagle fights with his beak in the same cause. Her enemies are overcome with terror, and are fleeing from her presence in hot haste; and with them Anger, Revenge, and Discord are driven away.

2*d Group*. AGRICULTURE. — In the centre sits Ceres, the Goddess of the Harvest, holding the horn of plenty in her left hand. America, with her head crowned with the liberty-cap, grasps the reins attached to a pair of fiery horses which are hitched to an American reaper and held in check by two stout laborers. Pomona with a basket of fruit stands by the side of Ceres, and Flora kneels near the reaper, gathering flow ers, while a child sports by her side. The background is a tasteful arrangement of American vegetation.

3d Group. MECHANICS.—Vulcan stands with his right foot resting on a cannon, and his right hand grasping a hammer which he leans on his anvil. Machinery, cannon balls, mortars, and other mechanical contrivances are scattered around, and five attendants are busy in preparing them for use.

4th Group. COMMERCE.—Mercury, the patron of travellers and merchants, is seated on a pile of bales and boxes, holding up a bag of gold to the gaze of Robert Morris, the Financier of the Revolution. On the right of the swift-winged deity are laborers engaged in loading a truck, and on the left two sailors point to a distant gunboat. There is a bitter sarcasm about this picture, which symbolizes not only the country's commercial greatness, but also its ingratitude. One seems to detect a wild yearning in the gaze which Robert Morris fixes upon Mercury's gold. The poor man needed the money badly, for after guiding his country safely through its pecuniary difficulties, he fell a victim to his own embarrassments, and died a bankrupt, in a debtor's prison, in which his grateful countrymen allowed him to languish.

5th Group. THE MARINE.—Neptune, in royal state, is seen emerging from the deep, gazing about him as if to seek some explanation of the mighty events which are going on upon the land and sea. Below him, Aphrodite, half risen from the waves, is about to drop into the ocean the Atlantic cable, which she has received from a winged cherub which hovers near her.

6th Group. The Arts and Sciences.—Minerva, armed with helmet and spear, stands in the centre, instructing a group on her left, collected around an electrical machine. These are Benjamin Franklin, Robert Fulton, and Professor Morse. They listen with rapt attention to her teachings. On her left is a group of school-boys being instructed by their teacher.

The painting covers an area of 4,664 square feet, and was executed by Signor C. Brumidi, a native of Italy, and a naturalized citizen of the United States. It cost the Government forty thousand dollars.

THE VIEW FROM THE DOME.

A stairway leads from the gallery below the picture to the base of the lantern, beyond which visitors are forbidden to ascend. A door admits us to the highest outer gallery of the dome. It requires a fatiguing journey to reach it, but the magnificent view to be obtained from it fully repays us for all our trouble. The air blows keen as we pass out upon the narrow balcony, for we are nearly three hundred feet above the ground. The view is magnificent. The whole city is at our feet, with its long lines of streets, its splendid public buildings, its parks and gardens and beyond is a panorama of unsurpassed beauty.

To the northwest the high hills in Virginia and beyond Georgetown stretch back to the horizon. The river, breaking from them, sweeps away to the southeast, and is crossed by the canal bridge at Georgetown and the Long Bridge at the foot of Maryland Avenue. On the Virginia side the heights are bold and picturesque. Arlington, once the home of the Rebel General Robert E. Lee, and now a Freedmen's village and National Cemetery, stands near the Virginia end of the Long Bridge. The heights here are crowned with massive earthworks, which were erected for the protection of the Capital during the war. They are very distinct to the eye, and with a good glass every detail of construction can be made out. Pennsylvania Avenue stretches out grandly before us, and at our feet, that portion extending from the Capitol to the President's House being handsomely built up. The various objects in the city can be distinctly made out, for the whole town is splendidly mapped out below us. To the westward the eye ranges over a vast tract of country in Virginia, and to the southwest the city of Alexandria, eight miles distant, is in full view. The Potomac, here over a mile wide, sweeps majestically by the city, and disappears amidst the southwestern woods which shut in the view. To the south are the Eastern Branch, the Navy Yard, the Insane Asylum, and beyond, the hills crowned with the red earthworks. To the north, the Baltimore Railroad is seen emerging from the woods and descending a steep grade towards the city. On all sides, long lines of fortifications greet the eye, each telling its mute but eloquent story.

In the early months of the war, when the Southern army occupied Mason's and Munson's hills, in Virginia, their colors could be seen from this balcony, and during the desperate struggles on the early Potomac the smoke of battle frequently hung over the distant woods, and the dull throbbing of the guns could be distinctly and painfully heard.

Descending as we came, we pause in the gallery under the fresco to notice the ingenious arrangement of the gas-lights. Four hundred and twenty-five burners are arranged in a circle around the base of the canopy, at distances of one inch apart, and over each one passes an incombustible wire connected with an electrical battery placed between the outer and inner shells of the dome, near the stairway, on our right as we go down. Upon reaching the old Senate lobby, after descending from the canopy, we pass into the rotunda again, and pause in the doorway to notice a large metal plate in the side of the wall, containing a number of knobs, each of which has its appropriate label cut in the plate immediately over it. These control the lighting apparatus of the dome and the two Houses of Congress. A pressure on one of the knobs opens a valve, and allows the gas to flow up to the burners, and a touch upon an adjoining knob causes an electric current to flash along the copper wire over the burners, and in an instant the whole dome is in a blaze of light. The effect of this illumination is very fine. The light falls brightly over every object, and when seen from without the dome seems almost on fire.

Passing through the rotunda, and leaving it by the western doorway, one enters a narrow passage which leads to

THE LIBRARY OF CONGRESS.

The three halls which contain this valuable library are located in, and occupy the whole of the western projection of the main building, and are among the handsomest and most elegant in the Capitol. The main hall opens on a portico of ten coupled columns, fronting the western park and the city, and commanding a charming view of the surrounding country The main hall is 91 feet long, 34 feet wide, and 38 feet high. It has two rows of galleries around it, on all four sides. These galleries are constructed of ornamental iron work, and are reached by spiral stairways set in recesses at the ends of the room. The ceiling is of iron and glass, and is both elegant and tasteful. The North and South halls open into the main hall, are placed at right angles to it, and are fitted up in the same style. The rooms are painted a light cream color and are handsomely ornamented with gildings. There is an air of quiet and repose about the apartments which is grateful and refreshing.

On the 24th of April 1800, Congress, at the suggestion of Mr. Jefferson, appropriated the sum of $5,000, to be expended by the Clerks of the two Houses, under the direction of a joint Committee, for books for the use of those bodies and the various officers of the Government. In 1802, regulations were adopted for the government of the library, and a librarian was appointed. When the British burned the Capitol in 1814, the entire collection, numbering 300 volumes, was destroyed.

Mr. Jefferson, with a view to remedy the loss, offered his own library to Congress. His collection was large and valuable, numbering about 7,500 books. His proposition was accepted by Congress in January 1815, and he was paid the sum of $23,950 for his library.

which was at once transferred to Washington, and placed in the Post Office building where Congress was sitting. In 1818 it was removed to the Capitol and temporarily placed in a room near the Supreme Court Room. In 1825, it was placed in the hall it now occupies. This was the nucleus of the present library.

In December 1851, the library numbered 55,000 volumes. On the 24th of December a defective flue set fire to that portion of the building, and the hall and 35,000 volumes were destroyed. Twenty thousand volumes, among which was fortunately the greater part of Mr. Jefferson's collection, were saved, in consequence of being in an adjoining apartment.

The library was at once temporarily removed to another room, and $10,000 appropriated for the purpose of replacing the works destroyed. In March 1852, $72,500 were appropriated for the repair of the hall, and the present library rooms are the result. An additional appropriation of $75,000 was made for the purchase of books in the same year. An annual appropriation varying from $8,000 to $15,000 is made for the purchase of miscellaneous and law books. The total cost of the three halls up to the present time has been $280,500.

"The portion of the Act of Aug. 10, 1846, requiring the deposit of a copy of a copyrighted book, map, etc., in the Libraries of Congress and the Smithsonian Institution, and for a long time previously practically disregarded by authors and publishers, was repealed Feb. 9, 1859. It was, however, re-enacted, March 3, 1865, so far as the obligation concerning a deposit in the Library of Congress was concerned; and 'An Act amendatory of the several Acts respecting copyrights,' approved Feb. 18, 1867, in default of compliance therewith, enjoins 'A penalty of twenty-five dollars, to be collected by the Librarian of Congress, in the name of the United States, in any District or Circuit Court of the United States, within the jurisdiction of which the delinquent may reside or be found.' A compliance with these requisitions is now strictly enforced."

In 1866 Congress authorized the transfer of the Library of the Smithsonian Institute to its own collection, which was thus increased by forty thousand volumes.

There are now nearly 170,000 volumes in the library, and the number is being daily enlarged by the operations of the copy-right law, and by judicious purchases. An excellently arranged catalogue has been printed, and can be consulted at any time while the library is open. The whole system is in charge of a joint Committee of the two Houses of Congress, but the regulations for its government are prescribed by the President of the Senate and the Speaker of the House. The library is kept open every day except Sunday, during the Session of Congress, from 9 A. M. until 3 P. M., and for the same time on Tuesdays, Thursdays, and Saturdays during the recess. Any one may consult the books in the hall, under certain prescribed regulations, but only the following persons are privileged to take them away; the President of the United States, the Vice President, the Members of the two Houses of Congress, Judges of the Supreme Court, Cabinet Ministers, the Diplomatic Corps, the Secretary of the Senate, the Clerk of the House, and the Agent of the Joint Committee on the Library.

The present librarian is Mr. A. R. Spofford, formerly of Cincinnati, a courteous and accomplished gentleman.

The following rules are required to be observed by all visitors to the library: —

"1. Visitors are requested to remove their hats.

"2. No loud talking is permitted.

"3. No readers under sixteen years of age are admitted.

"4. No book can be taken from the library.

"5. Readers are required to present tickets for all books wanted, and to return their books and take back their tickets before leaving the library.

"6. No reader is allowed to enter the alcoves."

THE NORTH WING.

Let us once more descend into the crypt of the old building, entering it by the western door. Turning to the left, we pass through a heavily-arched passageway under the lobby of the Supreme Court Chamber, into the new North, or Senate wing. All is silent in the old building, and the gas burns dimly and fitfully in the echoing passages; but as we pass through the glass doors, more bustle and animation greet us.

THE BASEMENT.

We enter a spacious corridor, paved with encaustic

tiles laid in mosaic, after the choicest Pompeiian and modern designs, and lighted by magnificent bronze chandeliers. The walls and ceilings are splendidly ornamented in fresco and distemper, the illustrations belonging to the natural history of North America, and being painted from life. Whole days may be spent in examining these splendid paintings, which are the work of Signor Brumidi. It would require a volume to describe the corridors accurately, and no one should by any means omit a visit to them. It is hard to tell which to admire the more, — the genius of the artist, or the fidelity with which he has copied Nature in her minutest detail.

There are fourteen committee rooms on this floor, each of which is designated by the name painted on the door. They are handsomely paved with encaustic tiles, or the floors are covered with luxurious velvet carpets. The walls are magnificently ornamented with appropriate paintings in fresco and distemper, and a massive bronze chandelier hangs from the ceiling, over a large table, surrounded by comfortable arm-chairs, placed in the centre of the room. The windows are curtained with heavy, rich hangings, and sofas, desks, chairs, and book-cases are arranged around the apartment. Each apartment has an air of taste and magnificence which must be extremely gratifying to the honorable gentlemen using it.

There is a restaurant on the east side of the corridor leading from the old building, in which an excellent repast can be procured at any time during the session of the Senate. Legislation seems to improve the appetite, and it is noticed that the chambers prove excellent customers to these places.

The folding room of the Senate is an establishment similar to that of the House,—which we have already described,—except that it is smaller, and burdens the mails with less rubbish. It is much handsomer than the House folding room, and is located in the southeast corner of the Senate basement.

HOW THE CAPITOL IS WARMED AND VENTILATED.

At the door of Room No. 59, in the southwestern end of the basement, we notice a card marked, "*Entrance to the Heating and Ventilating Apparatus.*" As we enter the door, a current of air rushes out, and warns us that we are about to enter a different region from that we have been exploring. Passing down the stone steps, we enter a narrow whitewashed passage, lighted with gas, and lined with rows of heavy iron doors, all of which are securely locked. Iron tubes or pipes extend in every direction overhead. There is no one to be seen, and a deep silence reigns over every thing,—broken only by the monotonous sound of machinery. Passing on in the direction of this sound, we see two men sitting in arm-chairs at the end of the passage. There is a door on each side of the passage, and an intricate arrangement of iron pipes overhead. These men are the assistant engineers in charge of the machinery. They are quiet and reserved, and understand their business thoroughly. They are very kind and obliging in showing and explaining the machinery as they are fully aware that their department is one of the most interesting features of the Capitol.

There are two small engines, one on the right and the other on the left of the passage, which are placed in rooms of a slightly lower level. The cylinders are upright, and the steam is supplied from the boilers in the furnace room. They work with a droning sound, and the click of the piston rods and cranks is deadened by an abundance of oil. These engines turn large fan-wheels, one of which is eighteen and the other twenty-four feet in diameter, and from which they are separated by glass windows. A door communicates with the fan chamber, to which visitors are admitted if they desire it; but the draught of air is so strong in this room, and the revolutions of the fan are so rapid, that one does not care to remain long in it. Opposite the engines are immense iron cases, or chambers, containing miles of coiled iron pipes. Steam is generated in boilers placed in another apartment, and is forced through these pipe coils, thereby producing a certain and regular degree of heat. By means of the fans, a current of fresh air is drawn into the chambers from without, and driven across these hot pipe coils until it is thoroughly warmed. Huge pipes then conduct it to all parts of the wing, the fan being sufficiently powerful to create a strong draught in the highest story of the building. In this way, an even and regular temperature is maintained in all parts of the Capitol. The fresh air, after being warmed, is constantly passing into the rooms and corridors through the registers, and the strong draught produces a thorough and perfect ventilation of the entire building.

The boilers and furnaces for generating the steam are located in an adjoining vault, which is placed at a lower level than the engine rooms, and which opens (in both wings) into the western court of the old building. The vaults would be insufferably hot at all times, and especially in warm weather, but for an excellent arrangement which keeps a current of cool air constantly passing through them.

In the summer the building is kept cool by shutting off the steam, and forcing the fresh air through the registers. The excellence of this system is manifest in every part of the Capitol. Many of the principal rooms have no natural means of ventilation, and would be damp and unhealthy but for this most ingenious arrangement.

Every thing is kept scrupulously neat and clean in this department. The machinery shines like polished gold and silver, and you might rub your pocket handkerchief over the floors of the engine-rooms without soiling it. The engineer has several assistants, and is provided with a handsomely fitted-up office, the perfect order and neatness of which attests the care and regularity with which his duties are discharged.

There is an apparatus in the House-wing basement, in Room 34, exactly similar to that we have described above. Besides warming their respective wings, these engines also supply heat and ventilation to the principal portions of the old building.

Returning as we came, we again pass through the corridors of the basement. Our attention is called to two handsome bronze stairways, leading to the Senate Chamber. These are for the Senators only, and are often very useful in enabling the honorable members to escape from the persecutions of their "dear constituents," and "gentlemen who have a little scheme on foot."

The eastern doors to the basement of each wing open upon a vaulted carriage-way, under the splendid porticos we have described. In wet weather, these carriage-ways are very useful, as they enable persons to avoid the rain and dampness in entering the Capitol.

Water-closets for gentlemen, both comfortable and convenient, will be found in Room No. 54.

THE SECOND FLOOR.

Two handsome marble stairways lead from the basement to the second, or main floor. They are situated in the southeastern and southwestern ends of the wing. They are continued, on a much more magnificent scale, from the second floor to the galleries and rooms of the third floor.

This portion of the two wings is on a level with the floor of the Rotunda, and contains the principal apartments of the Capitol. The main entrances are by the magnificent North and South Porticos, which are soon to be ornamented with the superb bronze doors designed for them. The doors of the Senate portico will illustrate the events of the life of Washington. The House doors are completed, and will be described farther on.

Entering from the portico, the visitor finds himself in a beautiful marble hall, the ceiling of which rests upon massive marble columns. The marble is vari gated, and the general effect is fine.

On the right of this hall is

THE POST OFFICE OF THE SENATE.

This is a large and handsomely frescoed apartment. The principal feature is a small and tasteful post office, constructed of black walnut and plate-glass. Each Senator has his private box, in which all mail matter for him is placed, subject to his order. Letters and parcels from any member or officer of the Senate are mailed here. The room is in charge of a postmaster appointed by the Senate. Mails are sent off and arrive at stated hours.

The office of the Sergeant-at-Arms of the Senate opens into this room.

On the left of the passage-way is the Stationery Room of the Senate. Here paper, envelopes, pens, ink, and other articles of stationery are kept for the use of the members and officers of the Senate.

The door at the end of the passage leads to the Senate Chamber, and, during the sessions of that body, is in charge of a doorkeeper. The door on the right leads us to

THE LADIES' RECEPTION ROOM.

This apartment is magnificently frescoed. The carpets and hangings are of the richest materials. Marble columns support the ceiling, and splendid mirrors adorn the walls. The furniture is elegant and luxurious, and a costly chandelier hangs in the centre. A door leads into the private passage in rear of the Senate Chamber, so that Senators can reach the apartment without passing through the public halls. Ladies wishing to speak with a Senator present their cards to the doorkeeper of this room, and await his pleasure in the reception room. The apartment is much frequented by "female lobby members," and by loungers in general.

Passing into the hall again, we cross it, and find ourselves at the foot of the stairway leading to the third floor. On our right hand is the famous statue of Benjamin Franklin, by Hiram Powers, a fine and life-like work. Passing by the stairs, we enter the south corridor of the Senate, which is spacious and handsomely ornamented. Half way down the corridor are two doors; the one on the right being the principal entrance to the Senate Chamber, and the other leading off to the old building. At the west end is a fine portrait of Mr. Lincoln, by Coggeswell. A bust of Chief-Justice Taney stands at the eastern end. An iron doorway admits us to the western corridor. The Senate Chamber is still on our right. The rooms on the left are the offices of the Secretary of the Senate and his clerks.

Upon reaching the north end of the corridor, and turning to the right, we enter the private passage in the rear of the Senate Chamber. The first door on our left standing open, we enter

THE VICE-PRESIDENT'S ROOM.

THE PRESIDENT'S ROOM.

This is a small, square apartment, but one of the gems of the Capitol. Its windows look out on the northern portion of the city, and are draped with elegant and tasteful curtains. The floor is covered with a rich carpet, and the furniture is simple but costly. The ceiling is vaulted, and is magnificently frescoed with representations typical of the history of the country. The walls are adorned with large mirrors and with portraits in fresco of Washington and his first Cabinet. At night a superb chandelier sheds a soft and pleasant light through the apartment.

The room is occupied by the President during his official visits to the Capitol. Towards the close of the sessions of Congress large numbers of bills are hurried through the two Houses, and brought to him here for his signature. Much valuable time is saved by having him so near.

THE VICE PRESIDENT'S ROOM

is at the opposite end of the private psssage-way. It contains a large portrait of Washington by Rembrandt Peale, and is handsomely ornamented and frescoed. It is much larger than the President's Room, but is more simply furnished. It is used by the Vice President of the United States, or, in his absence, the presiding officer of the Senate, who receives his friends and transacts much of his official business here.

THE MARBLE ROOM.

Lying between the President's and Vice President's

Rooms is a suite of sumptuous apartments—the most magnificent in the building—known as the Marble Room. The total length of the three rooms is about 85 feet, the width $21\frac{1}{2}$ feet, and the height $19\frac{1}{2}$ feet. The floor is an exquisite piece of mosaic in marble, and the ceiling is in panels of slightly colored Italian marble, and rests upon a series of magnificent white Italian marble pillars with elaborate capitals. The walls are adorned with large and superb mirrors, and are veneered with the finest specimens of Tennessee marble in the country. The windows are richly curtained, the furniture is exquisite, and the apartment is lighted by a large brass chandelier. The suite is used by the Senators as a retiring and private reception room. They are not altogether worthy of so much magnificence, as it is not uncommon to see cigar stumps on the floor and tobacco stains on the marble.

The private apartments of the two Houses of Congress are not open to any but invited guests during the sessions of those bodies, but visitors are permitted to examine them during the recess of Congress.

Returning to the west corridor, we notice near the foot of the stairway Stone's fine statue of John Hancock.

THE MARBLE STAIRS.

There are two stairways in each of the new wings, leading from the main floor to the gallery. They are amongst the chief beauties of the building, and are constructed of a fine quality of white and variegated marble, with massive balustrades of the same material.

Ascending the western stairway of the Senate wing we pause to notice the large painting on canvas, by Walker, representing the storming of the Castle of Chapultepec by the American army under General Scott, on the 13th of September, 1847. The scene represents the grim old castle in the background, which, together with its formidable outworks, is wreathed in smoke. A heavy fire is being maintained by the defenders, and the Mexican tricolor floats defiantly above the seemingly impregnable lines. The American forces are struggling, in the foreground, through the dense chaparal, and are steadily winning their way, step by step, towards the castle. The dead and wounded, and broken guns and artillery carriages lie about. An Indian woman, with her babe strapped to her back, is seen supporting the head of her dying husband, unmindful of the storm of battle which is raging around her. The picture represents the battle at the moment of the consultation held between General Quitman and several of the officers of his advanced division, when the troops had carried the outworks at the foot of the castle, and opened the way along the aqueduct towards the Garita de Belen. The conception is brilliant, and the execution fine. The painting cost $6,000, and was designed for the room of the Senate Committee on Military Affairs. This fact explains the singular shape of the canvas.

THE UPPER CORRIDOR,

on the third floor, extends around the entire wing. Opening into it are the doors of the rooms of Committees, a Document Room, and a ladies' retiring room. It is handsomely ornamented and tiled. The doors on the inner side lead into the galleries of

THE SENATE CHAMBER.

This magnificent chamber is 112 feet in length, 82 feet wide, and 30 feet high. The ceiling is constructed entirely of cast iron, deeply panelled, with stained glass skylights, and ornamented with foliage, pendants, and drops, of the richest and most elaborate description. The walls and ceiling are painted with strong, brilliant colors, and all the iron work is bronzed and gilded. A cushioned gallery extends entirely around the hall. That portion immediately over the chair of the Vice President of the United States is assigned to the reporters of the press, and a section enclosed by handsome iron railings, and immediately facing the Chair, is for the use of the members of the Diplomatic Corps. The rest of the gallery is divided into sections for ladies and gentlemen. A fine view of the hall can be obtained from any part of it. The space under the gallery is enclosed, and used as cloak rooms, etc. The gallery will seat one thousand persons.

Immediately opposite the main door of the Chamber is the chair of the Vice President of the United States, who presides over the Senate. It is placed on a platform of pure white marble, and behind a desk of the same material Just below this is a similar but larger desk, used by the Secretary of the Senate and his assistants, and at the foot of this table are the chairs of the short-hand reporters of the debates.

The floor rises in the form of an amphitheatre from the space in front of the Secretary's desk to the rear. Along these rows of steps, the registers are built in the floor, and keep the temperature of the Chamber at a fixed heat. The desks of the Senators are of oak, of a handsome and convenient pattern, and are arranged in three semicircular rows facing the Chair. A comfortable armchair is provided for each desk; and sofas and chairs for the convenience of Senators and those entitled to the privileges of the floor, are arranged around the sides of the hall. The choice of seats is determined by drawing lots.

During the day the glass ceiling allows a soft and pleasant light to pass into the chamber, and at night the gas jets, which are arranged above the skylights, shed through the beautiful hall a radiance which can scarcely be distinguished from the light of the sun.

Leaving the galleries, we pass around to the eastern stairway and admire its beauty. Our attention is called to a painting by Rembrandt Peale, which adorns the first landing of the stairway. It represents Washington on horseback, reconnoitring the position of the British Army at Yorktown, previous to opening his lines of approach. He is accompanied by Lafayeytte, Hamilton, Lincoln, Knox, and Rochambeau. This painting does not belong to the Government, though the Senate once voted $4,500 for its purchase.

THE SOUTH WING.

Leaving the North Wing by the south door, we pass through the corridor connecting it with the main building. This is a small but handsome passage The western side is occupied by a dealer in guide-books to the Capitol, diagrams of the two Houses, photographs, &c., and on the opposite side, cakes and pies are sold. We pass through the dark, circular lobby of the old Senate Chamber—reserving that historic hall for description in another chapter—and find ourselves again in the Rotunda. Crossing it, we are in the old South Wing. The room on our right was the old post office of the House, and is now used as a document room. The stairs leading to the gallery of the old hall are on our right also. The door on the left leads to the basement. The door in front opens into

THE OLD HALL OF REPRESENTATIVES.

This beautiful chamber is one of the most interesting apartments in the Capitol. It is semicircular in form, and the ceiling is vaulted. It is 95 feet in length, and the height from the floor to the apex of the vaulted ceiling is 60 feet. The ceiling is panelled and beautifully painted in imitation of that of the Pantheon at Rome. It is supported by twenty-four magnificent columns of American marble, which extend around the western side of the hall, and behind which are the galleries. A handsomely painted cupola rises from the centre of the ceiling and admits the light. At the south side, in the tympanum of the arch, is a colossal statue of Liberty, executed in plaster by Signor Causici, and beneath it is an American eagle in sandstone, modelled from life by Signor Valaperti. The Speaker's chair was formerly placed under this eagle. Over the door by which we enter from the Rotunda, is Franzoni's beautiful statue, representing History, with listening ear, recording the passing events in an open volume. She is standing in a winged car, the wheel of which rests on a globe ornamented with the signs of the zodiac. The wheel forms the face of a clock, the works of which are placed back of it. The whole is cut out of pure white marble, and forms one of the most beautiful ornaments of the Capitol.

The hall is now deserted. The galleries are soon to be removed, and the space in rear of the columns will be thrown open. The House held its sessions here from 1825 until the completion of the new South Wing a few years before the Rebellion, and some of the most interesting events in the history of the country have transpired herein. A great desire was expressed throughout the Union that the hall should be preserved, and Congress, in 1864, set it apart for statuary. By the terms of this law each State is to have the privilege of sending hither two statues of her most eminent sons. It is hoped that in this way a national collection of statues of our great men will be formed; but as yet no such contributions have been made. A copy of Houdon's fine statue of Washington is now the sole occupant of the hall.

Passing under the eagle's outspread wings, and leaving the hall by the southern door, we arrive at the corridor leading from the old building to the new South Wing. At the entrance we behold the famous

BRONZE DOOR.

This magnificent work of art is the most superb of its kind in the world. It was designed and modelled in Rome, in 1858, by Randolph Rogers, the American sculptor, cast at the Royal Foundry at Munich, by F. Von Müller, and completed in 1861. It weighs 20,000 pounds, and cost thirty thousand dollars. It is seventeen feet high, nine feet wide, and is folding or double. The casing is semicircular at the top, and projects about a foot in front of the leaves of the door. Around the casing extends a handsome border, emblematic of conquest and navigation. The key of the arch of the casing is ornamented with a fine head of Columbus, beneath which is the American Eagle with outspread wings. Four figures, representing Asia, Africa, Europe, and America, stand at the top and bottom of the casing. The upper right-hand figure represents Asia, the upper left-hand figure Africa, the lower right-hand figure Europe, and the lower left-hand figure America.

There are eight square panels in the door, besides the semicircular transom panel. Between these panels are ten heads, five on each leaf of the door, "representing historians who have written on his (Columbus') voyages, from his own time down to the present day, ending with Irving and Prescott." On the right and left of the panels are sixteen statuettes, set in niches, representing the most eminent of the contemporaries of the great discoverer. The names of these worthies are marked on the door, and the figures can be easily recognized. In describing them we shall begin with the lower right-hand figure, which is opposite the first part of the story told by the door.

The figure is that of JUAN PEREZ, Prior of the Convent of La Rabida, the most faithful of all Columbus' friends, and through whose influence he was enabled to state his scheme to the Spanish Queen.

The next above is CORTEZ, the Conqueror of Mexico.

The third is DON ALONZO DE OJEDA, a distinguished but unfaithful follower of Columbus.

The top figure is AMERIGO VESPUCCI, after whom the Continent is named.

At the top of the double row, between the two leaves of the door, are PEDRO GONZALES DE MENDOZA, Archbishop of Toledo, and Grand Cardinal of Spain, sometimes called, on account of his immense influence, the "third King of Spain," and POPE ALEXANDER VI. The Cardinal, who was an early patron of Columbus, stands on the right, and the Pope is on the left.

The figures immediately below them are FERDINAND and ISABELLA, King and Queen of Spain, the queen being placed on the right.

Below them are DONNA BEATRIZ DE BOBADILLA, Marchioness of Moya, one of the fast friends of Columbus, and CHARLES VIII., King of France. The artist was unable to find a likeness of the noble lady here represented, and gave to her the features of Mrs. Rogers, his wife.

HENRY VII., of England, and JOHN II., of Portugal, form the lowest pair, the English monarch being on the right. John of Portugal would not listen to Columbus' proposals; but Henry carefully weighed the scheme, which was presented to him by the brother of the discoverer. Before his answer was ready, however, the New World was found.

Martin Alonzo Pinzon stands at the bottom of the left row. He was the captain of the "Pinta," one of the little squadron of Columbus, and enjoyed the honor of being the first to see the "land" of the Western World. Eventually, he betrayed his friend and commander, and died from grief and mortification.

Above him is Bartholomew Columbus, the brother of the great man, and appointed by him Lieutenant-Governor of the Indies. This figure wears the face of the artist, Mr. Rogers, as it was impossible to procure a likeness of the subject.

Above him is Vasco Nunez De Balboa, who, crossing the Isthmus of Darien, with his followers, discovered the Pacific Ocean on the 29th of September, 1510.

Francisco Pizarro, the cruel conqueror of Peru, fills the topmost niche, and completes the group.

We come now to the exquisite pictures embraced in the panels of the door. The work is in *alto relievo*, the figures standing out boldly from the surface. Every detail is perfect, and the gazer's emotions of admiration are strongly mingled with wonder that such an elaborate design has been so faithfully and minutely executed. An oil painting or steel engraving could not more forcibly or perfectly tell the story.

The lowest right-hand panel begins the tale, the transom panel being the central scene.

Panel I. Columbus is expounding his theory of

finding the Indies by sailing due west, to the Council of Salamanca. This Council gravely deliberated the subject, and solemnly concluded that the project was "vain and impossible, and not becoming great princes to engage in on such slender grounds as had been adduced."

PANEL II. Weary and heart-sick, on foot, and leading his son, Diego, a mere lad, by the hand, Columbus sought shelter in the Convent of La Rabida, near Palos. He was without friends or money, and was in despair of having his grand scheme of discovery adopted by any potentate. The monks of the Convent received him kindly, and induced him to remain with them a long time. While here, he stated his plan and hopes to the prior, Juan Perez, who had been Queen Isabella's confessor. Here he also met Alonzo Pinzon, who accompanied him in his subsequent voyage. The prior at once became warmly enlisted in the scheme, and mentioned it to Donna Beatriz de Bobadilla, an attendant and favorite of the queen. The two brought the matter to the queen's notice, and pressed it so thoroughly that her Majesty sent Columbus a sum of money sufficient to enable him to appear at Court, and plead his cause in person. The scene embraced in this panel represents him setting out from the convent to wait upon the queen.

PANEL III. Represents Columbus laying his plan before the King and Queen of Spain. The queen leans forward with eagerness, but the king holds back coldly and doubtingly. The courtiers in the background regard the bold adventurer with looks of mingled scorn and incredulity.

PANEL IV. Is at the top of the right leaf of the door, and represents "The Departure from Palos." The admiral's ships lie waiting in the harbor, while he is standing on the shore, bidding farewell to his son, and confiding him to the care of his friend, the prior.

THE TRANSOM PANEL. This extends across the whole door, is semicircular in form and represents the admiral and his companions landing at San Salvador, and taking formal possession of the island. The banner of Spain is held aloft by Columbus, whose other hand holds a sword. Boats are coming in from the ships in the offing, and a group of natives crouch at the foot of a large tree, gazing at the new comers with wonder and fear.

PANEL V. Is at the top of the left leaf of the door, and represents the first intercourse between the Indians and the discoverers. One of the sailors is seen approaching the admiral, bearing on his shoulders an Indian girl whom he has captured and bound. Columbus sternly rebukes him for his cruelty, and orders the instant release of the girl.

PANEL VI. Represents "The Triumphal Entry into Barcelona." Columbus, having returned from the New World, bringing with him the proofs of his discoveries, is entering the City of Barcelona, amidst the plaudits and cheers of the assembled multitude. The admiral, on horseback, is seen in the foreground.

PANEL VII. Represents the wrongs of Columbus. Don Francisco de Bobadilla, having been sent to the New World, to investigate the charges brought against the admiral by his enemies, took sides against him, and sent him back to Spain in chains. The panel represents the arrival of the admiral in chains, on board the vessel which was to convey him to Europe The officers of the ship, filled with generous indignation, desired to relieve him of his fetters, but he replied, "No; I will wear them as a memento of the gratitude of princes."

PANEL VIII. Represents "The Death of Columbus." On the voyage home, Don Francisco de Bobadilla, and all his crew, were drowned, but the admiral reached Spain in safety, to find the charges against him cleared away. The queen was dead, however, and King Ferdinand was ungrateful to the man who had given a new world to Spain. The admiral was thus left without friends at court.

Landing near San Lucas, Columbus proceeded to Seville. He was poor in purse, and broken down in health, besides being feeble from age. He made repeated efforts to obtain redress for the wrongs done him, but failed in all. He died at Valladolid, May 20th, 1506, being about seventy years old.

The picture represents the chamber in which he died. His friends are gathered around his bed, the last rites of the Church have been received, and a priest holds aloft a crucifix, in order that his last earthly gaze may be fixed upon the symbol of his redemption. The world fast recedes from the dying eyes, the weak lips murmur "*In Manus tuas, Domine, commendo spiritum meum*," "Into Thy Hands, O Lord, I commend my spirit," and the great, grand soul passes into a blessed eternity.

Columbus was buried with great pomp in the Convent of St. Francis, in Valladolid. In 1513 his remains were removed to the Monastery of Las Cuevas, at Seville. In 1536, they were removed from Spain to St. Domingo, where they rested until 1796, when they were carried to Cuba, and interred with magnificent display, in the Cathedral at Havana.

Not yet, however, have they found their proper resting-place. That place is under the dome of the Capitol of the Great Republic of the New World.

The door is indescribably beautiful, and an accurate description of it is an impossibility. It must be seen to be appreciated.

We pass by the door, whose beauties tempt us to linger over it, and through the corridor connecting the new south wing with the main building. A telegraph office on our left affords communication with all parts of the country, and guide-books and photographs are offered for sale at a stand on our right. Leaving this, we enter

THE NORTH CORRIDOR

of the House wing. It is handsomely tiled and frescoed. Immediately in front of us is the principal entrance to the hall of the House, in charge of the efficient and accomplished door-keeper and his assistants. Turning to the left, we pass into the East Corridor, and find ourselves at the foot of one of the marble stairways leading to the gallery. Here stands Powers' famous statue of Jefferson. It is claimed to be an excellent likeness, and is wonderfully like the late General Randolph, of Virginia, who was his grandson, and said to be the image of him. Beyond it we find ourselves in the vestibule communicating with the magnificent Southeast Portico. This is the principal entrance to the wing, and will soon be ornamented with the beautiful bronze door we have described.

On the right of the vestibule is the

POST OFFICE OF THE HOUSE.

This establishment is similar to that of the Senate, but is larger and handsomer. It is conducted in the manner we have described in connection with the Senate Post Office. It opens into the East Corridor, and not into the vestibule.

The South Corridor, immediately in rear of the Hall of the House, is for the private use of Members, and is railed off from the other passages. It is carpeted, and has an air of comfort and elegance. Bronze stairways, similar to those of the Senate wing, lead from this passage to the basement, for the convenience of "Members only." The apartment at the eastern end of this passage is the

LADIES' RECEPTION ROOM.

It is beautifully furnished and carpeted, and the walls and ceilings are ornamented with fine frescoes. Ladies having business with Congressmen are shown into this apartment, while their cards are sent to the Member's seat in the Hall. If he desires to see the lady, he seeks her in the reception room. Lobbyists are well known to the attachés of the chamber, and could the silent walls speak, their revelations would create a sensation in the Federal City, and elsewhere.

The Office of the Sergeant-at-Arms of the House adjoins the reception room. It is handsomely ornamented and comfortably furnished.

THE SPEAKER'S ROOM

is immediately in the centre of the South Wing, and faces the south. It is entered by two doors leading from the private passage. It is a large, elegant apartment, and is for the private use of the Speaker of the House of Representatives. Its carpets and draperies are rich and elegant, and the furniture is costly and tasteful. The ceiling is frescoed, and the walls are adorned with portraits of nearly all the distinguished men who have been speaker of the House since the first organization of Congress.

The adjoining apartment on the west is for the private use of Members of the House. It is elegantly fitted up, and is used as a private reception room.

The western end of the wing is occupied with offices of the Clerk of the House of Representatives. Visitors are not admitted to these offices, or to those of the Secretary of the Senate, at any time, as the officials engaged therein are always busy with the discharge of their duties. Committee Rooms open into the various corridors, and are handsomely furnished and elaborately frescoed.

At the north end of the west corridor is a splendid marble stairway leading to the third floor and the gal

WESTERN TERRACE OF THE CAPITOL.

leries. The wall, from the first landing to the ceiling is ornamented with

LEUTZE'S GREAT PAINTING,

entitled, "Westward the Course of Empire Takes Its Way." It is lighted from a skylight in the roof, and is seen to the best advantage from the upper corridor.

The picture is painted in fresco, but the coloring is softer and more life-like than is often seen in such paintings. The surface is rough, but the work has been done with such a master-hand that it seems as if it were real life. Gaze at it for hours, and the eye will discover some new beauty every hour. However minute it may be, every detail is brought out with the utmost fidelity. The painting is the greatest work of art in the possession of the Government, and one of the grandest in the world.

The scene represents a train of emigrants crossing the Rocky Mountains. They have reached the summit of the range, from which a glorious view stretches out before them to the westward. The adventurers consist of the usual class of emigrants, men, women, and children. There are several wagons and a number of horses in the train. The faces of the emigrants express the various emotions which fill their hearts as they gaze upon the glorious scene before them. Some are full of life and vigor, and hope beams in every feature, whilst others are struggling with sickness and despair. The advance of the train has been momentarily checked by a huge tree which has fallen across their path, and two stout men, under the direction of the leader of the party, who is sitting on his horse, are engaged in hewing it away with axes. Two men have climbed to the summit of a neighboring rocky crag, on which they have planted the banner of the Republic, which is seen flapping out proudly from its lofty perch. In the foreground stands a manly youth, clasping his father's long rifle with a firm grasp, and gazing towards the promised land with a countenance glowing with hope and energy. His sister, hopeful as himself, is seated by her mother's side, on a buffalo robe which has been thrown over a rock. The mother's face is sad, but patient. She knows well the privations, toil, and hardships which await them in the new home-land, but she tries to share the enthusiasm and hope of her children. She clasps her nursing infant to her breast, and listens to her husband, who stands by and points her to the new country where they will all have a home of their own. Her face is inexpressibly beautiful. The rich, warm light of the rising sun streams brightly over the whole scene, and lends to it a magical glow. The legend, "Westward the Course of Empire Takes Its Way," is inscribed over the painting in letters of gold.

An elaborate illuminated border, illustrative of the advance of civilization in the West, surrounds the painting. It is in itself one of the most elaborate works of art in the Capitol.

Beneath the painting, and detached from it, is a view of the "The Golden Gate," the entrance to the harbor of San Francisco.

On the right of the picture is a portrait of Daniel Boone, below which are the lines:

"The Spirit grows with its allotted Spaces:—
The mind is narrowed in a narrow Sphere."

On the left of the painting is a portrait of Captain William Clarke, and the lines:

"No pent up Utica contracts our powers;
But the whole boundless Continent is ours."

From the "guide" of Mr. Wyeth, we learn that the process of affixing the painting to the wall is termed *Stereochrome*, and is sometimes called "Water-glass painting." "The wall is coated with a preparation of clean quartz sand mixed with the least possible quantity of lime; and after the application of this the surface is scraped to remove the outer coating in contact with the atmosphere. It is then washed with a solution of silesia, soda, potash, and water. As the painter applies his colors, he moistens his work by squirting distilled water upon it. When finished it is washed over with the silesia solution. The picture also in its progress is washed with the same solution, and the colors thus becoming incorporated in the flinty coating, the picture is rendered hard and durable as stone itself."

Leutze was paid $20,000 for this magnificent work. We leave the painting with regret, and pass into

THE UPPER CORRIDOR,

which extends entirely around the third floor. The doors on the outer side lead to rooms used by the Committees of the House, and those on the inner side to the galleries of the House. There are nine Committee Rooms opening into this corridor, all of which are splendidly fitted up. The only door on the North side leads to

THE LIBRARY OF THE HOUSE.

This apartment is situated over the corridor connecting the South Wing with the old building. It contains nothing but documents published by order of the House of Representatives, and is for the exclusive use of members.

THE HALL OF THE HOUSE OF REPRESENTATIVES.

Passing through one of the inner doors, we enter the galleries of this magnificent hall, and pause for a while to admire the beauty of its design and the comfort of its arrangements.

The hall is 139 feet long, 93 feet wide, and 36 feet high. It is of sufficient size to afford comfortable accommodations for the increased number of members a century hence. It has an area of 12,927 square feet. The galleries extend entirely around it, and will seat 1200 persons. The seats are cushioned, and present a handsome appearance. That portion opposite the Speaker's chair, is ornamented with a magnificent bronze clock. Immediately over the Speaker's chair, is the Reporters' Gallery, which is for the exclusive use of the Press. It is furnished with handsome private desks, one of which is assigned to the accredited Reporter for some particular journal for the entire session. Some twenty-five or thirty of the leading newspapers of the land are represented here.

The rest of the gallery is divided into sections for the members of the Diplomatic Corps, for ladies, and for gentlemen unaccompanied by ladies. These are separated from each other by iron railings.

The ceiling is of cast-iron, and is similar to that of the Senate Chamber, but handsomer. In the centre is a large skylight containing a number of panels ornamented with the coats of arms of the various States and Territories of the Union. The hall is lighted by means of this skylight. "An arrangement of movable metallic plates, on the principle of Venetian blinds, is placed under the sunny side of the respective roofs of the House and Senate, so that the same amount of light may be admitted all the time." The arrangement of the gas-lights is similar to that of the Senate Chamber. Fifteen hundred burners are placed over the glass of the ceiling, at a distance of an inch apart. Over each one of these passes an incombustible wire. The gas is turned on, an electric current flashed along the wire, and in an instant the hall is filled with a soft, pleasing light, which resembles that of the sun.

Opposite the principal door, are three desks of pure white marble, ranged one above the other. The highest is occupied by the Speaker of the House, the next by the Clerk of the House and his assistants, and the lowest by the official reporters of the debates.

The registers for warming the hall are built in the sides of the different steps into which the floor is divided, and openings in the wall permit the heated air to pass off. The engines which work the heating and ventilating apparatus, are situated in the basement, and are of such power that the air of the entire hall is renewed every five minutes.

The ceiling is magnificently painted, and the walls below the galleries are laid off in large panels, which are to be ornamented with paintings in fresco illustrative of the principal events of the history of the country. One of these panels has already been filled with a magnificent fresco, by Brumidi, illustrating an event which occurred at the Siege of Yorktown.

On the right and left of the Speaker's chair are full length portraits of Washington and Lafayette. The portrait of Washington was painted by Vanderlyn, by order of Congress, and that of Lafayette was presented to Congress by the great Frenchman himself, on the occasion of his visit to the United States in 1825. Both pictures were among the ornaments of the old Hall of Representatives.

The floor rises from south to north, like an amphitheatre. The seats and desks of the members (which are similar to those of the Senators) are arranged along this amphitheatre, in successive circles, facing the Speaker. There are at present 236 of these desks and seats in use. The desks and chairs are all of a handsome pattern, and make a very showy appearance. Seats are chosen by lot at the beginning of every session. The desk of the Sergeant-at-Arms is on the Speaker's right, that of the Door-keeper on his left.

The space under the galleries is enclosed and occupied by two cloak rooms for Members, a Barber Shop for Members, a Folding Room, and Document Room.

There is also a private room for the use of ladies, at the southeastern end of the ladies' gallery.

Leaving the gallery, we descend to the main floor by the eastern stairway, which is constructed of polished Tennessee marble, with splendid columns and balustrades of the same material. It is exactly similar to the western stairway, by which we reach the galleries. On the first landing hangs a fine portrait of General Scott, mounted on his war-horse, by Mr. Edward Troyes. It was painted by order of the Legislature of Virginia, but being unfinished at the time of the breaking out of the Rebellion, was left on the artist's hands. It is to be hoped that Congress will purchase it, as it is the best portrait of the old hero in existence.

THE BASEMENT.

Continuing our descent of the marble stairs, we find ourselves in the basement of the South Wing. We enter a handsome corridor running north and south, lighted by the windows at each end. To the left of the stairway is the vestibule leading to the carriage-way under the southeast portico. Passing westward, the first room across the corridor containing the stairway is fitted up with a row of water closets for gentlemen. The next room contains the

MEMBERS' BATHS.

These consist of a row of handsome closets, finished in black walnut, each of which contains a large bath tub, with hot and cold water for both plunge and shower baths, a wash-stand, and a water closet. The floor is laid with marble tiles, and every thing is upon the handsomest and most comfortable plan. The room is for the use of the members and officers of the House alone, and is one of the most luxurious establishments of its kind in the world. When not in use, it is always open to the inspection of visitors. The next door on the right of the passage leads into

DOWNING'S RESTAURANT.

This establishment occupies two rooms, and is entered from the passage we have been traversing, and from the central corridor. It is handsomely fitted up, and is carried on for the accommodation of the members, officials, and visitors. The proprietor, Mr. George T. Downing, is a gentleman of color, of middle age, and has decidedly the most elegant manners to be seen in the Capitol. He is from New York, where he is well known to all lovers of good living, and has opened in the Capitol one of the best restaurants in the Union. His bill of fare contains every delicacy of the season, and his dishes are served in a style which would not shame Delmonico himself.

THE CENTRAL CORRIDOR

traverses the basement from north to south, and joining the corridors of the old building, which communicate with those of the Senate wing, affords a continuous passage from one end of the Capitol to the other. In the House wing it is 24½ feet broad, and contains thirty monolithic fluted columns of white marble, with

DOWNING S RESTAURANT—CONGRESSM

N LUNCHING WITH THEIR FRIENDS.

capitals foliated with tobacco leaves and buds, which support a panelled ceiling of cast iron.

THE COMMITTEE ROOMS

on this floor are large and beautiful. There are thirteen of them. That on the south of the western entrance is the room of the Committee on Agriculture, and is one of the most beautiful apartments in the Capitol. It is magnificently furnished. The ceiling is arched, and is divided into four compartments containing representations of the four seasons. In the east is Flora scattering the flowers of Spring; in the south, Ceres holds sheaves of ripe grain; in the west, Bacchus is sporting amidst clusters of the vine; and in the north, Boreas brings storms of wind and rain.

The eastern wall is ornamented with a painting in fresco, representing "Cincinnatus Summoned from his Plough to be Dictator of Rome," and on the opposite wall is a companion picture, "Putnam Leaving his Plough to Fight for Independence." The paintings are all by Signor Brumidi.

THE STATUE OF FREEDOM.

Leaving the Capitol, which we have now explored,* we pass out into the grounds, and pause to gaze up at the magnificent bronze statue of Freedom, which surmounts the lantern of the dome, at an altitude of 300 feet above the ground. The statue was finally placed in its present position at 12 o'clock on the

* The old Senate Chamber will be described in the Chapter upon "The Supreme Court."

2d of December 1863, and was greeted with a salute of 35 guns from a field battery on Capitol Hill, and with similar salutes from all the defences of the city. It is 19 feet 6 inches high, and weighs 14,985 pounds. It cost the Government, before being raised to its present position, $23,796 82.

This magnificent statue was the last conception of the lamented Crawford. It represents a female figure in a royal robe, on whose head is placed a helmet cap ornamented with the wings and beak of an eagle. Her right hand rests upon a sheathed sword, the point of which touches the ground at her feet, and her left holds a wreath over a shield ornamented with the Stars and Stripes. Her face is uplifted, and her brow is encircled with a wreath of stars. The face is pure and queenly, and seems glowing with life and noble thoughts. It is one of the noblest works of its kind in the world.

The bronze cast was made by Mr. Clark Mills, at his foundry near Washington.

GREENOUGH'S STATUE OF WASHINGTON.

This statue is placed in the Capitol Park, opposite the Central Portico, east of the building. It represents Washington seated in majesty, his left hand holding a sheathed sword, and his right pointing to Heaven. His figure is naked to the waist, but the right arm and lower part of his body are draped. The figure is about twelve feet high, and the features are massive, but the likeness is correct. Lions' heads and acanthus leaves ornament the chair, against the back of which leans a small figure of Columbus, and one of an Indian Chief. The former suggests the origin and source of our civilization, the other our country in its primitive days.

On the right of the chair, in *basso-relievo*, Phaeton in his chariot, with its steeds, symbolizes the rising sun, with the crest representing the arms of the United States.

The following design, also in *basso-relievo*, ornaments the left side of the chair. The Genius of North America, in the guise of the young Hercules, is strangling the Serpent of Despotism. That of South America, as Iphiclus, crouches to the ground, fearing to enter upon the struggle.

On the back of the chair is the following inscription:

"SIMULACRUM ISTUD
MAGNUM LIBERTATIS EXEMPLUM,
NEC SINE IPSA DURATURUM."

HORATIUS GREENOUGH,
FACIEBAT.

which has been translated:

"This statue cast in Freedom's stately form,
And by her e'er upheld."

HORATIO GREENOUGH, Sculptor.

The statue is of one piece of marble, but is not pure white. Together with its pedestal, it weighs fourteen tons. On three sides of the pedestal are inscribed the lines, "First in War—First in Peace—and First in the Hearts of his Countrymen."

The statue has been much admired, and much

abused. Edward Everett considered it one of the greatest works of sculpture of modern times. Others have denounced it as unworthy of its place; and it is hard to say which are the more numerous, its admirers or those who condemn it.

It was finished in 1843, having been executed in Italy, and was brought to the United States in the ship of the line, Ohio, no merchant vessel being able to transport so large a single bulk. It cost Congress twenty-five thousand dollars.

THE CAPITOL GROUNDS.

The Capitol Park covers an area of several acres. Entering it at the western gate, on Pennsylvania Avenue, the broad walks lead us up several flights of stone stairs, by which we mount from terrace to terrace, until we reach the level of the basement of the building. The hill on which the Capitol stands is between eighty and ninety feet higher than the level of the western entrance. The terracing is handsomely finished in freestone, and gives to the grounds a very elegant appearance. That portion in front of the building is level, and is well laid off. The entire park is ornamented with handsome shrubbery and fountains, and enclosed with an iron railing.

THE COMMISSIONER OF PUBLIC BUILDINGS.

The Capitol, as well as all the other public buildings of the city are in charge of the Commissioner of Public Buildings, who has the care, also, of all the squares, parks, streets, and avenues, under the control of the Government. He is appointed by the President, and it is customary for him to attend at the White House as usher at receptions and State occasions. His office is in the west front of the Old Building of the Capitol, and he is assisted in his duties by several clerks. The position is one of great responsibility, and is always filled by a man of character.

THE CAPITOL POLICE.

form a force distinct from that of the city. They are uniformed, and are on duty in the building and through the grounds, day and night. They are charged with the peace and safety of the establishment, and are required to exercise the utmost vigilance over all parts of it. They are courteous and obliging to strangers, and readily furnish any information desired of them. They have their headquarters in the basement of the Old Building, where they have also a guard-room for the detention of offenders.

IV.

CONGRESS.

The Government of the United States is divided, by the terms of the Constitution, into three coördinate branches—the Legislative, the Executive, and the Judiciary. They are mutually dependent upon each other, and yet each is separate and distinct in itself, and independent of the others. It is the task of the Legislative to enact laws for the government of the country, the duty of the Executive to see that they are enforced, and the province of the Judiciary to pass judgment upon their constitutionality, if called upon to do so.

The Legislative being the initiatory branch of the working of the Government, we shall glance at it first:

The Congress of the United States consists of a Senate and House of Representatives, which bodies are required by the Constitution to assemble, at least once a year, on the first Monday in December, unless they shall by law appoint some other day. Every Congress expires by law at 12 o'clock on the 4th day of March, next following the commencement of its second session. A majority of each House is necessary to constitute a quorum for the transaction of business, but a smaller number may adjourn over from day to day. Either house may adjourn at pleasure, for a period not exceeding three days, but, for a longer time, it is necessary for the consent of the other house to be given. The members of both houses swear to support the Constitution, and, during their terms of office, are privileged from arrest, except for treason, felony, or breach of the peace.

THE SENATE.

The Senate is composed of two Senators chosen from each State by the Legislature, for six years; or, in case of a vacancy, appointed by the Governor, to serve until the next session of the Legislature. The Constitution requires that: "No person shall be a Senator who shall not have attained to the age of thirty years, and been nine years a citizen of the United States, and who shall not, when elected, be an inhabitant of that State for which he shall be chosen."

The Senators are the accredited representatives of the *States*, while the members of the Lower House represent the *people* of the Union.

The Vice-President of the United States is, by virtue of his office, the President of the Senate, and occupies the chair during the deliberations of that body; but the Senate also chooses a president *pro tempore*, who presides in the absence of the regular chairman. The Vice-President has no voice in the deliberations of the Senate, and cannot vote except in case of an equal division, when he has the casting vote. The deliberations of the body are open, except when some special occasion renders it desirable to sit with closed doors. In such case, a Senator offers a resolution that the galleries be cleared, and that the Senate go into secret session. The resolution is then submitted to a vote, and, if carried, the presiding officer warns all persons not connected with the body to leave the hall. Twelve o'clock, noon, is the regular time of meeting, but, late in the session, an earlier hour is generally appointed, in order to accomplish all the business before the house. The officers of the Senate are, a secretary, a sergeant-at-arms, a door-keeper, and assistant door-keepers. They are chosen on the second Monday of the first session of every Congress, but it is not usual to remove officers who have given satisfaction.

The Senate has the sole power to try impeachments, to confirm or reject the nominations of the Executive of persons to fill the various offices under the Government, and to ratify treaties with foreign powers. The Senators are generally men of middle age or advanced in years, and who have filled offices and positions of prominence and trust in their own States and in the Federal Government.

THE HOUSE OF REPRESENTATIVES,

or Lower House of Congress, is composed of members chosen once every two years by the people of the States. Each member is required to be twenty-five years old, seven years a citizen of the United States, and a citizen of the State in which he is chosen. The number of Representatives is limited to 233, and the apportionment of members to population is made every ten years, as soon as possible after the results of the last census are known. Delegates from the Territories are admitted to seats on the floor, but are not entitled to a vote, though they may take part in the debate.

All measures respecting the imposition and collection of taxes must originate in the House of Representatives. Other bills may originate in the Senate, but the consent of both Houses and the approval of the President, or the passage of the measure over the veto of the President, are necessary before any bill can become a law. Each House prescribes the rules for its government, and is the sole judge of the qualifications of its members. Occasionally one House will seek to interfere with the affairs of the other; but such conduct is sure to be met with a sharp rebuke from the offended body.

THE SENATE IN SESSION.

The Senators during their deliberations afford a marked contrast to the Representatives. In the Senate Chamber the proceedings are generally quiet and dignified; in the House noisy and without dignity. Perhaps the members of the Senate, having, as a general rule, passed beyond the frivolities of their younger contemporaries, and having arrived at that period of life when gravity and dignity are natural to man, deserve no great credit for this, after all. Certainly many of them are as bitter and violent partisans as any Member of the House, and there have been occasions when the Senate Chamber has been the scene of contests quite as exciting and disgraceful as any that have ever marked the annals of the House. These occurrences, however, are rare in the north wing of the Capitol. There are some fine-looking men in the Senate, but as a general rule the present members do not in any personal manner indicate their exalted positions.

As the hour for meeting approaches, the lobbies or corridors of the Chamber begin to fill up, visitors drop into the galleries, and Senators straggle into their seats. Finally Mr. Vice-President Wade appears in his seat, and is at once surrounded by members who desire to speak with him. At the moment for assembling, he brushes them by, rises in his place, raps the marble desk with his gavel, and calls the Senate to order. A prayer is offered, and the business of the day begins with the reading of the journal of the previous day's session.

The Senators at once fall to work at their task of paying no attention to what is transpiring in the hall. Some are engaged in conversation, some in writing, some in reading newspapers, the constant rattle of which must make any but old hands nervous.

A number of pages are scattered about the hall. They are sent to and fro by Senators at all times, without regard to what is going on. A Senator wishing to summon a page claps his hands together smartly, with a ringing sound which is heard all over the hall. It is said that a stranger to the place and its customs was once sitting in the gallery, absorbed in the debate, which was warm and rather personal. Suddenly a Senator struck his hands together for the purpose of summoning a page. Our innocent friend immediately supposed that this was designed for applause of the Senator speaking, with whose cause he sympathized warmly, and bringing his hands into play he made a vigorous clapping which threw the whole Senate into a roar of laughter.

A person unaccustomed to the scene is overwhelmed with astonishment at the utter indifference manifested by Senators towards the business of the house. Unless something of more than usual interest is transpiring, little or no attention is paid to any Senator who may have the floor. So deeply does every one seem to be interested in his own affairs, that it is surprising that any Senator should ever be able to vote intelligigently on the majority of the questions presented to the house. Indeed, it is no uncommon thing to see Senators so much absorbed in their private affairs, or in conversation, as to forget to answer to their names when the vote is taken by a call of the house.

PERSONAL SKETCHES.

From the gallery an excellent view can be obtained of the Senate in session. Diagrams are sold in the corridor connecting the North Wing to the old building, by means of which the occupants of the seats in the hall can be distinguished.

That sour-faced, sickly-looking gentleman occupying the chair of the presiding officer, is

SENATOR WADE,

of Ohio, the Acting Vice-President of the United

States, or as he is more familiarly known, "Old Ben Wade." Mr. Wade is in his sixty-ninth year, and is a native of Massachusetts. He began life as a school teacher, but soon after removed to Ohio, and turned farmer. Being of an ambitious nature, he studied law, and was admitted to the bar in 1828. Engaging actively from the first in politics, he has been successively Justice of the Peace, Prosecuting Attorney, State Senator, Judge of the Circuit Court, and United States Senator. He was elected President *pro tempore* of the Senate in March, 1867, and in this way became Acting Vice-President of the United States. He is now serving his third term in the Senate, which expires in March, 1869.

Old Ben's ambition to be President came very near being gratified when President Johnson was impeached last spring, and it is said that not a few of the honorable members of the august Court were sadly afraid of such a termination of the trial, as they feared that once in the White House, Old Ben would secure the Chicago nomination for himself.

As his countenance indicates, Mr. Wade is a man of strong feelings and prejudices, and if he is a good friend, he is also a good hater. He is not given to concealing his opinions of men and measures, but speaks them with a boldness and sharpness which has made him many enemies. He is a thin, wiry man, with a shrewd, nervous face. His voice is shrill, and is that of an invalid. He dresses in black, which gives him a melancholy appearance.

Mr. Wade was amongst the candidates for the

Chicago nomination, and is said to have been disappointed by his lack of success. He was very anxious to ascertain General Grant's political views during the stormy period of the past year, and endeavored to apply the pumping process to the reticent hero. "But," says he, in describing his interview, "whenever I'd talk politics to Gen. Grant, he'd talk horse to me, and I couldn't get a word out of him." Grant quietly remarked, upon hearing of this complaint, that he knew more about horses than Ben. Wade did about politics.

SENATOR MORTON

sits in the second seat from the central aisle in the front row, on the Vice-President's right. He is the Republican Senator from Indiana, and has recently come into prominence in consequence of his views and action respecting the financial question.

Three seats on his left, is

SENATOR POMEROY,

of Kansas, a large, fine-looking man, with a bold, high forehead and a bushy beard. Mr. Pomeroy is one of the leaders of the Republican party, and was particularly active and bold in his advocacy of the measures which terminated in the impeachment of President Johnson. He is a native of Massachusetts, and went to Kansas in 1854, in charge of a colony, as the agent of the New England Emigrant Aid Society. He has figured very prominently in the politics of his adopted State, and is now serving his second term in the Senate.

Two seats to his left is the desk of Mr. William

Pinckney Whyte, the new Senator from Maryland, a handsome man, and an accomplished orator. Mr. Whyte is the successor of

REVERDY JOHNSON,

our present Minister to England. Mr. Johnson was by common consent regarded as the ablest man in the Senate. He was a Democrat in politics, but was so extremely popular with and so much respected by his Republican colleagues that his nomination to the position he now holds was confirmed by the Senate without even the usual reference to a Committee.

We do not design referring to Mr. Johnson as a Senator, however, but have seized the occasion which the mention of his name offers to present the following characteristic anecdotes concerning him, which are related by one of his friends. The writer referred to, says:

"It is difficult to conceive upon what principles, or from what motive diplomatic, William of the State Department selected the gay old Reverdy for his agent to negotiate the Alabama claims. It is whispered here that the appointment came of an after-dinner talk, in which the choice old wines of Reverdy's cellar had more to do with the selection than the sober second thoughts of the Secretary. I do not know how much truth there may be in that suggestion, but I do know that the Hon. Reverdy and the Hon. Billy are open to the suspicion.

"Reverdy Johnson is one of the gayest old gentlemen in or about Washington. I crossed the Atlantic with him once, and, from the time we left port until we entered port, he kept the ship in an excited state over his jests and practical jokes. I was in no condition to enjoy them, for I was deathly sea-sick—so sick I could not stay below, but wrapped in blankets, remained, night and day, rain or shine, on deck. The Collins Line could roll somewhat, and when not rolling, any one of the lot could pitch with remarkable activity. I used to lay upon my back, and repeat all that I could remember to the discredit of old Ocean, and to me would come old Reverdy to worry my head with all sorts of queer suggestions. I told him one day, in response to a question as to what I was thinking about, that I was constructing, or studying the construction of a raft in case of accident.

"'Well,' he said, 'what's your idea?'

"'Do you see those two corpulent old ladies?' I replied.

"'Certainly.'

"'Well, I intend to lash them together and launch, as the ship goes down.'

"'What a lovely design,' he exclaimed, rapturously; 'and I'll get up my trunk and go with you. Do you know that a voyage at sea always brings up the old cannibal in my nature. I want to eat somebody. Now we'll get a carving-knife and cut out steaks, and eat as we sail.'"

"The next day he came to me with a very sad expression on his funny old face.

"'Do you know, P.,' he said, 'your raft is a no go; it won't work.'

"'Why, what's the matter?'

"'One end of our raft says that if any thing happens to this vessel she is going to lock herself up in her state-room.'

"'What is that for?'

"'She says she cannot bear the thought of being eaten by the monsters of the deep.'

"'She don't know that a monster is this minute eyeing her anxiously, with a carving-knife in his coat-tail pocket.'

"After that my friend got the poor old lady near me, and argued seriously upon the wickedness of not making a last effort for her life, by remaining on deck to the last moment. And with a comical look he would ask in an undertone, 'Where have you got your ropes, P.?'

"One night the engines suddenly stopped their tireless throbbing, and the ship lay rocking on the long swell in ominous silence. The wildest alarm ran through the vessel. So many painful accidents had recently occurred that any change brought apprehension. Reverdy was engaged in a quiet game of cards in the cabin. It was nearly midnight, and a majority of the passengers were in their state-rooms. Reverdy heard the alarm, and at once hastened to the state-room of a gentleman from New York, a banker by profession, and one so economical in his way—well, not to put too fine a point on it, so miserly, that Mr. Johnson especially disliked him. Pounding loudly on his door, he roared:

"'Get up, K., get up. Put on a clean shirt. You'll be in — in five minutes.'

"The poor man hurried on his clothes, all the while asking in intense alarm for the cause of the trouble.

"'Haven't you any baggage you want to save?' asked the joker.

"'Yes, yes,' and he seized hold of a long trunk.

"'Never mind your clothes, man; here, I'll help you.'

"And the two, one very *decollette* as to dress, staggered through the cabins and up the winding stairs to the deck. Then his tormentor told him to sit down until he learned something of the condition of affairs. Soon he returned with the welcome intelligence that it was a false alarm.

"'Now, K., you can't go through the cabins in that condition; they are full of ladies. Wait here until I get them out of the way.'

"He left the poor victim in bare legs, sitting on his treasure. The wind blew as it always will blow at sea, and his teeth chattered as the minutes wore away, and no friend returned. At last he procured a blanket from a servant, and, wrapped in this, stalked through the cabins, to find his tormentor quietly at his cards again, quite oblivious to the condition of things he had left on deck."

The old gentleman whose bald head glistens so brightly immediately behind Senator Pomeroy, is Senator Van Winkle, of West Virginia. The gentleman on his right is

SENATOR HENDRICKS,

of Indiana, the leader of the Democrotic party in the

Senate. Mr Hendricks bears his half-century of years well, and is still a young looking man. He is finely made, erect and square-shouldered, and possesses one of the most striking faces in the whole body. He is profoundly learned, a brilliant orator, fearless and eloquent in defence of his principles, and extremely popular with both parties in the Senate. He gained much eclat by his eloquent defence of President Johnson during the impeachment proceedings. He was recently defeated as the Democratic candidate for Governor of Indiana.

Senator Buckalew, of Pennsylvania, one of the ablest members of the body, sits next to him, and the second on the right of the Pennsylvania Senator, is

SENATOR SPRAGUE,

of Rhode Island. He seems a mere boy, as seen from the galleries, and even the glasses and moustache which he sports, fail to give him a manly look. He is the youngest member of the Senate, being only thirty-eight. He has a dissipated, *blasée* appearance, and is said to be rather a lively Senator. He is the Chairman of the Committee on Manufactures, being himself one of the wealthiest and most prominent factors in the Union. When he was only thirty-one years of age, he was elected Governor of his native State. He served, during the first campaign of the late war, with the First Rhode Island Regiment. He is one of the wealthiest men in the country, and is the husband of the eldest daughter of Chief-Justice Chase.

JOHN SHERMAN,

the vigorous young statesman of Ohio, and a brother of our great soldier, sits on Governor Sprague's right. Mr. Sherman is regarded as the coming financial genius of the Senate, and is now the head of the important Committee on Agriculture.

Just back of him, in the third seat from the centre aisle, sits

ROSCOE CONKLING,

of New York. Mr. Conkling is a comparatively new member, but is considered very promising. He is slow and heavy as a speaker, but is regarded as one of the working men of the Senate. He is tall and well made, and has a florid complexion, with light, sandy hair and beard. He resides in Utica, N. Y., which is also the home of Ex-Governor Seymour, the recent Democratic candidate for the Presidency. These gentlemen are brothers-in-law. This relationship gave rise to an amusing incident during the past campaign. A serenade was given to Governor Seymour, soon after his nomination, by the townspeople of Utica. Senator Conkling was at his brother-in-law's quarters at the time, and was soon called on for a speech. He complied with the request, and proceeded good-naturedly to state that he should not vote for his relative, as General Grant was his choice. An Irishman in the crowd, not understanding how men so closely allied could differ in their political views, and evidently thinking Mr. Seymour the bigger fish of the two, and entitled to the support of all his relatives, here cried out wrathfully, "Arrah! shut up, ye spalpeen. Youv'e gone back on your own brother-in-law." This sally was greeted by the throng with a shout of laughter, in which Mr. Conkling joined heartily.

GARRETT DAVIS,

of Kentucky, sits two desks on the left of Mr. Conkling, and by the side of the other Kentucky Senator, Mr. McCreery. Mr. Davis is regarded as the most querulous and critical member of the Senate. It is his fortune to dissent from almost every measure brought forward, and to assail it in no measured terms.

The seat of Mr. Saulsbury, of Delaware, is the second on the left of Mr. Davis. That gentleman is rarely to be seen in a sitting posture, however, as he passes the most of his time in pacing up and down the Chamber, being of too nervous a temperament to remain still for any length of time.

Three seats on his left is Mr. Patterson, of Tennessee, the son-in-law of President Johnson.

Senators Ferry, of Connecticut, Conness, of California, Morrill, of Vermont, and Anthony, of Rhode Island, are the prominent men occupying the front row of seats on the left of the Chair.

In the second row, the seat adjoining the central aisle is that of Senator Dixon, of Connecticut. Next to him, sits

SENATOR FESSENDEN,

of Maine, the Chairman of the Finance Committee,

and Judge Chase's successor as Secretary of the Treasury. He is sixty-three years old, but one of the finest-looking men in the Senate. His commanding abilities have made him one of the leaders of the Republican party, and his unspotted purity of character has given him more moral weight in the deliberations of the Senate than any other member possesses. Although a stern Republican, he voted for the acquittal of President Johnson in the impeachment trial, and not all the threats or blandishments of his party could move him in the slightest from what he regarded as the path of duty. Mr. Lincoln's estimate of him may be inferred from the following incident, related by Mr. F. B. Carpenter:

Mr. Chase had resigned, and it was necessary to select a successor. Mr. Lincoln decided to nominate Mr. Fessenden for the position. "The next morning he went to his office and wrote the nomination. John Hay, the Assistant Private Secretary, had taken it from the President on his way to the Capitol, when he encountered Senator Fessenden on the threshold of the room. As Chairman of the Finance Committee, he had called thus early to consult with the President, and offer some suggestions. After a few moments' conversation, Mr. Lincoln turned to him with a smile, and said: 'I am much obliged to you, Fessenden, but the fact is, I have just sent your own name to the Senate for Secretary of the Treasury. Hay had just received the nomination from my hand as you entered.' Mr. Fessenden was taken completely by surprise, and, very much agitated, protested his inability to accept the position. The state of his health, he said, if no other consideration, made it impossible. Mr. Lincoln would not accept the refusal as final. He very justly felt that with Mr. Fessenden's experience and known ability at the head of the Finance Committee, his acceptance would go far towards re-establishing a feeling of security. He said to him, very earnestly, 'Fessenden, *the Lord has not deserted me thus far, and He is not going to now*,—you must accept!'"

Two seats on his right sits the burly Massachusetts Senator Henry Wilson, whose immense frame looms up boldly when he rises to speak. Mr. Wilson's successful rise from a shoemaker's bench to the seat of a Senator of the United States affords a brilliant example to our young men, and splendidly illustrates this glorious feature of our system of Government.

LYMAN TRUMBULL,

of Illinois, sits two seats on Wilson's right. He was one of the original Republicans, when to bear that name required more patriotism and courage than it does now. He was the colleague of Stephen A. Douglas, and many a tilt have these two intellectual giants had in this beautiful Chamber. He is one of the ablest and most upright members of the Senate. He is a native of Connecticut, but removed to Illinois when a young man.

Mr. Frelinghuysen, the handsome New Jersey Senator, and one of the marked men of the Senate, sits on Judge Trumbull's left.

The tall, gray-haired man sitting two desks on Mr. Frelinghuysen's right, in the back row, is

SIMON CAMERON,

of Pennsylvania. Nearly fifty years ago, a barefooted boy floated down the Susquehanna River on a raft, and arrived at Harrisburg, Pennsylvania. He came from the northern part of the State, and belonged to a large family. He had all his earthly goods tied up in his red and yellow pocket-handkerchief. He sought employment immediately upon his arrival at Harrisburg, and at length after a good deal of difficulty obtained it in a printing-office, as apprentice. From an apprentice, he rose to be a journeyman; then to be a reporter in the State Legislature—then an editor.

The barefooted boy had thus worked his way against obstacles which only the poor know; but he at length began to realize the fruits of his patient toil and privation. He became printer to the State, and by frugal management was soon enabled to accomplish the object nearest to his heart—the establishment of his mother in a home surrounded with every comfort she could desire.

His brothers were his next care; and like Napoleon, he had a strong arm with which to aid them—an indomitable perseverance that nothing could successfully obstruct. In a few years they, too, with his sisters, were independent of the world. The once barefooted boy was in possession of affluence, and surrounded by a young and affectionate family.

But he did not stop here. He was the friend of

the friendless, the patron of merit, the encourager of industry. He rose in honor and in office, until the poor barefooted boy, who entered a printing-office hungry and weary, and laid down his little bundle on a pile of wet paper, was elected a Senator in the Congress of the United States, and afterwards chosen Secretary of War by President Lincoln. Such has been the life of Simon Cameron.

During his term in the War Department, General Cameron made many enemies, and the President was literally besieged with requests to remove him. Speaking of the visit of a delegation for this purpose, Mr. Lincoln said:

"They talked very glibly, especially a man named G——, from Boston, and I finally told them as much —adding, nevertheless, that I was not convinced. 'Now, gentlemen,' said I, 'if you want General Cameron removed, you have only to bring me *one proved* case of dishonesty, and I promise you his "head;" but I assure you I am not going to act on what seems to me the most unfounded gossip.'"

Zack Chandler, of Michigan, is in the second seat on Cameron's left, and Senator Nye, of Nevada, in the second seat on Chandler's left.

The next seat is that of

CHARLES SUMNER,

of Massachusetts.

The merits of no other Senator have been disputed as warmly as those of Mr. Sumner. He is confessedly one of the most accomplished men in the Senate. His enemies, however, charge him with being lacking in practical sense, and in natural ability—qualities which his friends claim for him in the highest degree. The late Count Gurowski said of him: "Sumner is a little afraid of losing ground with the English guardians of civilization. Sumner is full of good wishes, of generous conceptions, and is the man for the millennium. Sumner lacks the keen, sharp, piercing appreciation of common events. * * * Sumner attributes to envy his anomalous position with the best men on the Republican side. He cannot understand that it is his scholarly pretensions which render him unpalatable to his colleagues. His cold rhetoric falls powerless at their feet, and no Senator envies him his fertility in random quotations."

Mr. Sumner is the Chairman of the Committee of Foreign Affairs. His position naturally brings him into constant intercourse with the State Department, and it is said that a decided jealousy exists between Mr. Seward and himself. He was much esteemed by Mr. Lincoln; and, to his honor be it said, was one of the few friends who remained true to the widow and family of the martyr, after power and patronage had passed out of their hands.

SENATOR MORGAN,

of New York, sits on Mr. Sumner's left. He is one of the finest looking men in the body, and is very wealthy. As Governor of the State of New York, during the Rebellion, he rendered efficient service to the country, in furnishing men for the army. He is very popular in the Senate, in which body he possesses considerable influence.

SENATOR YATES,

of Illinois, sits on Mr. Morgan's left. He was Governor of his State at the time of the breaking out of the Rebellion, and was the first to assign General Grant to duty. It is his boast that he "made Grant," though the country does not thoroughly appreciate the boast. Mr. Yates has the appearance of a well-to-do parson, and would easily pass for one, were it not that his face too plainly indicates a certain weakness for which he feels called upon to apologize, periodically, to his "dear constituents." Mr. Yates is an able man, and is worthy of a better fate than that which he courts.

The last seat in this row is that of

SENATOR DOOLITTLE,

of Wisconsin. The name, in this case, is not indicative of the character of the man, as Mr. Doolittle is one of the most industrious men in the Senate. He is also a man of great ability, and unblemished integrity, and, to his credit be it said, will retire a poor man at the end of his term. He is a Democrat in politics, and was one of the ablest champions the President possessed during the recent impeachment proceedings.

CHOOSING SENATORS.

The post of United States Senator is one of the proudest in the Government, and its occupant is the dispenser of much power and patronage. Consequently, the position is much sought after. A vacancy is sure to cause a scramble amongst the politicians. All sorts of arguments and persuasions are brought to bear upon the various legislatures charged with the duty of making a choice of Senators. The newspapers for the coming year will be full of disclosures upon this subject, as a number of Senators are to be chosen before the spring. Some of the practices resorted to, to secure the elections, will be found to be not the most upright in the world.

THE HOUSE IN SESSION.

Some years ago, an English traveller wrote as follows, concerning the sessions of the House of Representatives in the old Hall:

"These beautiful chambers are calculated to make an impression very favorable to the dignity of the deliberative assemblies which occupy them; and the general appearance of the members does not materially impair it. Many of them have the appearance of English country gentlemen; and a considerable portion of them are lawyers, who carry in their faces those marks of intellectual exertion, which seem to plead some apology for having sacrificed little to the graces. Some of the members from the western country, indeed, would look a little queer in our House of Commons. The proceedings, both of the Senate and House of Representatives, seem to be conducted with great order and decorum, and with a courtesy and attention to the feelings of honorable gentlemen, which I was not prepared to expect. The style of their best speakers is fluent, forcible, and perspicuous; and in cases where it is not possible that their arguments should be sound, they seldom fail to be specious and acute. My friend, who would, I believe, be considered the first authority on the subject, told me that he considered their two prominent faults to be, a proneness to engage in dissertation, and to pursue the investigation of a difficult question, which had been started incidentally in the course of the debate, without ascertaining whether its solution was absolutely necessary to the original discussion. He regards the frequent change of members in the House of Representatives as inimical to the acquisition of that knowledge, or the formation of those habits, so desirable in a deliberative assembly; and deprecates the custom into which they have fallen of referring every thing to committees, as tending, in effect, to leave to the decision of a few, many questions which ought to be argued upon general principles, by the House at large.

"It is usual for ladies to attend when any interesting debate is expected. Ordinarily, they are admitted only into the gallery; but instances have occurred, when they have been allowed a seat on the floor. The reporters for the newspapers have a seat assigned them behind the Speaker's chair. Except when some remarkably good speaker has possession of the floor, the members, instead of attending to what is spoken, are busy in conversation, in writing letters, rapping the sand off the wet ink with their knuckles, rustling the countless newspapers which deluge the House, locking or unlocking their drawers, or moving up and down the avenues which divide the ranges of seats, and kicking before them, at every step, printed reports, letter covers, and other documents strewed on the floor. A couple of active little boys are always seen running to and fro with armfuls of papers, or carrying slips of writing from members to the Chair, or from member to member. Whenever any one rises to speak, who, there is reason to infer, from experience or from internal evidence, will be lengthy, one of these little Mercuries flies off for a glass of water, which he places on the orator's desk."

What Congress was then, it is now, except that the confusion and noise in the hall have increased. The number of pages has been multiplied several times, and are still kept quite busy. Sometimes the Speaker has hard work to preserve order in the House. Members are very unruly, and give the Chair a world of trouble. You see them obstructing the aisles, talking and laughing in a tone which is audible in any part of the hall, or sitting with their feet elevated on their desks, oftentimes fast asleep. If any thing of interest attracts them away from the hall, they leave it in such numbers that the House is often without a quorum, and the Speaker is forced to compel their attendance by the Sergeant-at-Arms.

DISGRACEFUL SCENES IN THE HOUSE.

There are bitter rivalries and heartburnings between the members, and these often lead to outbreaks as fierce and disgraceful as those which marked the old slavery contests before the war. As a general rule, the disputes on the floor are not carried into private life, and political enemies are often warm friends in private; but there are frequent instances where differences, not only between Republican and Democrat, but between men of the same party, have been followed by the fiercest and most uncompromising hostility at all times and in all places. The lie is given freely on the floor of the House, and members bandy the most insulting epithets with true bar-room proficiency. The disgraceful scenes which marked the quarrel of Messrs. Donnelly and Washburne, last summer, are of frequent occurrence in Congress. The Thirty-ninth Congress, which expired on the 4th of March, 1867, is famous as having been the most orderly and respectable body that has assembled in the Capitol for many years. Yet even in this model assemblage, the following shameful occurrences took place. The record is taken from Barnes' History of the Thirty-ninth Congress:

"On one occasion, Mr. Chanler, of New York, submitted a resolution, 'that the independent, patriotic, and constitutional course of the President of the United States, in seeking to protect, by veto power, the rights of the people of this Union against the wicked and revolutionary acts of a few malignant and mischievous men, meets with the approval of this House, and deserves the cordial support of all loyal citizens of the United States.'

"For introducing this resolution, the House voted to censure Mr. Chanler, as having attempted a gross insult to the House.

"Before the vote was taken, Mr. Chanler said: 'If by my defiance I could drive your party from this hall I would do so; if by my vote I could crush you, I would do so, and put the whole party, with your leader, the gentleman from Pennsylvania (Mr. Stevens), into that political hell surrounded by bayonets, referred to by him in his argument on Thursday last.' * * *

"In February, 1866, Mr. Rousseau, in the course of a speech on the Freedmen's Bureau Bill, made the remark, 'If you intend to arrest white people on the *ex-parte* statement of negroes, and hold them to suit your convenience for trial, and fine and imprison them, then I say that I oppose you; and if you should so arrest and punish me, I would kill you when you set me at liberty.'

"To this Mr. Grinnell, of Iowa, replied: 'I care not whether the gentleman was four years in the war on the Union side or four years on the other side, but I say that he degraded his State and uttered a sentiment I thought unworthy of a Union officer when he said that he would do such an act on the complaint of a negro against him.'

"To this Mr. Rousseau, on the following day, replied: 'I pronounce the assertion that I have degraded my State and uttered a sentiment unworthy of an American officer, to be false, a vile slander, and unworthy to be uttered by any gentleman upon this floor.'

"Some months after this, Mr. Rousseau, in a public speech delivered in New York City, denounced Mr. Grinnell as a 'pitiable politician' from Iowa. In a speech made in the House on the 11th of June, Mr

Rousseau said of Mr. Grinnell: 'I do not suppose that any member of this House believed a word he said. When a member can so far depart from what every body believes he ought to know and does know is the truth, it is a degradation, not to his State, but to himself.'

"'When any man,' replied Mr. Grinnell, 'I care not whether he stands six feet high, whether he wears buff, and carries the air of a certain bird that has a more than usual extremity of tail, wanting in the other extremity—says that he would not believe what I utter, I will say that I was never born to stand under an imputation of that sort.

"'The gentleman begins courting sympathy by sustaining the President of the United States, preparatory to his assault upon me. Now, sir, if he is a defender of the President of the United States, all I have to say is, God save the President from such an incoherent, brainless defender, equal in valor in civil and in military life. His military record—who has read it? In what volume of history is it found?'

"Mr. Rousseau determined to resent the insult which he conceived to be offered him in this speech by inflicting a bodily chastisement upon Mr. Grinnell. On the morning of June 14th, Mr. Rousseau informed a military friend of his purpose of flogging Mr. Grinnell. The person so informed procured a pistol and waited in the Capitol until the close of the day's session, in order to be present at the flogging and see 'fair play.' Two other friends of Mr. Rousseau, also armed with pistols, happened to be present when the scene transpired. While Mr. Grinnell was passing from the House through the east portico of the Capitol, he was met by Mr. Rousseau, who, in an excited manner, said. 'I have waited four days for an apology, for words spoken here upon this floor.'

"'What of that?' asked Mr. Grinnell.

"'I will teach you what of that,' said Mr. Rousseau, who then proceeded to strike Mr. Grinnell about the head and shoulders with a rattan, stopping occasionally to lecture him, and saying, 'Now, you d—d puppy and poltroon, look at yourself.'

"After receiving half a dozen blows, Mr. Grinnell exclaimed, 'I don't want to hurt you.' *

"'I don't expect you to hurt me, you d—d scoundrel,' said Mr. Rousseau, 'but you tried to injure me upon the floor of the House. And now look at yourself; whipped here; whipped like a dog; disgraced and degraded! Where are your one hundred and twenty-seven thousand constituents now?'

"A Committee was appointed to investigate this disgraceful affair. In just one month after the transaction, a report was presented, signed by Messrs. Spaulding, Banks, and Thayer, stating the facts in the case, and recommending the expulsion of Mr. Rousseau. They also presented a resolution to express disapproval of the reflections made by Mr. Grinnell upon the character of Mr. Rousseau. The 'views of the minority' were also presented by Messrs. Raymond and Hogan. They recommended that the punishment of

* The reader will not fail to be impressed with the exceedingly amiable manner in which Mr. Grinnell received his castigation.—*Author.*

Mr. Rousseau should be a public reprimand by the Speaker. After a protracted discussion, the House came to a final decision. The motion to expel, requiring two-thirds, failed by a few votes—the motion by which the Speaker was directed to publicly reprimand Mr. Rousseau was carried by a vote of 89 to 30. There were not enough in favor of the motion to disapprove of Mr. Grinnell's remarks, to call the ayes and noes. Mr. Rousseau endeavored to evade the execution of the sentence by sending his resignation to the Governor of Kentucky. The House declared that a Member could not dissolve his connection with the body under such circumstances, without its consent. On the 21st of July, the execution of the order of the House having been demanded, Mr. Rousseau appeared at the bar, when the Speaker said, 'General Rousseau, the House of Representatives have declared you guilty of a violation of its rights and privileges in a premeditated personal assault upon a member for words spoken in debate. This condemnation they have placed on their journal, and have ordered that you shall be publicly reprimanded by the Speaker at the bar of the House. No words of mine can add to the force of this order, in obedience to which I now pronounce upon you its reprimand.'"

PARTY DISCIPLINE

is very strict in Congress. Each party has an acknowledged leader, who directs its movements, and is most prominent in attacking or resisting the other party. Thaddeus Stevens was the leader of the Republican party for some years before his death, and any one who has ever seen the manner in which the grim old man conducted the affairs of his party, will bear out the assertion that he was a very tyrant. He could not bear the term "conservative Republican," and his severest denunciations were reserved for that wing of his party. In times of emergency he would call on every Republican in the House to sustain the party measures, and boldly defy any conservative to oppose them on pain of being "read out" of the Republican organization. At such times his manner would be expressive of the bitterest sarcasm, and his voice, cold and trenchant as steel, would strike terror to the hearts of his weaker followers. They had no choice but to obey him, as they knew he did not threaten in vain. During the impeachment proceedings he literally drove his party forward, and terrified the conservative members into the support of measures to which they were utterly opposed. He has left a void behind him, and his followers are casting about to-day for some one to fill his place. A recent Washington letter, says:

"There is a contest in progress between Messrs. Schenck and Washburne as to which of those two gentlemen shall have the leadership of the party in the House. It has always heretofore been the understanding and custom of that body that the Chairman of the Committee on Ways and Means should, by virtue of that position, be the recognized leader of his party in Congress. But when, on account of the uncertainties and disabilities of ill-health, old age, and other circumstances, which rendered the duties devolving upon the head of the Committee on Ways and Means too heavy and full of responsibility to be trusted to the late Thaddeus Stevens, it was thought advisable to make a division of the Committee, as it originally stood, and out of it take the Committees on Appropriations and Banks and Banking, to the former of which Mr. Stevens was designated as chairman, while Mr. Schenck was appointed as chairman of the original committee, then, as an act of courtesy simply to the Pennsylvania veteran, he was still allowed to retain the leadership of the House until his death.

"Now, since that event, the privilege would fall back, according to the old and established order, to Mr. Schenck; but Mr. Washburne, who has preceded Mr. Stevens as Chairman of the Committee on Appropriations, assumes to have become successor to the party leadership likewise, which was only continued to Mr. Stevens as a matter of general friendly consideration and respect. In consequence there is quite a contest between Schenck, to whom the privilege should lapse, according to custom, and Washburne, who is not content to walk in the dead man's shoes, but wants to have on his overshoes (which he thinks fit him) also. As the presumed mouthpiece of the incoming President he has a certain weight of authority on his side, but the quiet caution, firmness and business tact, shrewdness and vigor of General Schenck give him such advantages that, so far, it is a neck-and-neck run, with vibrations on either side and the chances, I am told, in favor of Schenck."

The leader of the Democratic party in the House is Mr. James Brooks, of New York, one of the proprietors and editors of *The Evening Express*, of that city He is a tall, fine-looking man, and one of the ablest and most accomplished parliamentarians in the House.

The men acting as leaders of their respective parties, are always on the alert. It is their business to prevent strife amongst their followers. For the sake of success, they exert themselves to heal these breaches when made, and are usually successful in preserving at least an outward appearance of harmony. The reader will remember the fierce quarrel between Messrs Butler and Bingham, which was smoothed over for the sake of success in the impeachment trial.

Party is supreme in both Houses of Congress, and legislation is shaped entirely with a view to perpetuate that supremacy. Congressmen support men and measures they dare not defend to their constituents, because they think such measures will benefit the party. No matter how injurious to the country at large a measure may be, if the party in power needs it, it is passed. Democrats and Republicans are alike guilty of such conduct. Members elect, fairly chosen by their constituents, not unfrequently find their seats contested by the beaten candidate, who is in sympathy with the party in power. Feeling sure that the lawfully expressed wishes of the district they represent will not be disregarded, they do not concern themselves about the effort to turn them out, and are startled by a report from the Committee on Elections that they are not entitled to their seats. The result is that they are unseated, and the contesting members, fairly beaten at the polls, put in their places, not because Congress wishes to enforce the will of the people sending Representatives to Washington, but because it wishes to secure one more vote for the party in power.

THE FRANKING SWINDLE.

One of the privileges accorded by law to the Members of Congress, is the right to send through the mails his correspondence, and other legitimate mail-matter, free of charge. In order to secure this free transportation, he must endorse his name and rank on the cover of the package. This privilege was originally designed to cover the official correspondence of Congressmen with officials of the Government, and with their constituents, but, of late years, it has been so much abused that it has been put to uses never dreamed of before. Packages occupying an entire mail-bag have been sent by Congressmen with tough consciences, as franked matter. It is said that sewing machines have been sent home to their wives by members in this way, during the existence of the privilege; and that certain members have sent their dirty linen home to be washed, under the cover of their franks, in order to save expense. Says the *New York Tribune*, of a recent date:

"We know that Mr. Brooks disseminates circulars advertising the *New York Express*, by means of his printed frank; and Mr. Demas Barnes sends out price-lists of his "Mustang Liniments" and "Soothing Syrups." Congressman O'Neill, of Pennsylvania, has recently been found franking all over the country a good thick pamphlet published by the Union League of Philadelphia, and labelling it, by a pleasing freedom of language, a "Pub. Doc." We dare say, the book contained a great deal more useful information than nine out of ten documents issued from the Government Printing Office; but it was not a public document, for all that, and if Mr. O'Neill wanted to send copies of it through the mail, he ought to have paid the postage, as any private gentleman would. During the last election canvass, it was common for Congressmen who were candidates for reëlection to frank ballots and addresses all through their districts; and we know of at least one case in which, by some process of legerdemain which we do not profess to understand, the printed frank of a candidate was used to cover the ballots of his opponent."

Whole tons of matter are sent through the mails in this way, every day, the cost of transporting which the people have to pay. No Congressman can spare the time to write his frank on all the documents and parcels he sends off, and the practice has become common of having a stamp of his frank made. This is easily managed, and is often loaned out to political organizations and to friends; and whole tons of matter which the law never designed to make free, are thus thrown into the mails at the public expense.

The following correspondence, which recently appeared in the *New York Tribune*, will explain one of the abuses of this system:

"*To the Editor of the Tribune.*

"SIR: An article in your paper of the 29th, from the Hon. W. S. Lincoln, demands a reply on our part, having been singled out as parties who have abused the franking privilege, or rather used it without permission. The charge is too sweeping, and would naturally lead the reader to suppose an intentional wrong by us. Let us present the facts. Being connected with a political organization where the facsimile frank of Mr. Lincoln was in constant use, and not entertaining a doubt but with his consent, as similar franks were used by nearly all the different political organizations, furnished with the consent of different members of both parties, in order to transmit documents, we simply did as many others, with this difference, that ours was a business that increased rather than diminished the postal revénue, our publications being sent, in a large degree, through the mails, and every circular sent tending to increase the demand and benefit the Department. A large number of the franked envelopes were left in our hands just before the close of the campaign, and in these our circulars were placed, and transmitted to different parties. As the use of the stamp referred to was authorized by the Hon. M. C. for the benefit of the committee, we certainly must claim exemption from the serious charges made by him. The general use of stamps of this character, authorized by so many different parties, of both political organizations, certainly is detrimental to the public service, but we are prepared to show that in this instance at least it has been beneficial, and therefore repel the charge made against us.

"DIMMICK & Co.

"NEW YORK, December 30, 1868."

" *To the Editor of the Tribune.*

"SIR: In answer to the card of Messrs. Dimmick & Co., and your notice of the same, allow me to say, that, in accordance with a custom long since established by Senators and Representatives, I franked envelopes for the organization known as the "Grant and Colfax Boys in Blue," during the last campaign, with the express understanding that they should be used only for political purposes. I knew the officers of this organization to be gentlemen of honor, and did not for a moment suppose any person connected with the same would violate this agreement. When, in November, I found that Messrs. Dimmick & Co. were "flooding the mails" with circulars under my frank, I had not even a suspicion that any member of that firm had ever had any connection with the "Boys in Blue." I received large numbers of these circulars through the Dead Letter Office, and reported them to the Postmaster-General, and to the Postmaster at New York, and certainly had no right to suppose this firm (which I had never heard of) was in any way connected with the organization alluded to. The fac-simile of members of Congress has been used all over the country for general political purposes, and certain parties have sought to take advantage of this to subserve their own interests, which proves the privilege to be liable to great abuse; therefore, let us abolish it.

"Very respectfully yours,

"W. S. LINCOLN.

"WASHINGTON, D. C., January 2, 1869."

The mails are at present flooded to such an enormous extent, with letters and documents stamped with the franks of Congressmen, that many disreputable persons have had forged stamps made, and use them constantly, for the purpose of circulating their own advertisements and circulars, as they well know that it will be, in nine cases out of ten, impossible for any post-office official to detect the forgery. Of course, Congressmen are not responsible for such acts as these, except so far as their own abuses of the franking privilege have opened the way for them.

CONGRESSIONAL BUNCOMBE.

Speech-making is a weakness of Congressmen. Every Senator or Member must make one speech during the session, if no more, in order that he may have it printed and sent home to his constituents; and every possible occasion is seized upon with avidity. For the honor of the country, nine out of ten of these speeches had better be unspoken. They are so many empty words; for the Congress of the United States, though it has many able men, does not, as a whole, represent the intelligence or the eloquence of the nation. There are few really good speakers in either body

CONGRESSIONAL "BUNCOMBE."

Perhaps the very best speeches that have been delivered in the House, for many months, were com prised in the bitter passage between Messrs. Donnelly and Washburne, last summer. The affair was outrage- ous, indecent; but there was genuine wit, fire, and eloquence on both sides.

The occasion of the death of a member of either House is seized upon for a display of words. This was forcibly demonstrated in the eulogies upon the late Thaddeus Stevens. The speeches, with one or two exceptions, would not have done honor to a village debating society; and even the best of them failed to paint the old man in his true character. All was fulsome flattery, from which he would have shrunk in disgust. He was no coward, either morally or physically, whatever his other shortcomings were, and he never tried to hide or gloss over his faults. Says a letter written from Washington, the day the eulogies were delivered:

"The Cave of the Winds has for hours been blowing a solemn dirge over the demise of Old Sarcastic, commonly called the Old Man Eloquent, or the Great Commoner. I suppose my friend Mungen might be styled the great uncommoner. What the old scratch makes people indulge in this sort of stuff bothers me. The old man eloquent is a quotation from Milton, and when first applied to John Quincy Adams was well enough, but it is not applicable to the late Thaddeus. He was seldom, if ever, eloquent. He was sarcastic and bitter, and could make the fur fly when so disposed; but to please, penetrate, and persuade, that was not his forte.

"He was a grand old man, in his way, but one would never find it out from the flood of sickening eulogy that rolled out to-day. Good Lord! when will we have done with these windy platitudes? How old Thad. would have grinned, had he been present, and how he would have collapsed the pots of honey with a few words of sarcasm edging the lump of truth! How a little truth about the old man would have startled the House! Had his daily and nightly life been photographed for a moment, how each member would have started, as if a slander was being newly promulgated! And yet, each mother's son of them all knew the story of his life. And so we make history. And in such history we lose the lesson and belittle the actor. Take these eulogies, and make up from them, if you can, the real life of Thad. Stevens, as he hobbled into the House from a night of cards, and hour after hour frightened and coaxed, and bullied and controlled the members, and controlled them along the path of humanity. His acts were grand, but his ordinary life was not grand, nor even good. And yet, taking it all in all, it was human, and when we see what he did, it is well to know, for his credit, that, to accomplish the good, he had to swing out from much that was bad in his own nature. When will these people learn, that while we sympathize with, and even love defective humanity, we cannot comprehend, nor admire, and far less love the gods of their poor creation.

"Poor old Thad.—he left a vacancy in the House of Representatives that cannot well be filled.

"'Who will carry me, boys,' he said, with his grim smiles, to the men who brought him to the Capitol for the last time on their shoulders, 'who will carry me when you are dead?'

"The grass is not yet green above his grave, and we are forgetting him in these high-wrought eulogies."

PERSONAL SKETCHES.

It seems strange, but it is a fact that there are proportionately more able men in the House than in the Senate. In referring to them it will be impossible to point them out by their seats, as it is very rare that they are seen in their proper places. They are scattered about the hall in such utter confusion that it is almost impossible to make use of any diagram.

SPEAKER COLFAX.

The Speaker, except when the House is in Committee of the Whole, is usually to be found in the Chair, though he too takes flight from his lofty perch occasionally. He generally dresses in black broadcloth, a style much affected by both Houses of Congress, and which gives to them a decidedly funereal appearance. None of Mr. Colfax's portraits do him justice. They make him too dark, for the sunny, genial expression of his face, which is enhanced by the light color of his hair and beard, is his greatest outward attraction. He has a bright and winning air, which makes you think him a happy man, as he no doubt is, having but recently won the Vice-Presidency and an accomplished wife. His personal dignity is very great, but has no haughtiness about it. His pleasant, cheerful expression won him during the recent campaign the nickname of "Smiler." He is nearly forty-six years old. He is a native of the city of New York, and was born a poor boy. He has reached his present position by his own unaided efforts, and next March will enter upon the duties of the second office in the gift of the people. He makes an excellent Speaker, and is very popular with both parties in the House. It is no slight task to preside over the deliberations of so unruly a body as the House of Representatives, but Mr. Colfax has for nearly six years discharged his duties with perfect success.

As a general rule, he follows the example of the Members of the House, and engages in conversation with some one. His inattention is only seeming, however, for he is closely watching the House all the while. A member no sooner rises than the Speaker's quick eye discovers him and announces his name. Let a dozen rise together, and the Speaker, although apparently engrossed in his conversation, will in nine cases out of ten single out the right man and assign the floor to him. Members rarely quarrel with his decisions, as they know them to be just. Long experience has taught the Speaker patience in dealing with the humors of the House. A moderate amount of disorder and confusion will draw from him only a slight rebuke, but frequently the noise increases to such a degree that the voice of the member on the floor is almost drowned. Again, the Members crowd the aisles to such an extent that the Chair cannot distinguish gentlemen rising to claim the floor from those who have no desire to speak. Then the Speaker becomes emphatic. Rap, rap, rap, goes the gavel on the marble block, but the sound is unheeded by the delinquents. "Gentlemen," exclaims Mr. Colfax, in persuasive tones, "must take their seats and cease their conversation in the hall." No attention is paid to the warning, and the gavel comes down again, louder than ever, Rap! Rap! Rap! "Gentlemen *must* take their seats, and *cease* their conversation in the aisles," the Speaker growing more excited. Still the noise and confusion go on, and the orator on the floor, used to such scenes, sits with exemplary patience on the corner of his desk to await the result. The Speaker rises to his feet sharply, and grasping his gavel firmly, strikes his block with all his force. Rap! Rap! Rap! how the sounds ring through the hall. Rap! Rap! Rap! "Gentlemen MUST take their seats, and CEASE talking." There's a ring of determination in the Speaker's voice now, but it accomplishes nothing, for the noise and confusion are worse than before. "If gentlemen do not act as requested, the Chair will be compelled to address each one personally." The threat is unheeded, and after a brief pause, Mr. Colfax speaks rapidly and distinctly, pointing to the offending M. C.'s with his gavel. "Will the gentleman from New York take his seat and stop talking? Will the gentleman from Massachusetts take his seat? Will the gentleman from Minnesota cease his conversation and return to his seat? *Will* the gentleman from Ohio sit down and stop talking?" &c., &c. These sharp, pointed rebukes fasten the attention of the House and galleries upon the offenders, and accomplish the desired result. Order is restored, and for a little while the Speaker is at peace.

THE BOY-SPEAKER.

A tall, sparely-made young man, with a ruddy face, a full beard under the chin, with hair immaculately brushed, and an abundance of linen showing in contrast to his Congressional black broadcloth, may be seen standing or sitting at the speaker's right hand. Though not handsome, he has a striking, manly face, very grave and thoughtful for one so young. He is William Todd, the Speaker's page, or, as he is frequently called, "The Boy-Speaker." He is always on duty by Mr. Colfax, and is of the greatest assistance to him. He is a thorough parliamentarian, and has all the rules and customs of the House at his fingers' ends. He really does a good deal of the speaker's work for him. He arranges his business for him in the morning, so that every thing may pass off smoothly, and is at his side to prompt him when a vexed question arises and demands the ruling of the chair. Mr. Colfax is prompt to acknowledge the aid rendered him by his young Mentor, and a warm friendship exists between the two.

Willie Todd's predecessor was Thaddeus Morris, who was Speaker Pennington's page in 1860, and virtual Speaker of the House of Representatives. "Mr. Pennington was a delightful old gentleman, ignorant of parliamentary practice, and he was elected by a compromise between the adherents of Sherman and Marshall, of Kentucky. Placed in his embarrassing chair, he found the great dog-pit of the House barking, like Cerberus, under him, and he took every ruling point and suggestion from Thaddeus most gracefully.

"Once, it is related, when young Morris had prepared every thing snugly for Pennington, outlined the order of business, prompted him completely, and left the course 'straight as the crow flies,' so that a wayfaring man, though a fool, need not go astray, he said to the Speaker, 'Now, go on.'

"'Now, go on,' cried Pennington, promptly, to the House; at which there was huge laughter."

The leadership of the House, having been made vacant by the death of Thaddeus Stevens, is now disputed by Messrs. Schenck and Washburne, the one of Ohio, the other of Illinois.

GENERAL SCHENCK,

is a short, thick-set man, now in his sixtieth year. He has held a number of important public positions, and is regarded as one of the profoundest men in the House. He has the boldness and vigor necessary for a leader, and adds to these qualities an impetuous enthusiasm which rarely fails to communicate itself to his hearers. He served with credit in the army during a portion of the war, and was especially distinguished during the late impeachment proceedings for the boldness and vigor of his attacks upon the President. He is not a pleasant adversary in debate, for he deals his blows right and left in the most merciless manner. His earnest, impassioned manner once gave rise to a very amusing story at his expense, which is thus related:

11

"Every one who has heard the Honorable Robert C. Schenck speak for the first time, in a case where his feelings were deeply interested, knows what a vivid impression his withering sarcasm and impassioned manner are calculated to produce upon persons unaccustomed to listen to animated debates.

"An unsophisticated Methodist farmer, who lived in a distant portion of the country, and whose avocation seldom called him 'to Court,' accidentally heard that Mr. Schenck was appointed '*Minister to Brazil*,' a country in South America. The terms 'Minister' and 'preacher of the Gospel,' were inseparably associated in his mind; and he took it for granted that Mr. Schenck had turned preacher, and had been sent off on a professional 'mission.'

"With this impression he went home. 'Wife,' he said, 'what do you think I heard at Dayton to-day? That little white-headed lawyer you have heard me speak of so often, has become converted, and turned preacher to a heathen nation way down in South America! If the Devil ever met his match, I guess he has got him now; for if grace don't change him too much, he'll give no rest to the reprobate for the sole of his foot until he leaves the country.'"

ELIHU B. WASHBURNE.

Mr. Washburne is a Representative from Illinois, but is a native of Maine. He is the oldest member of the House, and is often called "The Father of the House," having served in it continuously for nearly seventeen years. He is the Chairman of the Committee on Commerce, and is one of the working men of the House. He has a mania for economy, and steadily opposes the extravagant appropriations of the House. He is a warm friend of General Grant, and, as the General himself has gratefully remarked, stood by him when he needed friends most. It is not likely that Mr. Washburne will retain his place in the House after next spring, as he will doubtless receive some prominent position at the hands of his friend the new President. He is very popular in the House, and his relations with the members of both parties are generally of a pleasant nature. Last year he had a sharp tilt with Mr. Ignatius Donnelly of Minnesota, in which he met his match. Disgraceful as the affair was, it had its redeeming features, and proved beyond all question that the combatants were sharp debaters. Mr. Washburne resides at Galena, Illinois, and is a fine specimen of the Western statesman.

That burly, heavy man, waddling across the hall, with his hands full of papers, and his head slightly bent forward, is

BEN BUTLER,

of Massachussetts, the best abused, best hated, man in the House. He is a man of unquestioned ability, and would be a leader in any cause to which he might give his efforts. As a commander during the late war, he succeeded in the administrative duties of his position, but failed signally in the field. He conducted the prosecution of the President during the impeachment trial with a vigor and ability, and a spice of personal hostility, which won him much praise from the friends of the measure. The late Count Gurowski, in his diary (for January 28th, 1864) thus speaks of him: "Ben Butler would make an excellent President. He has all the capacities of a statesman. Butler can destroy and build up, organize and administer. He is bold, with keen insight, and with prompt, unerring decision. * * Butler's capacities as a civilian are superior, are all that are wanted to save the cause. If President, Butler would easily select good generals."

The Democratic party and the people of the South hate him with a bitter and intense hatred, so that, taking the whole country, it is hard to say which are the more numerous, his friends or his foes.

That fine-looking, swarthy man, with a keen, flashing eye and a military air, who looks more like an Indian than an American, is

JOHN A. LOGAN,

of Illinois. Logan is of Irish parentage, and one of the most brilliant men in the House. He served in the army with great distinction during the war, and rose to the rank of Major-General of Volunteers. He commanded the Fifteenth Army Corps during Sherman's grand campaign, and was regarded by that soldier as one of his best and most promising lieutenants. He was an old Democrat, and Stephen A. Douglas' right hand man. Some of his enemies have asserted that, at the beginning of the rebellion, he offered his services to Jefferson Davis, but was refused; but the best contradiction of these reports lies in the fact that Logan was one of the first to volunteer for the defence of the Union after the fall of Sumter He is now one of the leaders of the Republican party and acted as one of the managers of the late impeach ment proceedings. He is extremely bitter in his pre judices, an ardent partisan, and an eloquent speaker He is considered a rising man in his State, and is pos sessed of considerable influence in the House.

That sleek-looking gentleman, with the air and face of a Methodist preacher, is

SIDNEY CLARKE,

of Kansas, a native of Massachusetts, and an editor by profession. He is thirty-seven years old, but looks younger. Mr. Clarke served during the war as Assistant Provost-Marshal General for Kansas, Nebraska, Colorado, and Dacotah, a section of the country in which there was not much room for him to display his talents as a soldier. He is one of the leading Republicans in the House, and is a born agitator. He emigrated to Kansas in 1858, and settled in Lawrence, where he proved one of the most earnest and energetic advocates of Republican principles in the new State.

Sitting near the extreme right-hand side of the hall, and on the Speaker's left, is a tall, handsome, middle-aged man, whom a stranger would at a glance single out as one of the leaders of the House. He is

GENERAL BANKS,

of Massachusetts. Nathaniel P. Banks is now fifty-three years old, and has filled many positions of trust and honor in his eventful career. He is emphatically a self-made man, as he was the son of parents too poor to do more than educate him at the free schools. From a poor apprentice boy, he rose to be the editor of a newspaper, published first in Waltham, and then in Lowell, in his native State. His next step was into the Legislature, in 1848, at the age of thirty-two. He served in both Houses, and was chosen Speaker of the Lower House. He presided over the Convention of 1853, which revised the Constitution of Massachusetts, and for the next four years represented his State in Congress. He was elected Speaker of the House in 1855, and presided over the deliberations of that body with a grace and dignity which have never been surpassed. In 1857 he was chosen Governor of Massachusetts, and was re-elected to that office for three successive terms. He was a Major-General of Volunteers during the Rebellion. General Banks is a member of the important Committee on Foreign Affairs, and is possessed of great influence in the House. He is very popular with both parties, and socially, is one of the most brilliant ornaments of the Capital.

That tall, dark, wild-looking man, who sits in the front row of desks, almost at the left hand of the official reporters, is the Tennessee loyalist,

HORACE MAYNARD.

He is nearly fifty-five years old, and is gaunt and ungainly in appearance. He is one of the Southern Congressmen who stood firmly by the Government during the Rebellion, and suffered great losses for the sake of his loyalty. He had considerable difficulty in procuring the readmission of his State into the Union after the war, and was refused his seat at the assembling of the Thirty-ninth Congress. He is a native of Massachusetts, and went to Tennessee about 1840, as Professor of Mathematics, in the University of East Tennessee. He is a fierce partisan, and is a man of ability.

Immediately behind him sits

CHESTER D. HUBBARD,

of West Virginia. Mr. Hubbard is nearly the same age as Mr. Maynard, and like him is a New Englander, being a native of Connecticut. He removed to Wheeling, the present capital of his State, at the age of five years, when that place was a mere village, and has grown up and prospered with it. He served several terms in the Lower House of the Virginia Legislature, and was a member of the Virginia Convention of 1860. He opposed the ordinance of secession with such vigor that he was expelled from that body. His constituents then sent him to represent them in the Convention which formed the State of West Virginia, and in 1865 sent him to Congress. He is one of the working men of the House. He represents a large and important constituency, and is regarded as an able and upright man.

The next man back of Mr. Hubbard, is

IGNATIUS DONNELLY,

of Minnesota, a native of Philadelphia. He went to Minnesota in 1857, and two years later was elected

Lieutenant-Governor of the State, in which capacity he served two terms. He was elected to Congress soon after, and has been returned regularly ever since. Mr. Donnelly is a leading member of the Republican party, and a most unfaltering partisan. The reader will not forget Mr. Washburne's scathing attack upon him in the House last summer. He is thirty-seven years old, and looks like a fat, sleek parson of the modern school He affects a sombreness of dress, which contrasts strikingly with his natural jollity of manner. He is an excellent speaker, and is one of the prominent men of the House. He recently distinguished himself by his eulogy upon Thaddeus Stevens, which, though fine in itself, was not at all a truthful or fair estimate of the dead man. Listening to him, it was hard to believe that the voice now so mellow and soft, so gentle and tender, was the same that had rung through the House a few months before in such bitter denunciation, and grown harsh with the most withering sarcasm; the same voice that had both charmed and shamed the whole country by its brilliant outrageousness.

EX-GOVERNOR BOUTWELL,

of Massachusetts, sits not far from the gentlemen just named. He has been Governor of his native State for two terms, and was the first Commissioner of the Internal Revenue. He served as a member of the Judiciary Committee which was charged with the duty of collecting evidence upon which to base the accusations against the President, and served as one of the managers on the part of the House during the trial. He was distinguished for the intensity of his hatred of the President, and the bitterness manifested by him in his whole course—a bitterness and hostility which contributed in no slight degree to making the impeachment measures odious to the best men of all parties.

JAMES M. ASHLEY,

of Ohio, who may be termed the "father" of the Impeachment scheme, sits just back of Mr. Boutwell. He is a rugged-looking man, with the face of a fanatic. He is a native of Pennsylvania, and is forty-four years old. He has been a printer, a steamboat clerk, a lawyer, a boat builder, a wholesale druggist, and a member of Congress. He is a violent partisan, and while he may do for times such as the country has just passed through, is not one of those calculated to win much enduring success for his party.

JUDGE KELLEY,

of Pennsylvania, is another of the self-made men of the House, and is regarded as one of its ablest members. He is fifty-five years old, and is a rugged, hard-featured man. He has fought his way up from his apprenticeship in a jeweller's shop, single-handed, and with no one to help him. He studied law after coming of age, and was admitted to the bar in his twenty-seventh year. He at once plunged into politics as a Democrat, but left that party in 1856, as he could not sustain the repeal of the Missouri Compromise. He is now one of the first men in the Republican party, and possesses the confidence and esteem of his associates in a high degree.

GENERAL GARFIELD,

of Ohio, is another of the marked men of the House. He is thirty-seven years old, is a native of Ohio, and began life as a teacher. He made a brilliant record in the Western army during the Rebellion, and rose to the grade of Major-General of Volunteers. He is an eloquent speaker, and is in high favor with the President-elect.

JAMES F. WILSON,

of Iowa, sits in the last row of seats near the extreme right of the hall. He is a native of Ohio, and is forty years old. He removed to Iowa at the age of twenty-five, and has been in public life almost ever since. He is a little over the medium size, and does not indicate his abilities by his personal appearance. His hair grows low on his forehead, is cut short, is of an iron gray, and defies all the efforts of the comb to make it lie flat. He is the Chairman of the important Judiciary Committee, which collected the testimony upon which the impeachment articles were based, and was one of the Managers on the part of the House during the trial.

JOHN A. GRISWOLD,

of New York, sits nearly in the centre of the hall. He is forty-six years old, and is a banker and iron-factor. He was once Mayor of Troy, in which city he resides, and has been in Congress since 1862. He was one of the parties who built the famous iron-clad

"Monitor;" and subsequently built several other vessels of the same class. He was defeated in 1868, as the Republican nominee for Governor of New York, by Mr. Hoffman, the Mayor of New York City.

JOHN A. BINGHAM,

of Ohio, sits in the front row immediately on the right of the official reporters. He is nearly fifty-four years old, and begins to show his age. He has spent twelve years in Congress, and is one of the most learned men in the House. He is a profound lawyer, and was retained by the Government as Assistant Judge-Advocate in the trial of the assassination conspirators, in May, 1865. His connection with the trial led General Butler to denounce him on the floor of the House as the hangman of an innocent woman. A bitter quarrel ensued between Messrs. Butler and Bingham, and when Mr. Bingham was selected as one of the Managers of the Impeachment, he is said to have refused to serve with a man who had brought so foul a charge against him. Party spirit, that bane of the country, however, effected a temporary accommodation of the hostility between the two gentlemen, and Mr. Bingham assisted in the trial of the President, winning great credit with his party.

JAMES BROOKS,

of New York, sits near the central aisle of the hall. He is fifty-eight years old, and is a native of Maine. He was a clerk in a store at the age of eleven, a schoolteacher at sixteen, and at twenty-one graduated at Waterville College. After travelling and corresponding with the press for several years, Mr. Brooks found himself in the Maine Legislature at the age of twenty-five. The next year he removed to New York City, and established the "Daily Express," of which he is at present an editor and proprietor, his brother being his associate. He has been actively engaged in political life since his removal to New York, and has served several terms in Congress. He is an able and vigorous speaker, and usually commands the attention of the House when he has the floor. Although not formally recognized as such, he is generally regarded as the leader of the Democratic party in the House, and is decidedly one of the soundest men in the hall. A Republican historian styles him the "most plausible and best-natured of Democrats."

Not far from him sits, erect and attentive to what is passing in the hall,

FERNANDO WOOD,

of New York, who may be easily recognized by his tall, commanding figure, and his heavy white moustache, which contrasts strikingly with his dark hair. He is one of the finest-looking men in Congress, a circumstance of which he is well aware, and in which he takes considerable pride. One of his political enemies has drawn the following pen-portrait of him:

"Mr. Wood is about sixty years of age. His hair is dark, but his moustache snowy white. He is tall, slim, and very erect. However well he is dressed, there is always a seedy look about him, such as marks a well-dressed loafer. He wears black, has a clerical look, and would be mistaken anywhere for a professor in college. He has a perpetual smile on his face, which, cold and hollow, is well described by the word *smirk*. He dresses evidently with care, and with as much taste as he can command. He makes up well, has been carefully preserved, and before he allowed his gray moustache to grow looked scarcely forty years of age. There is an insincerity about him, which you feel whenever he speaks to you. In his dress and deportment he shows his shrewdness. He has nothing to hope for but from the debased of New York. To them he caters. His careful array and sanctified demeanor are the secret of his power. Wood understands human nature. The vile and ignominious want a champion, but they do not want him to look vile and ignominious. They want him to dress and walk with the best. They point to him when he is in public, and say, 'That's our champion. He is as smart and genteel, as handsomely dressed, and behaves himself as well, as any of them.' Wood understands this well. When he goes among his constituents in the lower part of New York he goes well made up. His black frock coat, buttoned up to the throat, displays his lithe and genteel form to advantage. His hat, of the latest style, is well brushed and glossy. His boots, of the newest fashion, are polished like a mirror. His gloves fit the hand, and, with a small switch or walking cane, he moves round among the purlieus of the city like a person from another world. So his constituents receive him. He is civil and bland, but icy. He speaks to the women, pats the little dirty urchins on the head with his dainty fingers; holds his levees in beer saloons, and Dutch groceries, and drinks lager with his friends out of the rude mugs, as if he was tippling champagne at the St. Nicholas. Everywhere he wears the same bland, treacherous smile; everywhere he is the same wily, treacherous politician."

That big, burly fellow, sitting back near the extreme left of the hall, is one of the most noted men in Congress. Few persons visit the hall without asking to have him pointed out. He is

JOHN MORRISSEY,

of New York. In place of any description of our own, we present to the reader the following sketch of him by a recent writer: *

"A few years ago John Morrissey was a resident of Troy. He kept a small drinking saloon of the lowest character. It was the resort of the low prize-fighters, gamblers, thieves, and dissolute persons of all degrees. So low, and dissolute, and disreputable was the place, that it was closed by the authorities. With other traits, Morrissey blended that of a prize-fighter of the lowest caste. Drunken, brutal, without friends or money, battered in his clothes and in his person, he drifted down to New York to see what would turn up. He located himself in the lowest stews of New York. At that time the elections in the city were carried by brute force. There was no registry law, and the injunction of politicians to vote early and vote often,

* Sunshine and Shadow in New York. By Mathew Hale Smith.

was literally obeyed. Roughs, shortboys, brutal representatives of the Bloody Sixth, took possession of the polls. Respectable men, who were known to be opposed to the corruption and brutality which marked the elections, were assaulted, beaten, robbed, and often had their coats torn from their backs. The police were powerless; often they were the allies of the bullies, and citizens had quite as much to fear from them as the rowdies. If the election was likely to go against them, and their friends presided over the ballot-box, and should signal the danger, a rush would be made by twenty or thirty desperate fellows, the boxes be seized and smashed, tables and heads broken, the voters dispersed, and the election carried by default.

"A local election was to take place in the upper part of the city. The friends of good order were in the majority, if allowed to vote. But it was known that the rowdies would come in force and control the election. A few voters got together to see what could be done, and among them the present General Superintendent of Police (of New York). It was suggested that force be met with force, the ballot-box be guarded, and the assailants beaten off by their own weapons. But where could the materials be found to grapple with the Plug-Uglies and their associates? Somebody said that Morrissey was in town, ready for a job, and that he could organize a force and guard the election.

"One day Mrs. Kennedy came to her husband, as he sat in his room, and said to him, 'There is an awful looking man at the door, who wants to see you. He is dirty and ragged, has a ferocious look, and is the most terrible fellow I ever saw. Don't go to the door, he certainly means mischief.' 'Is he a big, burly-looking fellow?' 'Yes.' 'Broad-shouldered, tall, with his nose turned one side?' 'Yes, yes,' said the impatient lady. 'O, I know who it is; it is John Morrissey; let him come in.' 'O, husband, the idea of your associating with such men, and bringing them to the house, too!' But the unwelcome visitor walked into the parlor. Now, John Morrissey, at Saratoga, in his white flannel suit, huge diamond rings, and pin containing brilliants of the first water, and of immense size; tall of stature, a powerful-looking fellow, walking quietly about the streets, or lounging at the hotels, but seldom speaking, is not a bad looking man. Seen in New York, in his clerical black suit, a little too flashy to be a minister, yet among bankers, merchants, or at the Stock Board, he would pass very well as one of the solid men of the city. But Morrissey, as he appeared that morning, was an entirely different personage. He had come from a long debauch, and that of the lowest kind. He was bruised and banged up. His clothes were tattered. The Island was all that seemed to be opened to him. With him a bargain was made to organize a force of fighters and bullies, sufficient to prevent the ballot-boxes from being smashed, and the voters from being driven from the polls. He said he could do it, for he was at home among the desperadoes. True to his appointment, he was at the polls before they were open. He was attended by about thirty as desperate-looking fellows as ever rode in a wagon or swung from Tyburn. He stationed his force, gave his orders, told each not to strike promiscuously, but, on the first appearance of disturbance, each to seize his man, and not leave him till his head was broken. There was no disturbance till twelve o'clock. The late Captain Carpenter was in charge. About noon, a huge lumber van drove up, drawn by four horses. It was loaded with the roughest of the rough, who shouted and yelled as the vehicle neared the curb-stone. Bill Poole, at that time so notorious, led the company. They were choice specimens of the men who then made the rulers of New York. Plug-Uglies, Bummers, Roughs of the Bloody Sixth, Short Boys, Fourth Warders, and men of that class, were fully represented. Bill Poole sprang to the side-walk. Captain Carpenter stood in the door. Addressing him, Poole said, 'Cap., may I go in?' 'O, yes, walk in and welcome,' Carpenter said, and in Poole went. He saw the situation at a glance. He measured Morrissey and his gang, turned on his heel, and passing out, said, 'Good morning, Cap., I won't give you a call to-day; drive on boys,' and on they went towards some polling place where they could play their desperate game without having their heads broken.

"This was Morrissey's first upward step. He washed his face; with a part of the money paid him he bought a suit of clothes, and with the balance opened a small place for play. He became thoroughly temperate. He resolved to secure first-class custom. To do this he knew he must dress well, behave well, be sober, and not gamble. These resolutions he car-

12

ried out. His house in New York is the most elegantly furnished of any of the kind in the State. It has always been conducted on principles of the highest honor, as gamblers understand that term. His table, attendants, cooking, and company, are exceeded by nothing this side of the Atlantic.

"He followed his patrons to Saratoga, and opened there what was called a Club House. Judges, senators, merchants, bankers, millionaires, became his guests. The disguise was soon thrown off, and the Club House assumed the form of a first-class gambling house at the Springs. Horse racing and attendant games followed, all bringing custom and profit to Morrissey's establishment. About this time the celebrated conspiracy was formed by politicians and railroad men to break down Harlem Railroad, and with it Commodore Vanderbilt. As a player Morrissey soon became familiar with Vanderbilt, who spent his summers at the Springs. In the extraordinary movements made by Commodore Vanderbilt to checkmate the conspirators, and throw them on their back, Morrissey was employed to play a conspicuous part. He made his appearance at the Stock Board, backed by Vanderbilt. He traded in Harlem, in a manner that astounded the old operators at the Board. He was allowed to share in the profits of that bold stroke which ruined thousands who had sold Harlem short. Morrissey is now worth half a million. He is still a gambler by profession, and carries on his establishments in Saratoga and New York."

In the Fall of 1866, Mr. Morrissey was elected to Congress from the Fifth District of New York. His election created no little surprise throughout the country, as it was well known that he was in no way qualified for the position. The reasons for his choice will no doubt remain amongst the political mysteries of the land. It is the only instance in which a man of similar antecedents ever occupied a seat in the American Congress."

There was a parallel case in the British Parliament about half a century ago. At that time, there lived in England a noted prize-fighter, named John Galley. In this capacity he made many friends amongst the nobility and the "fancy." Having acquired some money, he opened a "hell" in St. James street, London, within a few doors of Piccadilly. He next became a patron of the turf, and got into "good society" at Doncaster. Soon after this, he was elected to the House of Commons, as member for Friarsborough.

PERQUISITES.

The pay of a member of Congress is five thousand dollars per annum, and mileage. The latter item is intended to cover all the expenses of the regular journeys between Washington and the member's home, which consist of coming to the Capital at the beginning of the session, and going away at the end of it. This amounts to a considerable sum, and is paid to members should they remain in Washington during the entire year.

The perquisites of members form a considerable item in their compensations. Each may order large quantities of stationery for his private use ; and in this term "stationery," are embraced many articles of luxury and extravagance. Members receive knives, toothpicks, fans, combs, pocket-books, medicated paper, and other things; and it is even said that articles of clothing have been drawn by unprincipled members "as stationery." A recent report made in Congress, showed that the total cost of these luxuries to the tax-payers of the country amounts anually to an enormous sum; and it is difficult to understand how so much "stationery" can be conscientiously used by Congress, during a single session. In the single item of pocket-knives, it was shown that the number issued to members was sufficient to supply each one with a new knife, of the finest pattern, every week during the session. Whole tons of writing materials are issued —more, in fact, to each member, than it seems can possibly be used by him. Indeed, the waste and extravagance of members, in articles of "stationery," is abominable, and imposes a heavy load upon our already overburdened people. Members seem to think they are bound by no obligation to be economical of the public funds; and while they are careful to deny appropriations to really deserving objects, on the ground of economy, they never fail to minister to their own luxurious fancies, at the public expense. Not long since, the idea was seriously advanced, that it was the duty of the Government to build residences in the city for the Senators, and it is probable that the scheme would have grown in favor, had not the indignant whirlwind of public sentiment swept it away, at its birth.

All this extravagance is covered over by the general term, "contingent expenses" of the House or the Senate. In the House, the waste is shameful. Mr. W. J. Monker, of Washington, in a pamphlet published by him some time since, thus sums up the annual expenses of the House of Representatives:

Year ending June 30, 1864, . .	$353,630
Year ending June 30, 1865, . .	481,884
Year ending June 30, 1866, . .	462,438
Year ending June 30, 1867, . .	502,081
Year ending June 30, 1868, . .	725,555
Additional Compensation, . . .	100,000
Total, ...	$2,625,588

In the year 1868, the allowance of "stationery" was equivalent to $520 to each member. There were $5,086 worth of pens, many of them gold pens, used by the House and $5,620 worth of pen-knives. The House during the last session appointed a committee to examine into the charges of extravagance brought against it, but the committee made a white-washing report, glossing over the affair. Mr. H. McCulloch, of Maryland, from this same committee, also presented a minority report, showing that funds have been illegally and improperly disbursed, and declaring that the committee is not a proper committee to investigate such charges. He says: "It is like a member charged with corruption or fraud asking for a committee to investigate that charge, and, being appointed its chairman, to report on his own case."

It is useless to lay these charges of extravagance and waste at the door of any particular party. The whole country is cursed with such evils, and Congress is but true to its natural and national instincts.

SENATE CHAMBER—SCENE DUN

THE IMPEACHMENT TRIAL.

V.

THE LOBBY.

Every man, woman, and child in Washington, is a politician. The people inhale politics with the air they breathe, and talk and think of but little else. Every man seems to be under the impression that he has influence in some part of the Government, did he but choose to exert it; and as for the women—ah! they would like to see the official or Congressman they cannot win over. Many of the residents, of both sexes, do seek to exercise this influence, which may be either real or fancied, and their ranks are swelled every winter by fresh arrivals, from other parts of the country, of persons equally impressed with the idea that they, too, have influence with Congress, or the Government, which they mean to exert in every possible manner. These individuals constitute what is generally known as "the lobby," and are, in most cases, proficients in the ancient art of "log-rolling."

WHY SHREWD MEN AND WOMEN ARE SENT TO THE CAPITAL.

Pecuniary enterprises of all kinds, both legitimate and infamous, are springing up every day in all parts of the country. Strange as it may seem, very few of the greatest of these schemes have sufficient vitality of their own to carry them through to success; and the great majority rely upon subsidies of lands or money from the General or State Governments, or from both. No one will deny that it is both wise and expedient for Congress to encourage and aid the great improvements of the country, which are national in their character; but the American people are averse, as a general rule, to spending their money for the benefit of a private corporation, and are emphatically opposed to such a use of it on the part of Congress. The members of that body are well aware of this, and while they disregard it, conduct their operations in such a manner as to make it almost impossible to discover any of their acts except their votes.

The parties interested in the schemes for which Government aid is asked, begin their operations by supposing that they must have some energetic, active agent in Washington, to keep the scheme before Congress and the Government, and urge upon the members and officials a compliance with their demands. Forthwith, an agent with full powers is despatched to the Capital. This person is generally a man, but is sometimes a woman. Almost all important schemes, however, have agents of both sexes, who are persons of education, intelligence, and great powers of insinuation and fascination. Women make excellent lobbyists, as they are more plausible than men, and cannot be shaken off as rudely.

Upon reaching Washington, the lobbyists are not slow in getting to work. Much is left to their own discretion; but much more is done in obedience to "instructions from headquarters." The aid desired may be from the Government, or from Congress, or from both; and all sorts of artifices are resorted to to secure it. Officials are approached in every imaginable way, and, if no direct bribe is offered, the intriguer endeavors, generally with success, to gain the confidence and friendship of the party against whom his arts are directed. This accomplished, he broaches his scheme so delicately, and presses it so skilfully, that the official is won over before he knows it. If the man fails, the female lobbyist is called in to exert her arts, which are more potent than those of the sterner sex. Congressmen and officials are famous as being the most susceptible men in the world, and the fair charmer is generally successful. Men in public life are very obliging when they choose to be, and these women know how to win favors from them.

It is very common for the lobbyists to approach public men through their families. Mrs. A. or Mrs. B. will receive magnificent presents from persons who are but little more than casual acquaintances. Their first impulse is to return the articles, but they are so handsome, and just what they have been wanting so long, without being able to afford them out of their husbands' incomes—for the lobbyists are careful to inform themselves what will be most acceptable—and so, after a little struggle, they decide to keep the gifts.

Of course some especial civility must be shown the givers of the presents. This is done, and the first point of the lobbyist is gained. In a little while the wife is won over. She thinks the scheme an excellent one—and honestly thinks it, too—and will be *so* beneficial to the country! She does not like to meddle in her husband's affairs, but she will mention the matter to him. The better-half of the official being thus secured, the remainder can and does make but a feeble resistance, and his aid is secured for the scheme.

Now this is the mildest and most innocent feature of the lobby. Of course there is a sacrifice of principle, from which a Senator of old Rome would have shrunk; but men's consciences are tough to-day, and our official, won in this way, honestly thinks he has sacrificed nothing of his duty, and has only yielded to a demand which no fair-minded, liberal man can resist. Why, *he* has been won over merely by the arguments of his wife and his friends. *He* has not sullied his honor with the acceptance of any thing like a bribe, and there was his friend the Honorable John Smith, who is said to have been paid in money for his influence and his vote in behalf of the same scheme! So he goes to his rest with a quiet mind, and a clear conscience, and—his wife or his children enjoy the benefits of his Spartan virtue.

Mrs. Lincoln was much sought after by the lobbyists, who, knowing that they would not dare to hint at a bribe to the President, loaded her with flattery and presents. She was not deceived by them, however, and made good use of them to secure the reëlection of her husband. She once said to one of her friends, in discussing the matter: "I have an object in view. In a political canvass it is policy to cultivate every element of strength. These men have influence, and we require influence to reëlect Mr. Lincoln. I will be clever to them until after the election, and then, if we remain at the White House, I will drop every one of them, and let them know very plainly that I only made tools of them. They are an unprincipled set, and I don't mind a little double-dealing with them."

"Does Mr. Lincoln know what your purpose is?" asked her friend.

"No! He would never sanction such a proceeding, so I keep him in the dark, and will tell him of it when all is over. He is too honest to take proper care of his own interests, so I feel it to be my duty to electioneer for him."

It is whispered in Washington that votes for Congress are bought for so much money, or for an interest in the schemes for which they are asked. You will hear all sorts of charges brought against officials of all grades, all affecting the honesty of the man. These things are told you in confidence, and when you ask for proofs, you cannot get them. Your confidential friend has no wish to get into trouble with the "powers that be," so he puts you off by reminding you that he trusts to your honor not to reveal any thing he has told you. The majority of these confidences are mere idle rumors. Did you heed all of them you could not resist the conviction that every official and Congressman in the city is in the direct pay of the lobby. Now the truth is, that there are honest men in the Government as well as in private life. Who are the dishonest ones, it is hard to say. Accusations are plentiful; proofs are scarce.

The facts are, that both in Washington and throughout the whole country, the integrity of many men in public life is doubted. The public moneys are wasted. Measures are set on foot and carried out which do not commend themselves to the sober judgment of the people, and which ought not to be adopted by those in power, and the rumor is general throughout the whole country that these measures were carried through by bribery. It is furthermore believed throughout the country that men are sent to Congress, and put into the various departments of the Government for the especial purpose of carrying out the most iniquitous schemes, of preventing inquiry into them, and shielding from punishment those engaged in them. No one will deny that these feelings of distrust and suspicion do prevail all over the land. Their effects are very damaging to the country and to the cause of public morality. It is known that large sums of money are spent by the "rings," as they are called, for the purpose of securing Government aid for their schemes. It is rumored and generally believed that this money is spent in buying the aid of individual members of the Government. It is known that few public men above the position of clerks, can or do live upon their official salaries. They spend annually more than double the sum received from the Government, and many of them have no other visible source of income. It is said that the most of this splendor is paid for by the lobby, and that the majority of public men are always open to bribes. We make no charges against any one. We merely mention what is generally suspected and believed throughout the country at large; and that our statements as to this popular belief are true, no one will deny. We content ourselves by recalling to the reader's mind, the homely old adage, "*There must be some fire where there is so much smoke.*"

CONGRESSIONAL LOBBYING.

Congressmen are famous lobbyists, and rarely fail to carry their points. A member introduces a bill, which he is anxious to have passed. In order to secure votes for it, he solicits his friends in the House to which he belongs, as follows: "Jones, I have a bill before the House to build a lighthouse at the harbor of my town, which my constituents are particularly anxious to have passed. Now, if you'll vote for my bill, I'll vote for that you introduced a few days ago to clear out your harbor." Jones thinks "a fair exchange no robbery," and obligingly promises his vote, and thus a vote is secured for each bill. This is very harmless and innocent, except that it leads to a looseness in matters of legislation, which is apt to make members forgetful of the real interests of the country.

THE LOBBY AT WORK.

The correspondent of the *Cincinnati Gazette* writes as follows of the "Washington Lobby:"

"Though bleeding, cupping, and leeching have had their day in the medical profession, our political Solons not only hold on to them all with desperation, but act as if they believed their own salvation, at least, depended upon the frequency of the operation and the amount of blood drawn at each.

"The body bled is the National Treasury. The chief physicians who assist are Senators and Representatives of both parties.

"The lobby—that great army of blood-suckers—has occupied Washington in force. Two weeks' skirmishing with them has fully developed their line. This army has come to steal—to use plain terms. It has come to steal on the large scale. It feels that unless its measures can be perfected before this session ends, they will fail through Grant's opposition and veto, even if Congress is not honest enough to cast them aside. And so the movement on this Congress is one in force. And it will be well for the press of the country to watch it.

"Just now the danger to the Republican party is, that the corporations to which many of its prominent men lend themselves will ruin it. Andrew Johnson's Administration has been fearfully corrupt, but all of its stealings have not gone into the pockets of Democrats. Randall's Postoffice ring, the Indian ring, and the Whisky ring have been held up to the country as purely Johnson institutions. The Republican press has been comparatively silent as to schemes in which members of its own party were participants, or at least the names of Republicans have not been used in connection with them. If political expediency is a matter to be considered, then it was well to consider these things. But now the time has gone for withholding truth. Every one of the rings mentioned above had

Republican members, some of them Senators, some of them members of the House. The moment a word is written against any of them now, they begin to plead what might be called the 'injured innocence' dodge. But it is too late, gentlemen ; entirely too late. The people gave most of you very significant hints in your reduced majorities last November. A general denial and raising a hue-and-cry against those who attempt to expose you, shouting 'Conservative,' 'Copperhead,' or what not, will not save you. The only way through is to stop short. Don't offer any more bills on either floor, which, if they had their real titles, would be: 'A bill for the benefit of myself and John Smith,' or 'A bill to obtain —— millions of government money.' Let your committees smother those of this character already before them—and nearly every committee has some under consideration. And in all of them Republicans and Democrats are engaged in about the proportion of their numbers in the two Houses. If any thing, Republicans are more largely represented, because they have more power.

"THE RAILROAD LOBBY.

"At present perhaps there is more money in the various railroad schemes than in any other. And this thing is on a scale which the country does not comprehend, notwithstanding the constant talk about it. Thus far in the Fortieth Congress there have been *seventy-two* railroad bills introduced in the Senate alone. *Eight* were presented at the first short session, *fifty two* at the second session, and in the two weeks of the present session *eleven* have been reported and printed. And these last do not include four as gigantic as any which have been passed, yet to come. One is in preparation for which its friends are now gathering power, for the Northern Pacific, one for the Albuquerque line and its several connections; one for Mr. Pomeroy's little private Atchison Pacific—one of the nicest and fattest speculations ever concocted and worked through—having these special qualifications of nice and fat, on account of the small number to divide the spoils; one for two roads south and west from St. Louis, and two or three for Southern Pacific lines from Memphis, New Orleans, and points in Texas.

"In all this there are four lines across the Continent, with connecting roads enough to stretch out into two more; and then such little ventures as the Atchison and Denver lines by the score.

"Of all these bills, fully three-fourths were originated by Republicans. Four Senators brought in nearly half of them. Mr. Pomeroy reported eleven, Mr. Ramsey seven, Mr. Conness five, and Mr. Harlan four. Mr. Pomeroy did not confine his attention to any particular part of the country. He proposed one land grant through the rich lands about Port Royal, South Carolina, and another one of his measures was for the benefit of his Wisconsin brethren; but, not desiring to be reckoned as worse than an infidel, he made full provision for his own political household in Kansas. We find his name attached to a land grant for a railroad from Lawrence to the Mexican line; to three bills for roads from Fort Scott to Santa Fe; to a pleasant arrangement for the Southern branch of the Union Pacific Road—whatever that may be—and also to a land grant from Irwing, Kansas, to New Mexico and all for the national good, of course.

"These, it must be remembered, are such railroads as Northern companies, Northern lobby men, and Northern Congressmen have concocted. The word concocted is good for most, though a few are meritorious. The Southern States are just beginning to vote, and the scent of Southern men in Congress is now as keen in respect to all material interests as the Northern Congressman's nose. The reason is evident. Southern smelling is now done with Northern noses. Carpet bags have wrought this change for the South; and as a result, among the very first subjects to call out bills from Southern men are the railroad interests.

And heading the column, comes Mr. Senator Spencer, with a bill making a land-grant, not through the public domain on the plains, but through the States of Tennessee, Georgia, Alabama, Mississippi, and Louisiana, with permission to get all the "earth, stone, timber, and other materials" for the construction of its roads, off the public lands along its line, and then to receive ten sections of land to the mile, wherever they can find that amount within twenty miles of the line they may see fit to locate, and from Mobile, onward to the western boundary of Louisiana; if the land cannot be found within twenty miles of the road, these patriotic gentlemen are to be obliged to hunt it up within forty miles north of their line. As this is the first attempt on the part of a Southern Senator to follow in the paths already worn so smooth by his fellow Republicans from the North, it will be interesting to see what a fine start Senator Spencer, of Alabama, makes. Section second of his bill is in part as follows:

"SEC. 2. *And be it further enacted*, That, for the purpose of aiding in the construction of the railroad of said company, there be, and is hereby granted to said company, from the public lands of the United States, ten sections of land for each mile of railroad completed and placed in running order by said company, pursuant to its charter. That said lands are granted as follows: On the line of said railroad from the city of Chattanooga, in the State of Tennessee, to the city of Mobile, in the State of Alabama, every alternate section of public land designated by odd numbers, to the amount of ten alternate sections per mile, for each mile of said railroad from the said city of Chattanooga to the said city of Mobile, such alternate section of land to be selected within the limits of ten miles on each side of the centre line of said railroad; and if public lands sufficient for the purpose shall not be found within said limit of ten miles upon each side of said railroad, then the said alternate sections of land are hereby granted, and may be selected within the limits of twenty miles on each side of the centre line of said railroad. And on the line of said railroad from the city of Mobile, in the State of Alabama, to the western boundary of the State of Louisiana, every alternate section of public land, designated by odd numbers, to the amount of ten alternate sections per mile for each mile of said railroad, from the said city of Mobile to the western boundary of the State of Louisiana, such alternate section of land to be selected within the limits of ten miles upon each side of the centre line of said railroad; and if public lands sufficient for the purpose shall not be found within said limits of ten miles upon each side of said railroad, then the said alternate sections of land are hereby granted, and may be selected within the limits of forty miles north of the centre line of said railroad, excepting, however, from this grant, all mineral lands, and lands sold by the United States, or lands in which a preëmption or homestead claim may have attached at the time the line of said railroad shall have been located and established.'

"What will the railroad docket of the Senate not contain by the time the Southerners have brought up their side of the railroad jobs to the present proud height of their Northern friends, and shall have added to the Washington lobby, its own army of blood-suckers, plausible gentlemen of unquestioned honor, and thieves?—for it takes all these, and more, to make a lobby. What a nice thing it will be for taxpayers!

"All this presents the railroad interest merely in outline. Every bill deserves a separate letter to show the means used to get it before the Senate, the persons engaged in pressing it, and the parties to be benefited by it; and in due time the principal ones at least will get that chapter.

"When the railroad jobs are disposed of, then the deck is only cleared for action against jobs in general.

There are, aside from these, the Niagara Ship Canal with a coupon of twelve millions attached; the Com mercial Navigation Company, with half as much on its coupon; the bills and schemes for getting damages paid to Southern men for property destroyed during the war, in all hundreds of millions; and then the lobby upon the more modest sum of five millions due from Southern railroads, and in which radical Republicans from Tennessee are deeply interested. The Osage Treaty is a nice plum; and one new feature is, that some Kansas men who showed a vast amount of righteous indignation over it, before their reëlection, are, now that their places are assured, helping the swindle on. Alta Veta is coming up again, and to crown all things, if it is possible, the change in the Indian Bureau is to be so managed as to place the present Indian ring on a firmer foundation than ever.

"The Republican party can now afford to rectify the irregularities which have crept into all portions of the Government while the great political battle with Rebellion was going on. If those here, as its Congress, will not free themselves from such things, the party need not die if it only throws them overboard. There are honest men enough who can take their places. Let the press watch jobs when the recess closes and the outside lobby, which is here in force, begins to work through its Senators and Representatives."

Commenting upon the same subject, the *New York Herald* said, editorially:

"The corruptions which have grown up in the national government, from the general demoralizations of our late civil war, are fearful to contemplate. One hundred millions a year lost to the Treasury from the spoliations of the whiskey rings 'beats out of sight any thing in the line of whiskey frauds under any other government on the face of the globe; but on a corresponding scale with their field of operations, the Indian rings, the Post-Office and Interior Department rings, the tobacco rings, the frontier smuggling rings, and various other rings, insiders and outsiders, jobbers, contractors, government officials and private speculators, are pretty well up to the percentage of the enormous stealings of the whiskey rings. The latest developments, however, show, that in the grandeur and number of their schemes of spoils and plunder the Congressional rings of railroad jobbers throw into the shade all the other rings of the lengthy catalogue of confederate Treasury robbers.

"A Washington correspondent, who has been looking into the the business reports that one hundred and fifty-nine railroad bills and resolutions have been introduced in the Fortieth Congress (the term of which expires on the 4th March next, with that of President Johnson), and that twice as many more are in preparation in the lobby; that one thousand millions of acres of the public lands, and two hundred millions in United States bonds, would not supply the demands of these cormorants. In other words, their stupendous budget of railway jobs would require sops and subsidies in lands and bonds, which, reduced to a money valuation, swell up to the magnificent figure of half the national debt.

"Among the jobs of this schedule is the Atchison and Pike's Peak Railroad Company, or Union Pacific Central Branch, which, after having received government sops to the extent of six millions, puts in for seven millions more. Next comes the Denver Pacific Railway and Telegraph Company, which, having feathered its nest to the figure of thirty-two millions, puts in for a little more; and this company is reported to be a mere gang of speculators, 'without any known legal organization whatever'—a lot of mythical John Does and Richard Roes, who cannot be found when called for. Next we have the Leavenworth, Pawnee and Western Railroad Company, now known as the Union Pacific, Eastern Division, chartered by the Kansas Territorial Legislature, in 1855, subsidized with Delaware Indian reserve lands in 1861, and then in 1862, by a rider on the Pacific Railroad law, granted sixteen thousand dollars per mile in United States bonds, and every alternate section of land within certain limits, on each side of the road, and the privilege of a second mortgage. This is cutting it pretty fat. But it further appears that a clique of seceders from the old company illegally formed a new company, and, having by force of arms taken possession of the road, are pocketing the spoils which legally belong to the old company. All this, too, with the consent of the President, the Secretary of the Treasury, and Congress. Are they all birds of a feather, that they thus flock together?

"From another source we learn that some half dozen other Pacific branch or main stem railroads,

Northern and Southern, are on the anvil, involving lands and bonds by tens and twenties and hundreds of millions; that of all these schemes fully three-fourths come from the Republicans in both Houses; that Senator Pomeroy, of Kansas, has seven of these jobs on the docket; Senator Ramsey, of Minnesota, four Senator Conness, of California, five, and Senator Harlan, of Iowa, four. Senator Pomeroy, however, distances all competitors in the number and extent of his jobs; for, as it appears, they include a line from Kansas to Mexico, three bills for roads from Fort Scott to Santa Fé, in Texas, a South Carolina line through the Sea Island cotton section, two or three lines from the Mississippi River through to Texas, and 'a little private Atchison Pacific, one of the nicest and fattest speculations ever worked through.'

"Is not this a magnificent budget, and is not the audacity of these railroad jobs and jobbers positively sublime? Some of these schemes are in successful operation, but many of them are still in the caterpillar, or chrysalis, state, and there is a prospect that very few of this class will come out as the full-blown butterfly."

THE RESULT.

How many people in the United States believe that the schemes for which Government aid is asked are really worthy of assistance, or will be faithfully carried out? It is said that the railroads to which Government aid has been vouchsafed so liberally, are badly constructed, that the contracts on the part of the companies, have not been faithfully carried out, and that the public grants have been used only to enrich the stockholders. Yet in spite of this, in spite of all the lessons of the past, Congress continues to squander the public wealth as recklessly as if it had full faith in the honesty of the men it enriches. The people are groan ing under the burdens thus imposed upon them, and are uttering murmurs of no uncertain character. Mr. Washburne, of Illinois, in a speech recently delivered in Congress, uttered this indignant protest against the madness of his colleagues:

"With the unreconstructed States admitted into the Union, with full and equal protection for all men in all the States, and with MANHOOD SUFFRAGE secured by legislation or constitutional amendment, the minds of the people will turn to questions of finance, of taxes, of economy, of decreased expenditures, and honest and enlightened legislation, to questions of tariffs, and to questions of railroad, telegraph, and express monopolies, which are sucking the very life-blood of the people, to the administration of the revenue laws and to the robberies and plunderings of the Treasury by dishonest office-holders. Already the eyes of the people of this country are upon Congress. I may say they are upon the Republican majority in Congress, for that majority is now responsible before the country for the legislation of Congress. It can make and unmake laws in defiance and contempt of Executive vetoes. The Republican party triumphed in the last election because it was pledged to honesty and economy, to the upholding of public faith and public credit, and to the faithful execution of the laws. And those pledges cannot now be ignored without subjecting that party to the censure of the people. The condition of the country, the vast public debt, the weight of taxation, the depreciated and fluctuating currency, the enormous expenditures of public money, the mal-administration of the Government, the extortions of monopolies, press upon our attention with most crushing force. The people elected General Grant to the Presidency not only on account of the great and inestimable services he has rendered the country in subduing the rebellion; not only on account of his devotion to the great principles of the Republican party, but because they believe him to be emphatically an honest man and an enlightened statesman, who would faithfully administer the laws, without fear, favor, or affection. The time has come when we are imperatively called upon to take a new departure. Added to other terrible evils brought upon the country by the war for the suppression of the rebellion, is the demoralization incident to all great wars, and to the expenditures of vast and unheard of amounts of public money; to the giving out of immense contracts by which sudden and vast fortunes were made, the inflation of the currency, which engendered speculation, profligacy, extravagance and corruption, by the intense desire to get suddenly rich out of the Government and without labor, and the inventions and schemes generally to get money out of the Treasury for the benefit of individuals without regard to the interests of the Government. While the restless and unpausing energies of a patriotic and incorruptible people were devoted to the salvation of their Government, and were pouring out their blood and treasure in its defence, there was the vast army of the base, the venal and unpatriotic, who rushed in to take advantage of the misfortunes of the country and to plunder its treasury. The statute-books are loaded with legislation which will impose burdens on future generations. Public land enough to make empires has been voted to private railroad corporations; subsidies of untold millions of bonds, for the same purposes, have become a charge upon the people, while the fetters of vast monopolies have been fastened still closer and closer upon the public. It is time that the representatives of the people were admonished that they are the servants of the people and are paid by the people; that their constituents have confided to them the great trust of guarding their rights and protecting their interests; that their position and their power are to be used for the benefit of the people whom they represent, and not for their own benefit and the benefit of the lobbyists, the gamblers, and the speculators who have come to Washington to make a raid upon the Treasury."

Yet what do such appeals and protests accomplish after all? Congress is deaf to all the demands of the people. Members should remember that their official lives are in the hands of their constituents, who desire *honesty* as much as talent, and that their persistence in their extravagant schemes is regarded, by those who can make or unmake them, as strong proof of the charges affecting their integrity as men.

LOBBY MEMBERS.

VI.

THE RINGS.

THE organizations formed for the purpose of defrauding the Government of the revenue which a faithful execution of the law would bring to it, are termed "Rings." They consist generally of the manufacturers or importers of articles upon which revenue taxes are levied, and the officials whose duty it is to collect such taxes. A false return is made to the Government with the full knowledge of the official, and the greater part of the taxable article is sold, without the tax, at a heavy profit to the manufacturer. The official is well paid for his services, and the Government is swindled of its just dues.

One of the most formidable of these organizations is known as

THE WHISKEY RING.

Its heaviest operations are carried on in the great cities of the Union, but its branches are to be found whereever there is a distillery.

In 1863, the tax on distilled liquors was twenty cents per gallon; in 1864 the tax was, after March 7th, sixty cents per gallon; from July, 1864, until June, 1865, one dollar and fifty cents per gallon; and after June 1st, 1865, two dollars per gallon, which is the present rate. In 1863, with a tax of sixty cents, the revenue from liquors was $28,431,797.83; but in 1866, with a tax of $2.00, it fell off to $15,995,701.66 This was not because there was less whiskey made and consumed during the latter year, but because the Whiskey Ring had been actively at work, and had evaded the tax upon all possible occasions. During the session of 1866–67 the public press made such an outcry over these frauds, that Congress enacted a law making the sale of whiskey for less than $2.00 per gallon, *prima facie* evidence of an evasion of the tax, and ordering the instant seizure of such whiskey, as illicit. This excellent provision, however, was nullified by another clause which provided that, in case of seizure and forfeiture of illicit whiskey, it should be destroyed unless it would bring at the Marshal's sale at least two dollars per gallon. So much for the law.

Its passage had no effect whatsoever. Western grain whiskey continued to sell in New York for from $1.40 to $1.70. This was done openly, and with the full knowledge of the Government officials whose duty it was to seize and forfeit all whiskey offered for sale in the market for less than $2.00 per gallon. For more than two years these frauds have been carried on, and whiskey may be bought anywhere for less than the excise duty imposed by the law. Not one cent of tax is paid on this liquor, and millions of dollars are thus annually lost to the Government. The Revenue officers in many, if not in most cases, are aware of this, but are in the pay of the whiskey capitalists, whose immense wealth and influence are exerted for the purpose of swindling the Government.

A recent report made to the House of Representatives enumerates as follows some of the most popular methods of evading the law:

"FRAUDS BY GAUGERS.

"The recent act of Congress required that taxes should be paid on all whiskey then in bond before removal. Great frauds are committed through gaugers. To illustrate: One hundred barrels of whiskey were inspected a few days ago by Government gaugers. An honest Revenue officer, suspecting something wrong, called in a city gauger, who, on inspection, found it had been gauged 1,000 gallons short, thereby defrauding the Government of $500. When it is remembered there were nearly 20,000 barrels in one district, and in July last nearly 700,000 in the country, the loss to the Revenue must be enormous."

"FRAUDS BY DISTILLERS AND STOREKEEPERS.

"Unfortunately, there is always some defect in legislation or oversight in the regulations of the department which give the dishonest operator an advantage. In the case of estimated capacity the act is so loosely drawn that one of the most essential elements is left to the determination of the distiller, and the expert in fixing the estimate is compelled to fix the time of fermentation as given by the distiller. Consequently, distillers in New York fix the period at 48 hours; in Virginia at 96 and 120. In New York the time is fixed at 48 hours, the act requires the tub to stand empty 24 hours after every fermentation, making the time for each fermentation 72 hours. When it is notorious that some distillers do not let the tubs stand empty 24 hours, most ferment in less than 48 hours—from 24 to 36; the result is that distillers generally produce from one-quarter to one-third more than estimated capacity; and the fact that none of the distillers return more than the estimated capacity, clearly shows that the distillers defraud and the officers connive at it. Besides, the estimated capacity, reduced as it is by the time of fermentation, is only charged to the distiller at 80 per cent, so that he gains in the underestimate of capacity and the 20 per cent discount.

"No further proof is needed of the existence of fraud; if so, it is found in the fact that the price of whiskey has ruled below the cost of production and the legitimate tax.

"There is now but little illicit distillation; most of that was from molasses, which cannot be manufactured at the present market value of whiskey."

"FRAUDS THROUGH COMPOUNDING HOUSES.

"Rectifying establishments were found easy aids to fraud, and the present law provides that none shall be used within 600 feet of a distillery; some distillers, not to be restrained by so plain a provision of the act, resorted to the expedient of evasion by substituting compounding houses, a branch of business carried on to a moderate extent, not necessary to adjoin a distillery. The business is merely compounding some articles with raw whiskey, thereby giving it a different character and greater value, which, under the previous law, was classed with and known as rectifying, but, under the last, by a remarkable coincidence, almost too remarkable to be an accident, compounding shops are made a distinct class, and separated entirely from rectifying. It seems as if Congress, while removing rectifying houses, took especial pains to make another class of houses not prohibited, which are as easy adjuncts for fraud as the class they proscribed. Many Revenue officers were examined, and all concur in the opinion above expressed, as to the character of compounding houses, with the remarkable exception of the collector and deputy-collector of one of the New York Districts, who consider them entirely harmless, and without the power to defraud. The significance of this exceptional evidence will appear hereafter."

HOW THE GOVERNMENT AIDS THE RING.

Efforts are made to discover and bring to justice the perpetrators of these swindles, but they accomplish nothing. Complaints are made to the Treasury Department, and investigations are ordered, but nothing is done to check the evil. A Revenue officer dares not do his duty, in nine cases out of ten, because the "Ring" will procure his dismissal from his place for such display of honesty. Further than this, the "Ring" in some way manage to secure the appointment of officials who will aid them in their infamous schemes. The newspaper press of the whole land teems with instances of whiskey frauds, and the names of the guilty parties are often freely published, but still no one is brought to justice, and the frauds go on.

A prominent journal thus describes the state of affairs in the city of New Orleans:

"A gentleman who has just arrived in this city from New Orleans, and who, during his visit at that city, took particular pains to inquire into matters in connection with the collection of the revenue, reports the most appalling corruptions in all branches of that service. He says that, with but two or three exceptions, thieves and plunderers have, from the first, been in office in Louisiana, and that their subordinates have been sufficiently in collusion with them to enable them to carry out their schemes and robbery; that officers of different districts have been leagued together in perpetrating and covering up the immense cotton frauds amounting to millions. He says that there were over forty licensed distilleries running in New Orleans during the last fiscal year, and that the Government did not *collect tax enough to pay the salaries of the storekeepers.* No distiller has ever yet been prosecuted in Louisiana, to a final conviction. Bonded warehouses for liquors have been robbed of thousands of barrels. Warehouses were burned down where the liquors had been previously stolen. Bonds of Collectors have been wholly worthless, the securities when accepted being notoriously insolvent. Warehouse bonds have been largely of the same character. He reports that the Judge of an important court is openly denounced as unfaithful to his trust, and that the U. S. District Attorney is charged with being in the "ring," and that the defendants in certain wine lawsuits soon to be tried in that city have openly boasted that they have so "fixed" things that the Government can never obtain a verdict in the U. S. Court. The Secretary of the Treasury has been advised by merchants of high standing in New Orleans that gross frauds were committed last winter and spring in the Custom-House, and that Custom-House officers and Internal Revenue officers have colluded together in the fraudulent shipments of whiskey; that men holding small salaried offices have suddenly become rich, some buying plantations and valuable stock, others valuable city property, some spending tens of thousands upon fast women, and others losing still larger sums at the gaming-table and horse-races, while yet another, as rumor has it, is enabled to pay $40,000 to get elected to a high Congressional post, filling certain New Orleans offices from top to bottom with the negro legislators, and paying them $3 a day for doing nothing. The gentleman who is here and gives this information, says that all these matters have been reported over and over again to the Secretary of the Treasury, and the other authorities concerned, but that nothing has been done to stem the tide of corruption that is sweeping over the whole of that country, except to send down a mere boy from the Treasury Department, who writes back to Washington telling of the vast amounts of money that he could get if he would only join teams with the revenue officers."

Bad as the "situation" is in the Crescent City, the other great cities of the country do not present a much better picture when compared with it.

CONGRESS AND THE RING.

It is a notorious fact that the excise laws are full of imperfections, all of which are in favor of the Ring, and afford it great protection and encouragement in its efforts against the Government. Steps have been taken to bring about such changes as shall secure a thorough and honest collection of the revenue. These efforts meet with an uncompromising hostility on the part of the Whiskey men. They are willing to spend any amount of money in order to continue their dishonest practices, and keep their agents in Washington. The newspapers of the land do not hesitate to charge Members of Congress with corrupt practices in connection with these agents. It has been but recently stated that the failure of a certain United States Senator to secure his reëlection during the present winter would be very disastrous to the Whiskey Ring. Efforts are made in Congress to investigate the frauds, and committees report that the whole affair is very simple, greatly exaggerated, and easily remedied. The worst feature is that the men who compose or head these committees are those who are openly charged by the press with being in the pay of the "Ring." If innocent, these Members are placed in false positions by serving on these committees. If guilty, it is not to be expected that they will voluntarily criminate themselves. It is due to the country that these investigating committees should consist of men who have not been so assailed, and whose integrity has not been even suspected. There are such men in Congress, and their services in this connection are much needed.

Yet, in spite of the indifference and denials of Treasury officials and the "whitewashing reports" of Congressional Committees, the facts remain plain to all observers. The whiskey frauds continue. The whiskey men grow rich. The revenue from whiskey is known to be out of proportion to the activity in the whiskey trade, and the Government is swindled out of millions of dollars every year. These facts need no comment. Every intelligent man will form his own opinion with reference to them. The prevailing sentiment throughout the country is that this branch of the Revenue Service is rotten to the core, and that those in power do not desire a fair investigation of it.

AN HONEST INSPECTOR VS. THE RING.

A New York Detective relates the following incident, which will show the desperate measures resorted to by the whiskey men to continue their frauds:

"Last winter was a trying time for the owners of the distilleries and rectifying houses. There were three or four special agents of the Internal Revenue Department in New York, who held special authority from the Commissioner of Internal Revenue to seize all distilled spirits and all establishments engaged in the distillation or rectification of spirits suspected of fraud. The city swarmed with detectives and 'spotters' (a name given to those employed by the government to watch distilleries and rectifying houses), and no amount of money or influence could make the business of a dealer in spirits secure.

"The special authorization to seize, was generally given to men who used the power to extract money from the dealers in spirits, or as a menace to other Internal Revenue officers. One officer, however, an ex colonel of volunteers, made seizure after seizure of the largest liquor establishments in the city. He pounced upon the liquor-dealers unawares, acted independently of the detectives, or rather had his own system of gaining information independent of the government. It was noticed, that he rarely seized without securing a large amount of spirits, and almost always made a strong case for the government. This man the liquor dealers and their lawyers could neither bribe, intimidate, nor control, and many consultations were held by those engaged in the fraudulent manipulation of spirits, to mature a plan to get rid of him. It was finally arranged that the owners of a certain distillery in the upper part of the city, then in charge of the United States Marshal, should get authority from a Deputy Commissioner of Internal Revenue to keep up steam in their premises. Keepers in the interest of the distillers were put in charge of the premises. Some of the worst characters known to the police were chosen for the business, with orders to attack the ex-colonel of volunteers, should he attempt to force an entrance. In this way a very troublesome officer would be disposed of, while it was hoped that the death or maiming of the Colonel would intimidate others.

"A detective was bribed to report the case to the Colonel, and to offer to accompany him, in order to conduct him into the premises by a back entrance, near which the cut-throats in pay of the distillers would be in waiting. I went to the Colonel's house when I had sufficient evidence of the plot to warrant me in disclosing it, to warn him of his danger, but he was reported to me as dining with a friend and engaged to return to his house at ten o'clock P. M. I called again at this hour and waited until after eleven for his return. Fearing that the Colonel would make the seizure without returning to his home, I went to his office, hoping that he had made it a place of rendezvous for his men before starting on his expedition, upon which, by this time, I felt certain that he was bent. When I arrived at the office and had aroused the watchman in charge, I was informed that the Colonel had started only a few minutes before, with three or four men, and that he had taken a 'jimmy' and other tools to force an entrance. It seemed to me that the best thing to do was to go to the nearest police precinct, take three or four policemen, and repair at once to the distillery. I knew the revenue officials were about to seize, and if I could not get there in time to save the government officers, at least I could arrest the assassins. When I arrived near the premises I met some men who said that they were revenue officers, and had just been fired on, and that some of their comrades were there in actual collision with what I knew to be a party of assassins. As we pushed on breathless and entered the back gate, I heard the expressions, 'Look out for him!' 'Do you see him!' 'Look out for his knife in his left hand!' As I came on the rear of the scoundrels, I could just see the Colonel, who had managed to get into a dark niche and held his adversaries at a disadvantage, for they were huddled under a gaslight. How the Colonel had escaped assassination I don't know, but his opponents were evidently bewildered, and suddenly gave themselves up to the police. I heard afterwards that when the revenue officers entered, the men in the building were playing a game of poker, and thus a fierce altercation was going on as to the comparative honor of the thieves, and when called out to attack the revenue officers blows were being exchanged, so that when called to confront the Colonel, they were suspicious of one another, and at cross-purposes.

"This, together with the Colonel's coolness, and adroitness in keeping in the shade, undoubtedly saved his life."

Besides the Whiskey Ring, there are other organizations whose headquarters are in Washington, and whose object is to make money by swindling the Government out of its dues. They represent capitalists speculating in cotton, tobacco, and other bonded goods; in articles furnished to the Indians on the frontier by the Government; and in government contracts of various kinds. They are conducted in a manner similar to that in which the Whiskey Ring is operated. The Indian Ring has become so notoriously corrupt that General Grant and the army officers have urged upon

Congress the duty of transferring it from the Department of the Interior to the Department of War as a means of protecting the Indians from the outrages practised upon them by the contractors.

VII.

THE PRESIDENT.

HAVING glanced at the Legislative Department of the Government, let us now turn to the Executive.

The Constitution of the United States requires that "the Executive power shall be vested in a President of the United States of America. He shall hold his office during the term of four years, and, together with the Vice-President, chosen for the same term, be elected as follows:

"Each State shall appoint, in such manner as the Legislature thereof may direct, a number of electors, equal to the whole number of Senators and Representatives to which the State may be entitled in Congress; but no Senator, or Representative, or person holding an office of trust or profit under the United States, shall be appointed an elector. The electors shall meet in their respective States, and vote by ballot for President and Vice-President, one of whom, at least, shall not be an inhabitant of the same State with themselves; they shall name in their ballots the person voted for as President, and in distinct ballots the person voted for as Vice-President; and they shall make distinct lists of all persons voted for as President, and all persons voted for as Vice-President, and of the number of votes for each, which lists they shall sign and certify, and transmit, sealed, to the seat of the Government of the United States, directed to the President of the Senate. The President of the Senate shall, in the presence of the Senate and House of Representatives, open all the certificates, and the votes shall then be counted; the person having the greatest number of votes for President shall be the President, if such number be a majority of the whole number of electors appointed; and if no person have such majority, then, from the persons having the highest numbers, not exceeding three, on the list of those voted for as President, the House of Representatives shall choose immediately, by ballot, the President. But in choosing the President, the votes shall be taken by States, the representation from each State having one vote; a quorum for this purpose, to consist of a member or members from two-thirds of the States, and a majority of all the States shall be necessary to a choice; and if the House of Representatives shall not choose a President, whenever the right of choice shall devolve upon them, before the fourth day of March next following, then the Vice-President, elected by the Senate shall act as President, as in the case of the death or other constitutional disability of the President. The person having the greatest number of votes as Vice-President shall be the Vice-President, if such number be a majority of the whole number of electors appointed; and if no person have a majority, then, from the two highest numbers on the list, the Senate shall choose the Vice-President; a quorum for the purpose shall consist of two-thirds of the whole number of Senators, and a majority of the whole number shall be necessary to a choice. But no person constitutionally ineligible to the office of President shall be eligible to that of Vice-President of the United States.

"The Congress may determine the time of choosing the electors, and the day on which they shall give their votes, which day shall be the same throughout the United States.

"No person except a natural-born citizen, or a citizen of the United States at the time of the adoption of this Constitution, shall be eligible to the office of President; neither shall any person be eligible to that office who shall not have attained to the age of thirty-five years, and been fourteen years a resident within the United States.

"In case of the removal of the President from office, or of his death, resignation, or inability to discharge the powers and duties of the said office, the same shall devolve on the Vice-President, and the Congress may by law provide for the case of removal, death, resignation, or inability, both of the President and Vice-President, declaring what officer shall then act as President, and such officer shall act accordingly, until the disability be removed, or a President shall be elected.

"The President shall at stated times receive for his services a compensation, which shall neither be increased nor diminished during the period for which he shall have been elected, and he shall not receive, within that period, any other emolument from the United States, or any of them.

"Before he enter on the execution of his office, he shall take the following Oath or Affirmation:

"'I do solemnly swear (or affirm), that I will faithfully execute the office of President of the United States, and will, to the best of my ability, preserve, protect, and defend the Constitution of the United States.'"

The President is, by virtue of his office, Commander-in-Chief of the Army and Navy, and of the Militia of the several States, when in the active service of the United States. He has the power to pardon and grant reprieves, except in cases of impeachment. He appoints all officials of the Government, and, constitutionally, has the power to remove them when he deems it his duty to do so. He negotiates treaties with foreign Powers, and conducts the official intercourse of this Government with them. He executes, or causes to be executed, the laws of Congress, and from time to time lays before that body such information as he deems proper, respecting the state of the country, and recommends such measures as he judges necessary and expedient.

THE INAUGURATION.

The President enters upon his duties on the fourth of March next following his election by the people. The Constitution merely requires him to take the oath already given, but does not prescribe the hour, place, or manner of taking it, and there is no law of Congress regulating the inaugural ceremonies. The oath of office could be legally administered by any magistrate, but it is usual for the Chief-Justice of the United States to act upon such occasions.

Owing to the absence of any set form for the inaugural ceremonies, different customs have prevailed at different times. A review of these will be entertaining.

George Washington was first inaugurated President in New York City, on the 1st of May, 1789. He was escorted from his residence in Broad Street to the City Hall, which occupied the site of the present U. S. Sub-Treasury, where Chancellor Livingston administered the oath of office to him in the presence of the people. In 1793, he entered upon his second term by taking the oath in the Senate Chamber, in the presence of the two Houses of Congress and other dignitaries. John Adams was inaugurated in 1797, by taking the oath of office in the House of Representatives, at noon on the 4th of March. He delivered an inaugural address from the Speaker's Chair, before taking the oath.

Thomas Jefferson was the first President inaugurated in the City of Washington. He delivered an inaugural address, and took the oath of office in the Senate Chamber at noon on the 4th of March, 1801. He delivered no address upon the occasion of his second inauguration, but merely subscribed to the oath in the presence of Chief-Justice Marshall, and Judges Patterson, Cushing, and Washington of the Supreme Court. James Madison took the oath of office and delivered his inaugural address in the hall of the House of Representatives, on the 4th of March, 1809, and on the occasion of his second inauguration was merely sworn in at the Capitol by Chief-Justice Marshall.

Upon the election of Mr. Monroe, in 1816, it was resolved to make the inaugural ceremonies more imposing. On the 4th of March, 1817, the Vice-President was first sworn in, and then Mr. Monroe appeared on an elevated platform in front of the Capitol, delivered his inaugural address, and took the oath of office, which was administered by the Chief-Justice in the presence of an immense multitude. A salute of artillery was then fired, and the new President retired to the White House. When reëlected, Mr. Monroe could not be sworn into office on the 4th of March (1821), as that day happened to fall upon Sunday. As no legal oath can be administered on Sunday, the inauguration was postponed until the 5th, which proved a very tempestuous day. Mr. Monroe then simply took the official oath before Chief-Justice Marshall. On the 4th of March, 1825, John Quincy Adams delivered his inaugural, and took the oath of office in the Hall of the House of Representatives. On the 4th of March, 1829, Andrew Jackson delivered his inaugural address from the eastern portico of the Capitol, and took the oath of office in the presence of an immense multitude. On the occasion of his second inauguration, four years later, the ceremonies were conducted in the Hall of Representatives. Martin Van Buren was inaugurated on the 4th of March, 1837. The Vice-President was first sworn in, when he took the Chair as Presiding Officer of the Senate. At noon, Mr. Van Buren, accompanied by General Jackson, the retiring President, entered the Senate Chamber, from which the party repaired to the east portico of the Capitol, in front of which an immense multitude had gathered. Here Mr. Van Buren delivered his inaugural address, and took the oath of office at the hands of Chief-Justice Taney. On the 4th of March, 1841, General Harrison left his quarters, mounted on a magnificent white war horse, and was escorted to the Capitol by a brilliant throng. He at once repaired to the Senate Chamber, where the new Vice-President, John Tyler, had been sworn in. Repairing to the eastern portico, he delivered his inaugural, after which the oath of office was administered by Chief-Justice Taney. General Harrison survived his election only a few weeks. He was succeeded by Mr. Tyler, the Vice-President, who, although he deemed his oath as Vice-President a sufficient qualification for his new position, yet immediately took the Presidential oath before the Chief-Judge of the Circuit Court of the District of Columbia. James K. Polk was inaugurated in 1845, with an imposing display, the Vice-President, George M. Dallas, being first sworn in. The ceremonies took place in the eastern portico of the Capitol, and were followed by a levee at the White House. General Taylor was inaugurated on the 5th of March, 1848, the 4th chancing to fall upon a Sunday, and making the second day in the history of the country when the Republic has been without a President. He delivered his inaugural from the East Portico, and took the oath before Chief-Justice Taney, with the usual ceremonies. General Taylor died July 9, 1850, and on the 11th Mr. Fillmore, the Vice-President, took the Presidential oath in the House of Representatives.

Upon arriving in Washington for the purpose of entering upon the duties of his office, General Pierce took lodgings at Willard's Hotel. On the 4th of March, 1853, he was waited upon by the retiring President, Mr. Fillmore, and the Hon. Jesse D. Bright and Hon. Hannibal Hamlin, who had been appointed a Committee for that purpose by Congress, and was conducted to the Capitol by a splendid escort, in which detachments of the regular troops of the United States and a force of Volunteers took part. He delivered his inaugural, and took the oath before Chief-Justice Taney, from the East Portico, after which he held a levee at the White House. On the 4th of March, 1857, James Buchanan was escorted from his lodgings at Willard's Hotel to the Capitol, where the oath was administered to him in the Senate Chamber, by the Hon. James M. Mason, President *pro. tem.* of the Senate. Mr. Buchanan then repaired to the East Portico, where he delivered his inaugural address in the presence of an immense multitude.

On the 4th of March, 1861, Abraham Lincoln was inaugurated President. Rumors of plots to assassinate him were so plentiful, that it became advisable for him to pass through the State of Maryland with the utmost secrecy. He reached Washington in this way before any one but his most trusted friends were aware of his movements. Threats against his life were openly made after his arrival, and it became necessary to station a strong force of regular troops throughout the city, so as to make sure of the preservation of order and peace. The military arrangements were directed by General

Scott in person. Mr. Lincoln was conducted to the Capitol with great display. He was received by the Senate, and escorted to the East Portico, where he delivered his address, and took the oath before Chief-Justice Taney. His second inauguration, March 4, 1865, was accompanied with one of the finest displays ever witnessed in Washington. The ceremonies took place in the East Portico of the Capitol. The morning was dark and lowering, but as the President placed himself in front of the venerable Chief-Justice to pronounce the solemn vow, the sun burst from behind the heavy clouds, and shone down upon him with all its brilliancy.

The next occasion of this kind will be the inauguration of General Grant, and will be one of the most magnificent displays ever witnessed in America.

WHAT IT COSTS THE PRESIDENT TO LIVE.

The official salary of the President is fixed by law at twenty-five thousand dollars per annum, or one hundred thousand dollars for his term of four years. At the beginning of each term Congress makes an appropriation for refurnishing the Executive Mansion. The kitchen and pantry are supplied to a considerable extent by the same body. Congress pays all the employees about the house, from the private secretary to the humblest bootblack; it provides fuel and lights; keeps up the stables; and furnishes a corps of gardeners and a garden to supply the Presidential board with fruits, flowers, and vegetables. Besides this, the President receives many presents from private parties.

Many persons suppose that these allowances ought to be enough to enable him to live comfortably. They are mistaken, however. The President is required by public opinion to live in a style consistent with the dignity of his position and the honor of the country, and such a mode of life imposes upon him many very heavy expenses. Besides this, he is expected to be liberal and charitable towards persons and meritorious causes seeking his aid, and "their name is legion." He cannot give as a private individual; his donation must be large. The expense of entertaining the various officers of the Government, members of Congress, and Foreign Ministers is enormous; so that, when all things are considered, it is a wonder how the President can live decently upon the small allowance made him by Congress, especially at the present time when prices are so high, and the currency so much depreciated. One hundred thousand dollars per annum would not be too much to allow him.

THE PRESIDENT'S VISITORS.

Access to the President may be easily had by any person having legitimate business with him, or wishing to pay his respects to the Chief Magistrate of the Union, but, as His Excellency's time is valuable and much occupied, interviews are limited to the shortest possible duration. Visitors, upon such occasions, repair to the reception-room adjoining the President's private office, send in their cards, and await His Excellency's pleasure.

Besides granting these private interviews, the

President holds public receptions or levees at stated times during the sessions of Congress.

His official title is "Mr. President," but courtesy has added that of "His Excellency." It is worthy of remark that none of the Executive officers of the States of the Union, except the Governor of Massachusetts, have any legal claim to the titles, "His Excellency" and "Your Excellency."

All sorts of people come to see the President, on all sorts of business. His immense patronage makes him the object of the efforts of many unprincipled men. His integrity is subjected to the severest trials, and if he come out of office poor, as happily all of our Presidents have done, he must indeed be an honest man. His position is not a bed of roses, for he cannot hope to please all parties. His friends exaggerate his good qualities, and often make him appear ridiculous, while his enemies magnify his faults and errors, and slander and persecute him in every imaginable way. Pitfalls are set for him along every step of his path, and he must be wary indeed, if he would not fall into them. The late President Buchanan once said that there were at least two persons in the world who could not echo the wish experienced by each American mother, that her son might one day be President, and that they were the retiring and the incoming Presidents, the first of whom was worn and weary with the burden he was laying down, and the other for the first time fully alive to the magnitude of the task he had undertaken.

CABINET MEETINGS.

The Cabinet Ministers in our Government are the Secretaries placed at the heads of the various Departments. They are the constitutional advisers of the President, but he is not obliged to be governed by their advice. It is customary, however, to lay all important matters before them for their opinions thereupon, which are submitted in writing at the request of the President, and for this purpose regular meetings of the Cabinet are held at stated times in a room in the Executive Mansion, provided for that purpose. It is located on the second floor of the mansion, and is plainly but comfortably furnished.

The relations existing between the President and his Cabinet are, or ought to be, of the most friendly and confidential nature. They are well set forth in the attitude maintained upon this point by Mr. Lincoln. Says Mr. Raymond, his biographer: "He always maintained that the proper duty of each Secretary was to direct the details of every thing done within his own Department, and to tender such suggestions, information, and advice to the President, as he might solicit at his hands. But the duty and responsibility of deciding what line of policy should be pursued, or what steps should be taken in any specific case, in his judgment, belonged exclusively to the President; and he was always willing and ready to assume it."

VIII.

THE WHITE HOUSE.

THE Executive Mansion is situated on Pennsylvania Avenue, near the western end of the city, and is surrounded by the Treasury, State, War, and Navy Departments. The grounds in front are handsomely ornamented, and in the rear a fine park stretches away to the river. The location is attractive, and commands a magnificent view of the Potomac, but it is not healthy. Ague and fever prevails in the Spring and Fall, and renders it any thing but a desirable place of residence. The building is constructed of freestone painted white —hence its most common name, the "White House." It was designed by James Hoban, and was modelled after the palace of the Duke of Leinster. The cornerstone was laid on the 13th of October, 1792, and the house was ready for occupancy in the Summer of 1800. It was partially destroyed by the British in 1814. It has a front of one hundred and seventy feet, and a depth of eighty-six feet. It contains two lofty stories of rooms, and the roof is surrounded with a handsome balustrade. The exterior walls are ornamented with fine Ionic pilasters. On the north front is a handsome portico, with four Ionic columns in front, and a projecting screen with three columns. The space between these two rows of pillars is a covered carriage way

THE WHITE HOUSE—REAR VIEW.

The main entrance to the house is from this portico through a massive doorway, which opens into the main hall. The garden front has a rusticated basement, which gives a third story to the house on this side, and by a semicircular projecting colonnade of six columns, with two flights of steps leading from the ground to the level of the principal story.

THE INTERIOR OF THE WHITE HOUSE.

Entering by the main door, the visitor finds himself in a handsome hall, divided midway by a row of imitation marble pillars, and ornamented with portraits of former Presidents. Passing to the left, you enter the magnificent banqueting hall, or, as it is commonly called,

THE EAST ROOM,

which occupies the entire eastern side of the house. It is a beautiful apartment, and is handsomely furnished. It is used during the levees and upon great state occasions. The President sometimes receives here the congratulations and respects of his fellow-citizens, and is subjected to the torture of having his hand squeezed out of shape by his enthusiastic friends. It's a great pity that some one of our Chief Magistrates has not the moral courage to put a stop to this ridiculous practice of hand-shaking. The East Room is eighty-six feet long, forty feet wide, and twenty-eight feet high. It has four fire-places, and is not an easy room to warm.

Adjoining the East Room are three others, smaller

in size, the whole constituting one of the handsomest *suites* in the country. The first, adjoining the East Room, is the *Green Room*, the next the *Blue Room*, and the third the *Red Room*. Each is handsomely furnished, the prevailing color of the apartment giving the name.

THE RED ROOM

is elliptical in form, having a bow in rear, and is one of the handsomest in the house. It is used by the President as a general reception-room. He receives here the official visits of the dignitaries of the Republic, and of foreign ministers. Previous to the completion of the East Room, this apartment was used for all occasions of public ceremony.

The building contains thirty-one rooms of considerable size. West of the Red Room is the large dining-room used upon State occasions, and adjoining that is the small dining-room, ordinarily used by the President and his family. The stairs to the upper story are on the left of the main entrance, and are always in charge of the door-keeper and his assistants, whose business it is to see that no improper characters find access to the private portion of the house.

The north front has six rooms, which are used as chambers by the family of the President, and the south front has seven rooms — the ante-chamber, audience-room, cabinet-room, private office of the President, the ladies' parlor, and two others, used for various purposes.

THE LADIES' PARLOR

is situated immediately over the Red Room, and is of the same size and shape. It is for the private use of the ladies of the President's family, and is the hand somest and most tastefully furnished apartment in the house.

There are eleven rooms in the basement, which are used as kitchens, pantries, butler's-room, &c. The house is built in the old style, and has an air of elegance and comfort extremely pleasing to the eye. The furniture is, as a general rule, costly, but a little more taste might have been exhibited in its selection and arrangement.

THE FIRST MISTRESS OF THE WHITE HOUSE.

Mrs. John Adams came to Washington with her husband in November, 1800, and at once took possession of the Executive Mansion. Her impressions of it are thus described by herself in a letter to her daughter, written soon after her arrival. She says:

"The house is upon a grand and superb scale, requiring about thirty servants to attend and keep the apartments in proper order, and perform the ordinary business of the house and stables—an establishment very well proportioned to the President's salary. The lighting the apartments, from the kitchen to parlors and chambers, is a tax indeed, and the fires we are obliged to keep to secure us from daily agues, is another very cheering comfort. To assist us in this great castle, and render less attendance necessary, bells are wholly wanting, not one single one being hung through the whole house, and promises are all you can obtain. This is so great an inconvenience, that I know not what to do or how to do. The ladies from Georgetown and in the city have many of them visited me. Yesterday I returned fifteen visits. But such a place as Georgetown appears! Why, our Milton is beautiful. But no comparisons; if they put me up bells, and let me have wood enough to keep fires, I design *to be pleased.* But, surrounded with forests, can you believe that wood is not to be had, because people cannot be found to cut and cart it. * * * We have, indeed, come into a *new country.*

"The house is made habitable, but there is not a single apartment finished, and all within side, except the plastering, has been done since B. came. We have not the *least fence, yard, or convenience without,* and the great unfinished audience-room I make a drying-room of, to hang up the clothes in. * * * If the twelve years, in which this place has been considered as the future seat of government, had been improved, as they would have been in New England, very many of the present inconveniences would have been removed. It is a beautiful spot, capable of any improvement, and the more I view it, the more I am delighted with it."

OLD TIMES AT THE WHITE HOUSE.

Mr. Cooper thus describes a dinner at the White

House, to which he was invited, during its occupancy by Mr. Monroe:

"On this occasion, we were honored with the presence of Mrs. Monroe, and two or three of her female relatives. Crossing the hall, we were admitted to a drawing-room, in which most of the company were already assembled. The hour was six. By far the greater part of the guests were men, and perhaps two thirds were Members of Congress. * * * There was very great gravity of mien in most of the company, and neither any very marked exhibition, nor any positively striking want, of grace of manner. The conversation was commonplace, and a little sombre, though two or three men of the world got around the ladies, where the battle of words was maintained with sufficient spirit. * * * To me the entertainment had rather a cold than a formal air. When dinner was announced, the oldest Senator present (there were two, and seniority of service is meant) took Mrs. Monroe, and led her to the table. The rest of the party followed without much order. The President took a lady, as usual, and preceded the rest of the guests.

"The drawing-room was an apartment of good size, and of just proportions. It might have been about as large as the better sort of Paris *salon* in a private hotel. It was furnished in a mixed style, partly English and partly French. * * * It was neat, sufficiently rich, without being at all magnificent, and, on the whole, was very much like a similar apartment in the house of a man of rank and fortune in Europe. The dining-room was in a better taste than is common here, being quite simple, and but little furnished. The table was large and rather handsome. The service was in china, as is uniformly the case, plate being exceedingly rare, if at all used. There was, however, a rich plateau, and a great abundance of the smaller articles of table-plate. The cloth, napkins, &c., &c., were fine and beautiful.

"The dinner was served in the French style, a little Americanized. The dishes were handed round, though some of the guests, appearing to prefer their own customs, coolly helped themselves to what they found at hand. Of attendants there were a good many. They were neatly dressed, out of livery, and sufficient. To conclude, the whole entertainment might have passed for a better sort of European dinner-party, at which the guests were too numerous for general or very agreeable discourse, and some of them too *new* to be entirely at their ease. Mrs. Monroe arose, at the end of the dessert, and withdrew, attended by two or three of the most gallant of the company. No sooner was his wife's back turned, than the President reseated himself, inviting his guests to imitate the action. After allowing his guests sufficient time to renew, in a few glasses, the recollections of similar enjoyments of their own, he arose himself, giving the hint to his company, that it was time to rejoin the ladies. In the drawing-room, coffee was served, and every body left the house before nine."

AN OLD TIME LEVEE.

"On the succeeding Wednesday, Mrs. Monroe opened her doors to all the world. No invitation was necessary, it being the usage for the wife of the President to receive company once a fortnight during the session, without distinction of persons.

"We reached the White House at nine. The court (or rather the grounds) was filled with carriages, and the company was arriving in great numbers. On this occasion, two or three additional drawing-rooms were opened, though the frugality of Congress has prevented them from finishing the principal reception-room of the building. I will acknowledge the same sort of surprise I felt at the Castle Garden *fête*, at finding the assemblage so respectable in air, dress, and deportment.

"The evening at the White House, or drawing-room, as it is sometimes pleasantly called, is, in fact, a collection of all classes of people, who choose to go to the trouble and expense of appearing in dresses suited to an ordinary evening party. I am not sure that even dress is much regarded; for I certainly saw a good many there in boots. The females were all neatly and properly attired, though few were ornamented with jewelry. Of course, the poor and laboring clases of the community would find little or no pleasure in such a scene. They consequently stay away. The infamous, if known, would not be admitted; for it is a peculiar consequence of the high tone of morals in this country, that grave and notorious offenders rarely presume to violate the public feeling by invading society.*

"Squeezing through the crowd, we achieved a passage to a part of the room where Mrs. Monroe was standing, surrounded by a bevy of female friends. After making our bow here, we sought the President. The latter had posted himself at the top of the room, where he remained most of the evening, shaking hands with all who approached. Near him stood all the Secretaries, and a great number of the most distinguished men of the nation. Individuals of importance from all parts of the Union were also here, and were employed in the manner usual to such scenes.

"Besides these, one meets here a great variety of people in other conditions of life. I have known a cartman to leave his horse in the street, and go into the reception-room to shake hands with the President. He offended the good taste of all present, because it was not thought decent that a laborer should come in a dirty dress on such an occasion; but while he made a trifling mistake in this particular, he proved how well he understood the difference between government and society. He knew the levee was a sort of homage paid to political equality in the person of the first magistrate, but he would not have presumed to enter the house of the same person as a private individual, without being invited, or without a reasonable excuse in the way of business.

"There are, no doubt, individuals who mistake the character of these assemblies, but the great

* This was nearly fifty years ago.—*Author.*

majority do not. They are a simple, periodical acknowledgment that there is no legal barrier to the advancement of any one to the first association in the Union. You perceive, there are no masters of ceremonies, no ushers, no announcings, nor, indeed, any let or hindrance to the ingress of all who please to come; and yet how few, in comparison to the whole number who might enter, do actually appear. If there is any man in Washington so dull as to suppose equality means a right to thrust himself into any company he pleases, it is probable he satisfies himself by boasting that he can go to the White House once a fortnight, as well as a governor or anybody else."

ETIQUETTE.

The social observances of the White House are prescribed with the utmost exactness. At the commencement of Washington's administration, the question of how to regulate such matters was discussed with great earnestness. It was agreed that the exclusive rules by which European courts were governed, would not entirely suit the new Republic, as there were no titled personages in America, and as the society of our country was organized on a professed basis of equality. Washington caused the following articles to be drawn up:

"In order to bring the members of society together in the first instance, the custom of the country has established that residents shall pay the first visit to strangers, and, among strangers, first comers to later comers, foreign and domestic; the character of stranger ceasing after the first visits. To this rule there is a single exception. Foreign ministers, from the necessity of making themselves known, pay the first visit to the [cabinet] ministers of the nation, which is returned.

"When brought together in society, all are perfectly equal, whether foreign or domestic, titled or untitled, in or out of office.

"All other observances are but exemplifications of these two principles.

"The families of foreign ministers, arriving at the seat of government, receive the first visit from those of the national ministers, as from all other residents.

"Members of the legislature and of the judiciary, independent of their offices, have a right as strangers to receive the first visit.

"No title being admitted here, those of foreigners give no precedence.

"Differences of grade among the diplomatic members give no precedence.

"At public ceremonies, to which the government invites the presence of foreign ministers and their families, a convenient seat or station will be provided for them, with any other strangers invited, and the families of the national ministers, each taking place as they arrive, and without any precedence.

"To maintain the principle of equality, or of *pêle mêle*, and prevent the growth of precedence out of courtesy, the members of the executive will practise at their own houses, and recommend an adherence to the ancient usage of the country, of gentlemen in mass giving precedence to the ladies in mass, in passing from one apartment were they are assembled into another."

These rules were too arbitrary and exacting to give satisfaction, and society was not disposed to acknowledge so genuine an equality amongst its members. For some years, disputes and quarrels were frequent and bitter. In the winter of 1819, John Quincy Adams, then Secretary of State, addressed a letter to Daniel D. Tompkins, the Vice-President, stating that he had been informed that the members of the Senate had agreed amongst themselves to pay no first visits to any person except the President of the United States. He declared that he repudiated the claim on the part of the Senators, and that he would pay no first calls himself as being due from him or his family. Mr. Adams was severely criticised for his aristocratic views, and the controversy went on as warmly as before. The result, a few years later, was, that all parties interested agreed upon a code, which is now in force, and which may be stated as follows, as far as the White House is concerned:

THE CODE.

The title of the Executive is *Mr. President.* It is not proper to address him in conversation as *Your Excellency.*

The President receives calls upon matters of business at any hour, if he is unengaged. He prefers that such visits should be made in the morning. Stated times are appointed for receiving persons who wish to pay their respects to him. One morning and one evening in each week are ususually set apart for this purpose.

During the winter season, a public reception, or levee, is held once a week, at which guests are expected to appear in full dress. They are presented by the Usher on such occasions, and have the honor of shaking hands with the President. These receptions last from eight until ten o'clock.

On the 1st of January and the 4th of July, the President holds public receptions, at which the Foreign Ministers present in the city appear in full court dress, and the officers of the Army and Navy in full uniform. The Heads of Departments, Governors of States, and Members of Congress are received first, then the Diplomatic Corps, then officers of the Army and Navy, and then the doors are thrown open to the public generally for the space of two hours.

The President, as such, must not be invited to dinner by any one, and accepts no such invitations, and pays no calls or visits of ceremony. He may visit in his private capacity, however, at pleasure.

An invitation to dine at the White House takes precedence of all others, and a previous engagement must not be pleaded as an excuse for declining it Such an invitation must be promptly accepted in writing.

THE PRESIDENT'S RECEPTIONS.

The levees held by the President differ in nothing from those of Mr. Monroe's time, described a few pages back, except that the East Room is now finished, and the whole magnificent suite of apartments is used. The *élite* of the land are present, but the *infamous* are also there in the persons of those who live by plundering the public treasury.

The President stands in one of the smaller parlors, generally in the Red or Blue Room. He is surrounded by his Cabinet, and the most distinguished men in the land. Near him stands his wife, daughter, or some relative representing the mistress of the mansion. Visitors enter from the hall, and are presented to the President by the Usher, who first asks their names, residences, and avocations. The President shakes each one by the hand cordially, utters a few pleasant words in reply to the greetings of his guest, and the visitor passes on into the next room, to make way for those behind him. Before doing so, however, he is presented to the lady of the house, to whom he pays his respects also. This regular routine goes on for the space of two hours, when it is brought to an end, the President devoutly thanking Heaven that it does not last all night.

These levees are no doubt very interesting to the guests, but they are the bugbears of the President and his family. The former is obliged by custom to shake hands with every man presented to him, and when the levee is over, his right hand is often bruised and swollen. It is said that some of the Presidents have suffered severely from this species of torture, and that General Harrison's death was to some degree hastened by it.

The semi-annual receptions of the President—New Year's Day and the Fourth of July—are brilliant affairs. At a little before eleven o'clock in the morning, the approaches to the Executive Mansion are thronged with the splendid equipages of the various Cabinet officers and Foreign Ministers. The entrance at such times is by the main door, and the exit through one of the large north windows of the East Room, in front of which a temporary platform is erected. The customs upon such occasions vary slightly with each administration. In the description given here, the order observed at the last reception of the President, January 1, 1869, is followed.

The East Room and the other parlors are handsomely decorated with flowers and other ornaments, the full Marine Band is in attendance to furnish music for the promenaders in the East Room, and a strong police force is present to preserve order when the people are admitted *en masse.*

At a few minutes before eleven o'clock, the President and the ladies of the White House, in full dress, take their places in the Blue Room, the President standing near the door leading into the Red Room, and the ladies in the centre of the Blue Room. The President is attended by either the Commissioner of Public Buildings, or the Marshal of the District of Columbia, whose duty it is to present the guests to him. A gentleman is also appointed to attend the ladies for the purpose of presenting the guests to them.

Precisely at eleven o'clock the doors are thrown open, and the reception begins. The Cabinet Ministers and their families are admitted first, and after they have passed on into the East Room, through the Green Parlor, the Secretary of State remains and presents the

Foreign Ministers and their families. They are fol lowed by the Justices of the Supreme Court and their families. Then come the Senators and Representatives in Congress and their families. The next in order are the officers of the Army, then the officers of the Navy and Marine Corps, in full uniform, and then the officials of the District of Columbia. These personages generally occupy the first hour. The doors are then opened to the public, and the next two hours are devoted to receiving them. Several thousand persons are presented during this period. They say a few pleasant words to the President, receive a brief reply, and pass on.

The promenaders in the East Room often linger in that apartment during the whole reception. The scene is brilliant, the toilettes are magnificent, the uniforms and court dresses attractive, and the music fine. At a little after two o'clock the parlors are deserted, and the gay throng has sought other attractions.

Besides these public levees, the ladies of the White House hold receptions at stated periods, to which invitations are regularly issued. The President sometimes appears upon these occasions, but is under no obligation to do so.

During the first two years of the administration of Mr. Lincoln, he always selected a lady to join the promenade with him at his evening receptions, thus leaving his wife free to choose an escort from the distinguished throng which always surrounded her on such occasions. This custom did not please Mrs. Lincoln, who resolved to put a stop to it. She declared the practice absurd. "On such occasions," said she, "our guests recognize the position of the President as first of all; consequently, he takes the lead in every thing; well, now, if they recognize his position they should also recognize mine. I am his wife, and should lead with him. And yet he offers his arm to any other lady in the room, making her first with him, and placing me second. The custom is an absurd one, and I mean to abolish it. The dignity that I owe to my position, as Mrs. President, demands that I should not hesitate any longer to act."

The spirited lady kept her word. Ever after this, she either led the promenade with the President, or that dignitary walked alone or in company with some gentleman.

It has long been the custom for the President to give a series of state dinners during the session of Congress, to which the various Members of that body, the higher Government officials, and the Diplomatic Corps are invited. In order to be able to entertain each one of these celebrities it is necessary to give about two dinners per week. The custom was not much observed during Mr. Lincoln's administration, though it has been revived by his successor. A recent writer gives the following account of the cause of the change:

"The day after the levee (January 2, 1862) I went to the White House. Mrs. Lincoln said to me:

"'I have an idea. These are war times, and we must be as economical as possible. You know the President is expected to give a series of state dinners every winter and these dinners are very costly. Now

I want to avoid this expense; and my idea is, that if I give three large receptions, the state dinners can be scratched from the programme. What do you think of it?'

"'I think you are right, Mrs. Lincoln.'

"'I am glad to hear you say so. If I can make Mr. Lincoln take the same view of the case, I shall not fail to put the idea into practice.'

"Before I left her room that day, Mr. Lincoln came in. She at once stated the case to him. He pondered the question a few minutes before answering.

"'Mother, I am afraid your plan will not work.'

"'But it *will* work, if you only determine that it *shall* work.'

"'It is breaking in on the regular custom,' he mildly replied.

"'But you forget, father, these are war times, and old customs can be done away with for the once. The idea is economical, you must admit.'

"'Yes, mother, but we must think of something besides economy.'

"'I do think of something else. Public receptions are more democratic than stupid state dinners—are more in keeping with the spirit of the institutions of our country, as you would say if called upon to make a stump speech. There are a great many strangers in the city, foreigners and others, whom we can entertain at our receptions, but whom we cannot invite to our dinners.'

"'I believe you are right, mother. You argue the

point well. I think that we shall have to decide on the receptions.'

"So the day was carried. The question was decided, and arrangements were made for the first reception. It was now January, and cards were issued for February."

These receptions were discontinued after the first one, until 1864, in consequence of the death of little Willie Lincoln, the President's son, which plunged the entire household into the deepest grief.

IMPERTINENT GOSSIP.

The President and his family are much annoyed by the impertinent curiosity of which they are the objects. There are scores of persons in Washington, some of whom are doubtless well-meaning people, who are so ignorant of the common decencies of society, as to seek to lay bare before the public every incident of the private life of the family at the White House. The whole city rings with gossip upon this topic, much of which finds its way into the columns of the newspaper press in various parts of the land, to the great annoyance of its victims. There are people who can tell you how the President gets out of bed in the morning, how he dresses, breakfasts, picks his teeth, what he talks about in the privacy of his family, and a thousand and one other such private details, until you turn from your informant with the most intense disgust. It is said that much of this comes from the servants employed in the Executive Mansion, who seem to think it adds to their importance to retail such scandal.

During Mr. Lincoln's administration the gossips of Washington were especially busy. They managed to find out almost every thing that transpired in his family. The poor man could scarcely open his lips without his lightest and most confidential remarks being echoed and repeated at every fireside in Washington. Mrs. Lincoln was terribly persecuted in this way. Doubtless she had her faults—a perfect woman being a rarity—but the gossips made her out a monster of conceit and vulgarity. It was in vain that those who knew her best contradicted such reports. The gossips were the more numerous, and by far the more active. She was watched with a vigilance that would have made her life insupportable had she been a woman of less independence, and even her sacred grief as mother and wife in the two great afflictions which fell upon her in Washington, was not respected. Her milliners and *modistes* were urged to reveal the secrets of her wardrobe, the mysteries of her toilette (held more sacred by modern matrons than those of the *Bona Dea* were by the mothers of Rome) were penetrated, and each fresh discovery was laid before the public with the utmost unscrupulousness.

Nor must it be supposed that such pitiful gossip was to be heard only in the lower walks of society. The *élite*, the most exclusive of the city, were the busiest and the most merciless. Your fine ladies, whose womanly pride was equalled only by their charity, were eager to search out and reveal the secrets of the White House. And not only women engaged in this contemptible business, but men, gray-haired, bearded, and bewhiskered men, high in the service of the State and in the confidence of the President, debased themselves and degraded their manhood by endeavoring to surpass their wives and daughters in such gossip.

Every year this goes on, and every new occupant of the White House is subjected to such persecutions.

DEATH IN THE WHITE HOUSE.

Until a few years ago, it was a happy reflection with our people that Death had but twice invaded the White House since its doors were first opened to receive the ruler of the nation. Presidents Harrison and Taylor died there, but their predecessors and successors had left it as they had entered it.

During Mr. Lincoln's term, however, the King of Terrors twice crossed the threshold, and spread sorrow throughout the palace. The first of these occasions was the death of Willie Lincoln, a younger son of the President. The child was a great favorite with his father, who was terribly stricken by his loss. The late N. P. Willis has left the following description of the scene at the White House on the day of the funeral:

"On the day of the funeral I went, before the hour, to take a near farewell look at the dear boy; for they had embalmed him to send home to the West—to sleep under the sod of his own valley—and the coffin-lid was to be closed before the service. The family had just taken their leave of him, and the servants and nurses were seeing him for the last time—and with tears and sobs wholly unrestrained, for he was loved like an idol by every one of them. He lay with eyes closed—his brown hair parted as we had known it—pale in the slumber of death; but otherwise unchanged, for he was dressed as if for the evening, and held in one of his hands, crossed upon his breast, a bunch of exquisite flowers—a message coming from his mother, while we were looking upon him, that those flowers might be preserved for her. She was lying sick on her bed, worn out with grief and overwatching.

"The funeral was very touching. Of the entertainments in the East Room the boy had been—for those who now assembled more especially—a most life-giving variation. With his bright face, and his apt greetings and replies, he was remembered in every part of that crimson-curtained hall, built only for pleasure—of all the crowds, each night, certainly the one least likely to be death's first mark. He was his father's favorite. They were intimates—often seen hand in hand. And there sat the man, with a burden on his brain, at which the world marvels—bent, now, with the load at both heart and brain—staggering under a blow like the taking from him of his child! His men of power sat around him—McClellan, with a moist eye, when he bowed to the prayer, as I could see from where I stood; and Chase and Seward, with their austere features at work; and Senators, and ambassadors, and soldiers, all struggling with their tears—great hearts sorrowing with the President, as a stricken man and a brother."

The parting between father and son was not so

long as had been expected. But three years elapsed, and the lifeless form of the murdered President was borne into the East Room, and laid in sorrowful state, amidst the agonized mourning of a great people. In almost the same spot where he had stood to look his last upon the face of his dear boy, all that was mortal of the Martyr lay, all unconscious of the wild storm of grief that was raging over the land for him. Around him gathered the magnates of the Republic, men rich in honors, wisdom, and experience, all terrified, dumb with dismay. The firm hand was gone from the helm, and, for a while, the ship of State drifted helplessly upon the dark waters which encompassed it. Then, with standards draped and drooping, bells tolling, and cannon booming a mournful dirge, the body was borne away from the great hall, through the crowded cities of the land, each of which showered its highest and proudest honors upon it, while the whole nation mourned as it had never mourned before since Washington died, and laid in the tomb in that great Western land, with which his fame is so inseparably connected.

A NEW WHITE HOUSE.

Measures have been actively set on foot to secure the erection of a new mansion for the President. The great age of the present building and the unhealthiness of the location are serious objections to it. The Commissioner of Public Buildings has frequently declared that it is almost impossible to keep it in proper repair, and that it would be far cheaper to erect a new mansion than to put upon this one all the improvements it needs. A bill has been introduced in Congress for this purpose, and as that body is well aware of the importance of and necessity for a change, the measure will doubtless pass both Houses without any difficulty.

IX.

THE JUDICIARY.

THE third coördinate branch of the Government is the Judiciary, which consists of a Supreme Court, Circuit Courts, District Courts, and Court of Claims. Our purpose is to deal only with the courts sitting in Washington City.

THE SUPREME COURT.

The Supreme Court of the United States is the highest and most august legal tribunal in the land. It consists of a Chief Justice and eight Associate Justices, all of whom are appointed by the President, and hold office during good behavior. Five of these constitute a quorum for the transaction of business. The Court holds one session annually, commencing on the first Monday in December, and sits daily during the term, Sundays excepted, from 11 A. M., until 3 P. M. The Justices, besides sitting annually in Washington, are each judges of the Circuit Courts. Their circuits embrace the various States of the Union, which are fairly divided amongst them, and after the adjournment of the Supreme Court, they begin to hold their Circuit Courts.

The officers of the Supreme Court are the Attorney-General, a clerk, deputy clerk, reporter, marshal, and crier. The attorneys and counsellors practicing in this Court are few in number, and are men of high character and great ability. They must have had three years practice in the Supreme Court of the State in which they reside, and must be men of fair private and professional reputation.

The Supreme Court has exclusive jurisdiction over all civil controversies in which a State is a party, except in those between a State and its own citizens. In cases between a State and citizens of another State, or aliens, its jurisdiction is original, but not exclusive. The trials of issues in fact are by jury, but most of the cases brought before it are decided by the Court. It has appellate jurisdiction from the State and Circuit Courts, in cases which are provided for by law.

THE COURT ROOM.

The Court formerly sat in the hall now used for the law library, but, in 1860, moved into its present hall, which was the old Senate Chamber. The hall is small, but one of the handsomest in the Capitol. It is semicircular in form, is seventy-five feet long, forty-five feet high, and forty-five feet wide in the centre, which is its widest part. A row of handsome green pillars of Potomac marble extends across the eastern, or rear side of the hall, and the wall which sweeps around the western side, is ornamented with pilasters of the same material. The ceiling is in the form of a dome, is very beautiful, and is ornamented with square caissons of stucco. A large skylight in the centre of the room lights the chamber.

A handsome white marble clock is placed over the main door, which is on the western side. Opposite, from the eastern wall, a large gilded eagle spreads his wings above a raised platform, railed in, and tastefully draped, along which are arranged the comfortable arm-chairs of the Chief Justice and his associates, the former being in the centre. Above them is still the old "eastern gallery of the Senate," so famous in the history of the country. The desks and seats of the lawyers are ranged in front of the Court, and enclosed by a tasteful railing. The floor is covered with soft, heavy carpets; cushioned benches for spectators are placed along the semicircular wall, and busts of John Jay, John Rutledge, Oliver Ellsworth, and John Marshall, former Chief Justices, adorn the hall. After the political feeling of the present time dies out, a bust of Chief Justice Taney will no doubt complete the group.

With the exception of a few of the internal arrangements, which have been changed to suit the convenience of the Court, the room is very much as the Senate left it. It is one of the most famous halls in the land. Here were uttered those matchless specimens of eloquence, which the Senators of to-day can admire, but not equal. Here Clay, Calhoun, Webster, Hayne, Douglas, and their peers, lived their great, historic lives, and built up those splendid monuments to their fame, which shall last until the latest age of time. The place seems haunted with the memories of the great men who have tenanted it. Close your eyes, and you can imagine them all in their places again. What times were those! and what giants the little hall held then! Will such days or such men ever come to us again? The mantles of our great dead have fallen upon none of their successors, and the dead are greater than the living.

Sitting in the old hall, not long since, listening to the arguments in the "Legal Tender Case," we were carried back to the old days when a nobler and less sordid strife took place under the beautiful dome. Unconsciously the scene came back more and more forcibly, and the black-robed justices and the smooth-tongued advocates faded from our view. The hall seemed once more full of the great departed. The old desks and the red leather arm-chairs were once more in their semicircular rows, but the Senators had lost their careless, inattentive air, and were leaning forward in rapt attention, hanging breathlessly upon the orator's every word. Even the gaunt, stern face of the great Carolinian in the Vice-President's chair glowed with an answering fire, as the charmed words stirred his soul, and for once took captive his intellect. And the orator, how his tall form towered above the heads of those who surrounded him—intellectual giants all; how the large ox eyes glowed with a divine radiance, and how the grand voice rolled its volumes of eloquence through the chamber. He is closing his oration, and he pauses for a moment, and sends one sweeping glance around the hall. Even his political opponents are subdued, and they draw nearer so that they may not lose one single word. He is pleading for that Union, that Constitution he loved so well, and of which he was so proud, and, ceasing to speak to those within the sound of his voice, pours forth his grand appeal to posterity, at which the heart throbs now as thrillingly as then, though nearly forty years have passed away since the words were spoken:

"I have not allowed myself, sir, to look beyond the Union to see what might lie hidden in the dark recesses behind. I have not coolly weighed the chances of preserving liberty when the bonds that unite us together shall be broken asunder. I have not accustomed myself to hang over the precipice of disunion, to see whether, with my short sight, I can fathom the depth of the abyss below; nor could I regard him as a safe counsellor in the affairs of this government, whose thoughts should be mainly bent on considering, not how the Union may be best preserved, but how tolerable might be the condition of the people, when it should be broken up and destroyed. While the Union lasts, we have high, exciting, gratifying prospects spread out before us, for us and our children. Beyond that, I seek not to penetrate the veil. God grant that in my day, at least, that curtain may not rise! God grant that on my vision never may be opened what lies behind! When my eyes shall be turned to behold for the last time the sun in heaven, may I not see him shining on the broken and dishonored fragments of a once glorious Union; on States dissevered, discordant, and belligerent; on a land rent with civil feuds, and drenched, it may be, with fraternal blood! Let their last feeble and lingering glance rather behold the gorgeous ensign of the Republic, now known and honored throughout the earth, still full high advanced, its arms and trophies streaming in their original lustre, not a stripe erased or polluted, not a single star obscured, bearing for its motto no such miserable interrogatory as 'What is all this worth?' nor those other words of delusion and folly, 'Liberty first, and Union afterwards;' but everywhere, spread all over in characters of living light, blazing on all its ample folds, as they float over the sea and over the land, and in every wind under the whole heavens, that other sentiment, dear to every true American heart—'Liberty *and* Union, now and forever, one and inseparable!'"

THE COURT IN SESSION.

The chamber of the Supreme Court is one of the pleasantest places in the Capitol. The interest which attaches to the old hall, is not lessened by the grave and dignified appearances of the black-robed justices, and the quiet deportment of the members of the bar. Coming from either the House or the Senate, you seem to have entered another world. Everything is so calm and peaceful, so thoroughly removed from the noise and confusion of the political strife going on in the other parts of the Capitol, that the change is indeed delightful.

The Court consists of the Chief-Justice, Salmon Portland Chase, of Ohio, and Associate Justices Samuel Nelson, of New York; Robert C. Grier, of Pennsylvania; Nathan Clifford, of Maine; Noah H. Swayne of Ohio; Samuel F. Miller, of Iowa; David Davis, of Illinois; and Stephen J. Field, of California. There is one vacancy, which will doubtless be filled during the next administration. A more dignified and imposing body of men it would be hard to find. They represent well the majesty of the land.

At eleven o'clock in the morning, the door just back of the judges' platform is thrown open, and the Marshal of the Court enters, walking backward, with his gaze fastened upon the door. Upon reaching the centre of the chamber, he pauses, and cries in a loud voice,

"The Honorable, the Judges of the Supreme Court of the United States."

All present in the chamber immediately rise to their feet, and remain standing respectfully. Then, through the open door, headed by the Chief-Justice, enter the members of the Court, one by one, in their large, flowing robes of black silk. There is something very attractive about these old men, nearly all of whom have passed into the closing years of life. They ascend their platform, range themselves in front of their seats, and the Chief-Justice makes a sign to the "Crier," who immediately makes the following proclamation:

"O yea! O yea! O yea! All persons having business before the Honorable, the Judges of the Supreme Court of the United States, are admonished to draw near and give their attendance, for the Court is now in Session. God save the United States, and this Honorable Court!"

The Judges and other persons take their seats, and the business of the day begins.

THE CHIEF-JUSTICE.

The Chief-Justice of the United States is the highest legal officer in the Republic. His position is one of the proudest in the world, and he is looked upon by the people with more confidence and respect than any other member of the Government. It has rarely been the case that the maddest of politicians have ventured to question the integrity of the Court, and the Chief-Justice has almost always been safe from political persecution.

The office has been filled from the first by men of high character and great ability. The first Chief-Justice was John Jay, of New York, appointed September 26, 1789. In 1794, Chief-Justice Jay resigned his position to accept the post of Envoy Extraordinary to England.

President Washington then appointed John Rutledge, of South Carolina, in 1795, during a recess of the Senate. Mr. Rutledge presided at the August term of the Court in 1795, but in the following December, the Senate refused to confirm his nomination. William Cushing, of Massachusetts, at that time one of the Associate Justices, was then appointed and confirmed by the Senate, in January, 1796, but he declined to serve.

Oliver Ellsworth, of Connecticut, was then appointed. He was confirmed by the Senate March 4, 1796. At the close of the August term, 1799, he resigned his position, in order to accept the appointment of Minister Plenipotentiary and Envoy Extraordinary to France. In 1800, John Jay, of New York, was again appointed by the President, and confirmed by the Senate; but he declined to serve.

CHIEF-JUSTICE MARSHALL.

John Marshall, of Virginia, was appointed by President John Adams, in January, 1801, and confirmed by the Senate. At the time of his appointment, he was Secretary of State. He continued to act in both capacities until the close of President Adams' term in March, 1801. He died in 1835.

Judge Marshall was justly considered one of the purest and most learned Judges that ever sat on the bench. He had served on the personal staff of Washington during the Revolution, and was a man of the finest attainments. He was noted for his plainness of person and address, and his child-like simplicity and freshness of character. His exceeding carelessness of dress once caused the landlord of a public house to refuse to entertain him, mine host being suspicious that he did not have money enough to pay his bill.

One day a Mr. P., from the country, came to Richmond, Va., for the purpose of looking after a case of his, which was to be argued before the Court of Appeals. Standing in the porch of the Eagle Hotel, one morning, he asked the landlord to recommend to him some good lawyer, capable of undertaking the case. At this moment, Marshall, then a young man, sauntered up, dressed carelessly in a plain suit of linen. His hat was held under his arm, and was filled with cherries, which he was eating as he walked along the street.

He stopped a moment to exchange greetings with the landlord, who pointed him out to Mr. P. as the best man to conduct his case. The old gentleman, however, refused to engage him, declaring his belief that a man so careless as to his appearance could not be a good lawyer. He went to the office of the Clerk of the Court, and was recommended by that official to employ Marshall, but he again refused to do so. An old gentleman, Mr. V. by name, and a lawyer by profession, now entered. His remarkable appearance, powdered wig, and handsome dress, made such an impression on Mr. P. that he at once engaged him to conduct his case. The Court was opened a few minutes later, and in one of the first cases called, Mr. V. and Mr. Marshall both appeared. Mr. P. discovered his mistake. Mr. V. was a man of little ability or force, while Marshall was a giant in intellect. He at once sought ought the young lawyer, confessed to him his error, and the causes which led to it. He told him he had come to Richmond with one hundred dollars, as his lawyer's fee. He had paid Mr. V., and had only five dollars left. If Marshall would consent, he would cheerfully give him this sum for assisting in the case. "Marshall, pleased with the incident, accepted the offer, not however, without passing a sly joke at the *omnipotence* of a powdered wig and black coat."

"The venerable Captain Philip Slaughter was a messmate of Marshall during the Revolution. He says Marshall was the best tempered man he ever knew. During their sufferings at Valley Forge, nothing discouraged, nothing disturbed him; if he had only bread to eat it was just as well; if only meat it made no difference. If any of the officers murmured at their deprivations, he would shame them by good-natured raillery, or encourage them by his own exuberance of spirits. He was an excellent companion, and idolized by the soldiers and his brother officers, whose gloomy hours were enlivened by his inexhaustible fund of anecdote.

"For sterling honesty no man ever exceeded Marshall. He never would, knowingly, argue in defence of injustice, or take a legal advantage at the expense of moral honesty. A case of the latter is in point. He became an endorser on a bond amounting to several thousand dollars. The drawer failed, and Marshall paid it, although he knew it could be avoided, inasmuch as the holder had advanced the amount at more than legal interest."

Upon one occasion he was standing in the market in Richmond, Va., with his basket containing his purchases on his arm, when he was accosted by a fashionable young gentleman who had just purchased a turkey. The young man's foolish pride would not allow him to carry the fowl through the streets; and, taking the Judge for a countryman, he asked him to carry it home for him. The request was promptly granted; and, when the young man's home was reached, he offered the supposed countryman a shilling for his trouble. The money was courteously refused; and, upon asking the name of the person who had rendered him the service, the young man was not a little astonished and chagrined to learn that his thanks were due to the Chief-Justice of the United States.

A bet was once made that the Judge could not dress himself without exhibiting some mark of carelessness. He good-humoredly accepted the wager. A supper was to be given him, upon these conditions: If his dress was found to be faultlessly neat upon that occasion, the parties offering the wager were to pay for the entertainment; but if they detected any carelessness in his attire, the expense was to fall upon him. Upon the appointed evening, the guests and the Judge met at the place agreed upon; and, to the surprise of all, the Judge's dress seemed faultless. The supper followed, Judge Marshall being in high spirits over his victory. Near the close of the repast, however, one of the guests, who sat next him, chanced to drop his napkin, and, stooping down to pick it up, discovered that the Judge had put on one of his stockings with the wrong side out. Of course the condition of affairs was immediately changed, and amidst the uproarious laughter of his companions, the Chief-Justice acknowledged his defeat.

The following incident in his life is said to have occurred at McGuire's hotel, in Winchester, Virginia:

"It is not long since a gentleman was travelling in one of the counties of Virginia, and about the close of the day stopped at a public house to obtain refreshment, and spend the night. He had been there but a short time before an old man alighted from his gig, with the apparent intention of becoming his fellow-guest at the same house. As the old man drove up, he observed that both of the shafts of the gig were broken, and that they were held together by withes formed from the bark of a hickory sapling. Our traveller observed further that he was plainly clad, that his knee-buckles were loosened, and that something like negligence pervaded his dress. Conceiving him to be one of the honest yeomanry of our land, the courtesies of strangers passed between them, and they entered the tavern. It was about the same time that an addition of three or four young gentlemen was made to their number—most, if not all of them, of the legal profession. As soon as they became conveniently accommodated, the conversation was turned by the latter upon an eloquent harangue which had that day been displayed at the bar. It was replied by the other that he had witnessed, the same day, a degree of eloquence no doubt equal, but it was from the pulpit. Something like a sarcastic rejoinder was made to the eloquence of the pulpit; and a warm altercation ensued, in which the merits of the Christian religion became the subject of discussion. From six o'clock until eleven, the young champions wielded the sword of argument, adducing with ingenuity and ability, everything that could be said, pro and con. During this protracted period, the old gentleman listened with the meekness and modesty of a child; as if he was adding new information to the stores of his own mind · or perhaps he was observing, with philosophic eye, the faculties of the youthful mind, and how new energies are evolved by repeated action; or, perhaps, with patriotic emotion, he was reflecting upon the future destinies of his country, and on the rising generation, upon whom these future destinies must devolve; or most probably, with a sentiment of moral and religious feeling, he was collecting an argument which—characteristic of himself—no art would 'be able to elude, and no force resist.' Our traveller remained a spectator, and took no part in what was said.

"At last one of the young men, remarking that it was impossible to combat with long and established prejudices, wheeled around, and with some familiarity exclaimed, 'Well, my old gentleman, what do you think of these things?' If, said the traveller, a streak of vivid lightning had at that moment crossed the room, their amazement could not have been greater than it was with what followed. The most eloquent and unanswerable appeal was made for nearly an hour, by the old gentleman, that he ever heard or read. So perfect was his recollection, that every argument urged against the Christian religion was met in the order in which it was advanced. Hume's sophistry on the subject of miracles was, if possible, more perfectly answered than it had already been done by Campbell. And in the whole lecture there was so much simplicity and energy, pathos and sublimity, that not another word was uttered. An attempt to describe it, said the traveller, would be an attempt to paint the sunbeams. It was now a matter of curiosity and inquiry who the old gentleman was. The traveller concluded it was the preacher from whom the pulpit-eloquence was heard—but no—it was the *Chief-Justice of the United States.*'

CHIEF-JUSTICE TANEY.

Judge Marshall was succeeded by Roger Brooke Taney, of Maryland, who was nominated by President Jackson, and confirmed by the Senate in March, 1836. He died in Washington on the 12th of October, 1864. He was a man of pure character, vast learning and great legal ability, and in every way a fitting successor to John Marshall. His decision in the Dred Scott Fugitive Slave case, made him very unpopular with the anti-slavery party, and he was unjustly and cruelly assailed for it. He was too honest not to decide according to his convictions of duty, and too fearless to care for the opposition raised against him.

Mr. Samuel Tyler, of Maryland, has recently prepared a memoir of him. The correspondent of a western journal * relates the following incidents of the Judge's life, upon the authority of that gentleman.

"Judge Taney, as you know, was a man of originally tall stature, being upward of six feet high, but a delicate constitution had so been affected by his close and studious habits that in the generation in which he was most familiar to ourselves he had become bent and warped, so that his skin was like a cracked parchment, his stature bent, and he walked with difficulty and tardiness. Nevertheless his hair remained nearly of its original color; his eyes were bright, and his attenuated legs, and arms, and chest were always dignifiedly clothed.

"Mr. Tyler, an author, as I have said, whose books

* Cincinnati Commercial.

have been published by the house of Lippincott, at Philadelphia, is a spirited and amiable Maryland gentleman, from Frederick. With John M. Carlyle he divided the confidence of Judge Taney, and, therefore, I feel that in relating the incisive passage of our conversation, I am perhaps bringing out some feature of Chief-Justice Taney's life which may be useful to the age, which is in doubt as to the real motive principles of his extraordinary career. Of this career civilization will judge independently. I reproduce, merely, the verdict of a friend.

"'Was Judge Taney rich, Mr. Tyler?'

"'No, sir; always poor. He lived in Blagden row —the row of stuccoed houses nearly opposite the City Hall. They are four-storied; an irony balcony runs above the first story; two windows adjoin the hall door. His daughters, at this day, live upon copying reports and papers from the Department of the Interior. One of them, I believe, is unmarried; another a widow. They are in as nearly a state of indigence as I care to classify ladies so tenderly reared. The Judge himself said to me, during the war, that he lamented his narrow means, because he wanted to take another newspaper, and could not afford it.'

"'He had not always lived there?'

"'No, sir. He resided in Baltimore, after he quitted Frederick, down to a comparatively recent period. His birthplace was on the Chesapeake Bay, below Annapolis, and his grandparents were English Catholics, who settled in this country about 1700. You know that his public offices were Attorney-General of Mary land, Secretary of the Treasury, and, at last, Chief Justice. He has often told me that the first was the only office he ever coveted. His pride of State was very strong. He loved Maryland, and wished to be interred at Frederick, where he passed the majority of his private life.'

"'And is he buried there?'

"'Yes, sir; beside his wife, who was the sister of Francis Scott Key, author of the "Star-Spangled Banner." There it has been proposed to erect a monument to his memory. There lie all those members of his family whom he loved in his lifetime. There, sir, I met the Chief-Justice first, one of his townsmen.'

"'What papers did he take, sir? You have alluded to his love of contemporary reading.'

"'He took the New York papers, the *National Intelligencer*, the *Globe*, the *Edinburgh*, *North British*, *Quarterly*, and *Westminster Reviews* and the *London Times*, regularly down to his death. He read every article in them also.'

"'Was he much of a *reconteur?*'

"'Yes, upon subjects disconnected with himself; but being Chief-Justice he seemed to hold his personal affairs in a jealous regard, being fearful that they might become public and so compromise his professional opinions. To me, even, whom he had selected to write his life, if I found it worthy enough, he would seldom talk upon those concerns which I was curious to know.

"'In what year was Judge Taney appointed Chief Justice?'

"'In 1836, sir. There never was a country so

fortunate in its Chief-Justices as the United States The two terms of Marshall and Taney, put together, extend over sixty years.'

"'Taney had not literary abilities, like Marshall.'

"'Yes, he had abilities, but he was such a thoroughly devoted lawyer, who refused to express opinions, literary or otherwise, which might seem to obtain the sanction of the name of the Chief-Justice, and, although he read much, he seemed to compress his mind and utterances into legal channels merely, and looked upon his court with an eye single. Efforts were made to drag him into politics at many periods of his life, notably during the Douglas-Breckinridge campaign.'

"'What case was that, Mr. Tyler?'

"'Well, sir! One Mr. Hughes, of Hagerstown, an intimate friend of Judge Taney, wrote to the Judge in the heat of that political campaign, saying that it was affirmed all through the country that Judge Taney had declared himself in favor of Mr. Douglas for the Presidency. Consequently, the Irish Catholic voters were going pell-mell for Mr. Douglas. And Mr. Hughes, who believed the contrary to be the predilections of the Chief-Justice, wrote to the latter for permission to deny that he had expressed himself in support of the Little Giant, as he was called.'

"'What did the Chief-Justice reply?'

"'He wrote, in a letter which I possess, to this effect—very nearly in these terms:

"'Sir: I am Chief-Justice of the United States. As such, since the year 1836 I have *never cast a vote!*

I never permit any retainer or under-officeholder of mine to converse with me upon candidates and their prospects. I never give advice or render service voluntarily or involuntarily, upon any side. And so particular am I, sir, that my name shall never appear, with my consent, appended to any politics, that I refuse to permit you to deny that I am for or against any body at this juncture. If any man has affirmed any thing on the credit of my name, I hold to my neutrality so tenaciously that I refuse to let my name be used for any denial, even of an unauthorized falsehood.'

"'There were probably other instances of his political neutrality?'

"'Yes. I recollect that at one time the marshal of his court, being a stout partisan, wanted to go to the polls in his official capacity, to keep order, for the Democrats were hard pressed, and required both physical aid. The Chief-Justice said to him: 'Mr. Marshal ——,'—he always gave every man his official term, and insisted upon being entitled to his own name officially, in like manner; 'Mr. Marshal, you can go to the polls, sir, like every citizen, but if you go as marshal of my court, you go at your peril!'"

CHIEF-JUSTICE CHASE.

Upon the death of Judge Taney, President Lincoln was overwhelmed with solicitations from the friends of various public men, each one urging that the vacancy should be filled by the appointment of his favorite. After a careful consideration of all the claims presented to him, Mr. Lincoln adhered to his original idea and on the 6th of December, 1864, nominated Salmon Portland Chase, of Ohio, to be Chief-Justice, which nomination was unanimously confirmed by the Senate, and Mr. Chase was sworn into his office on the 15th of December, 1864. Says Carpenter, in his interesting narrative of his "Six Months at the White House," "Notwithstanding his apparent hesitation in the appointment of a successor to Judge Taney, it is well known to his most intimate friends, that 'there had never been a time during his Presidency, when, in the event of the death of Judge Taney, he had not fully intended and expected to nominate Salmon P. Chase for Chief-Justice.' These were his very words uttered in connection with this subject."

Judge Chase had been a member of Mr. Lincoln's Cabinet during his first term, and had conducted the affairs of the Treasury Department with a genius and vigor which had secured the confidence of the capitalists and people of the country in the bonds of the Government, even when the military situation seemed hopeless. During the political campaign of 1864, he was brought forward prominently as the candidate for the Presidency of the extreme Radical wing of the Republican party, who were dissatisfied with Mr. Lincoln, and there came near being a very serious rupture between Lincoln and Chase, a consummation for which certain self-styled patriots labored most devoutly. Fortunately for the country, their efforts did not succeed. Says Mr. Carpenter, "The Hon. Mr Frank, of New York, told me that just after the nomi nation of Mr. Chase as Chief-Justice, a deeply interesting conversation upon this subject took place one evening between himself and the President, in Mrs. Lincoln's private sitting-room. Mr. Lincoln reviewed Mr. Chase's political course and aspirations, at some length, alluding to what he had felt to be an estrangement from him personally, and to various sarcastic and bitter expressions reported to him as having been indulged in by the ex-Secretary, both before and after his resignation. The Congressman replied that such reports were always exaggerated, and spoke warmly of Mr. Chase's great services in the hour of the country's extremity, his patriotism, and integrity to principle. The tears instantly sprang into Mr. Lincoln's eyes. 'Yes,' said he, 'that is true. We have stood together in the time of trial, and I should despise myself if I allowed personal differences to affect my judgment of his fitness for the office of Chief-Justice.'"

Judge Chase is a native of New Hampshire, and a member of the famous New England family of that name. He is a nephew of the great Bishop Chase, of Ohio, and was partly reared by him. He is sixty-one years old, and is splendidly preserved. Personally he is one of the most imposing men in the country. His head is grand and massive, and his features are striking and intellectual. The likenesses on the Treasury notes are admirable, and will give the reader an excellent idea of the man. In point of ability Judge Chase has few equals, and no superiors in the land. He fills his exalted position with a grace and dignity peculiarly gratifying to his countrymen, who, without respect to party, are justly proud of his fame.

SALARIES.

The salary of the Chief-Justice is $6,500, that of each Associate Justice $6,000, and that of the Attorney-General, $8,000. The officers of the court receive salaries proportionate to their positions and services.

THE ATTORNEY-GENERAL.

The Attorney-General is the Legal Adviser of the President, and the counsel for the Government in all suits in the Supreme Court, in which the United States are concerned. It is his duty, when required by the President or requested by the heads of departments, to give his opinion, which is generally submitted in writing, upon any matter concerning their departments. He is required to be learned in the law, and to take an oath to discharge faithfully the duties of his office. He is a member of the President's Cabinet, and is allowed an assistant, three clerks, and a messenger.

THE COURT OF CLAIMS.

This Court meets in the hall under the Library of Congress. It was organized by act of Congress, on the 25th of February, 1855, and consists of three judges, appointed by the President, subject to the confirmation of the Senate. Two judges constitute a quorum for the transaction of business. They hold office during good behavior. All claims against the Government, brought before either House of Congress, may be referred to this Court, by which they are heard and determined. A record of the proceedings is kept, and reports of the same are made to Congress at the beginning of each session, and monthly until Congress adjourns. Sessions are held during the sitting of Congress, and also during the recess of that body, if there is sufficient business before the court to require it. The court sits Monday, Tuesday, Wednesday, and Thursday, and on pressing occasions, on Friday. Saturday is used by the judges for consultations.

The officers of the court are a solicitor and two assistant solicitors, to represent the Government, appointed by the President, and by and with the advice and consent of the Senate, and a clerk, assistant clerk, and a messenger appointed by the court.

X.

THE DEPARTMENT OF STATE.

THE building temporarily used for the Department of State, is located in the upper part of Fourteenth street West. It was originally erected for the Protestant Orphan Asylum, but has been leased by the Government for a term of years. When the magnificent extension of the Treasury Building is completed, the State Department will be installed in that portion of it at the corner of Pennsylvania avenue and Fifteenth street West.

The department was organized by act of Congress in July, 1789. The law for this purpose styled it the "Department of Foreign Affairs," and placed it in charge of an official, to be called the "Secretary of the Department of Foreign Affairs," who was to discharge his duties "*conformably to the instructions of the President.*" As his powers were derived from Congress, he was required to hold himself amenable to that body, to attend its sessions, and "explain all matters pertaining to his province." In September, 1789, Congress changed the title of the department to the "Department of State," and made a definite enumeration of the duties of the Secretary.

HOW THE ARCHIVES WERE SAVED.

In August, 1814, the British army burned the

building used by the State Department. The public archives had been removed previous to this to a place of safety, and were thus preserved from destruction. In his "Historical Sketch of the Second War of the United States," Ingersoll thus describes the manner in which they were removed:

"The day before the fall of Washington—a day of extreme alarm—on the 23d of August, 1814, the Secretary of State wrote to the President: 'The enemy are advanced six miles on the road to the wood-yard, and our troops retreating; our troops on the march to meet them, but in too small a body to engage; General Winder proposes to retire till he can collect them in a body. The enemy are in full march for Washington, and have the materials prepared to destroy the bridge.—Tuesday, nine o'clock. You had better remove the records.' Before that note was received, Mr. John Graham, chief clerk in the Department of State, and another clerk, Mr. Stephen Pleasanton, bestirred themselves to save the precious public records of that Department. The clerk then in charge of most of those archives was Josiah King, who accompanied the Government from Philadelphia to Washington. By the exertions of these clerks, principally Mr. Pleasanton, coarse linen bags were purchased, enough to contain the papers. The original Declaration of Independence, the Articles of Confederation, the Federal Constitution, many treaties and laws as enrolled, General Washington's commission as Commander-in-Chief of the Army of the Revolution, which he relinquished when he resigned it at Annapolis (found among the rubbish of a garret), together with many other papers, the loss of which would have deeply blackened our disgrace, and, deposited in the Tower at London, as much illustrated the British triumph —all were carefully secured in linen bags, hung round the room, ready, at a moment's warning, for removal to some place of safety. Wagons, carts, and vehicles of all sorts were in such demand for the army, whose officers took the right of seizing them, whenever necessary, to carry their baggage, provisions, and other conveniences, that it was difficult to procure one in which to load the documents. That done, however, Mr. Pleasanton took them to a mill, over the Potomac, about three miles beyond Georgetown, where they were concealed. But, as General Mason's cannon-foundry was not far from the mill, though on the Maryland side of the river, apprehension arose that the cannon-foundry, which the enemy would of course seek to destroy, might bring them too near the mill, and endanger its deposits. They were, therefore, removed as far as Leesburg, a small town in Virginia, thirty-five miles from Washington, whither Mr. Pleasanton, on horseback, accompanied the wagon during the battle of Bladensburg. From Leesburg, where he slept that night, the burning city was discernible, in whose blaze the fate of his charge, if left there, was told on the horizon. * * * Mr. Pleasanton took them [the papers] in several carts to the mill, where the carts were discharged; he slept at the Rev. Mr. Maffit's, two miles from the mill, and next morning got country wagons in which he, on horseback, attended the papers to Leesburg, where they were put in a vacant stone house prepared for him by the Rev. Mr. Littlejohn. That fearful night was followed by the next day's tornado, which, at Leesburg, as at Washington, uprooted trees, unroofed tenements, and everywhere around superadded tempestuous to belligerent destruction and alarm.

"Many of the records of the War, Treasury, and Navy Departments were destroyed; some were saved, less by any care than by the tempest, which arrested hostile destruction before its completion, and drove the enemy from the Capital. After their departure, several of the written books of the departments were found in the mud, soaked with water from the rain which so opportunely fell—which, by drying them in the sun and rebinding them, were recovered. Great numbers of books and papers, however, were irrecoverably lost."

ORGANIZATION.

The head of the Department is the Secretary of State. His subordinates are an Assistant Secretary of State, chief clerk, superintendent of statistics, translator, librarian, and as many clerks as are needed.

THE DIPLOMATIC BUREAU

has charge of all the official correspondence between the Department and the Ministers, and other agents of the United States residing abroad, and the representatives of foreign powers accredited to this Government. It is in this Bureau that all instructions sent from the Department, and communications to commissioners under treaties of boundaries, &c., are prepared, copied, and recorded; all similar communications received by the Department are registered and filed in this Bureau, and their contents are entered in an analytical table, or index.

THE CONSULAR BUREAU

has charge of all correspondence, and other business, between the Department and the Consuls and Commercial Agents of the United States. Applications for such positions are received and attended to in this Bureau. A concise record of all its transactions is kept by the clerk in charge of it.

THE DISBURSING AGENT

has charge of all correspondence, and other business, relating to any and all expenditures of money with which the Department is charged.

THE TRANSLATOR

is required to furnish translations of such documents as may be submitted to him by the proper officers of the Department. He also records the commissions of the Consuls and Vice-Consuls, when not in English, upon which exequaturs are based.

THE CLERK OF APPOINTMENTS AND COMMISSIONS

makes out and keeps a record of all commissions, letters of appointment, and nominations to the Senate; makes out and keeps a record of all exequaturs, and when in English, the commissions on which they are issued. He also has charge of the Library of the Department, which is quite large and valuable.

THE CLERK OF THE ROLLS AND ARCHIVES

has charge of the "rolls," by which are meant the enrolled acts and resolutions of Congress, as they are received by the Department from the President. When authenticated copies thereof are called for, he prepares them. He also prepares these acts and resolutions, and the various treaties negotiated, for publication in the newspapers and in book form, and superintends their passage through the press. He distributes through the United States the various publications of the Department, and receives and answers all letters relating thereto. He has charge of all treaties with the Indian tribes, and all business relating to them.

THE CLERK OF AUTHENTICATIONS AND COPYRIGHTS

is in charge of the seals of the United States and of the Department, and prepares and attaches certificates to papers presented for authentication; receives and accounts for the fees; keeps a register of books and publications for which copyrights have been granted, and records the correspondence of the Department, except the diplomatic and consular letters. He also has charge of all correspondence relating to territorial affairs.

THE CLERK OF PARDONS AND PASSPORTS

prepares and records pardons and remissions of sentences by the President; and registers and files the papers and petitions upon which they are founded. He makes out and records passports; and keeps a daily register of the letters received, other than diplomatic and consular, and the disposition made of them. He also has charge of the correspondence relating to his business.

THE SUPERINTENDENT OF STATISTICS

prepares the "Annual Report of the Secretary of State and Foreign Commerce," as required by the acts of 1842 and 1856.

THE SECRETARY OF STATE

receives eight thousand dollars salary, and is a member of the President's Cabinet. Strictly viewed, all the Cabinet Ministers are equal as regards their positions, but custom has assigned the Secretary of State the first rank in the Cabinet—a position corresponding to that of the Prime-Minister of European Governments. He conducts all the intercourse of this Government with those of foreign countries, and is often called upon to take a prominent part in the administration of home affairs. The duties of the office require the highest ability in the occupant, and the Secretaries of State have always been amongst the first statesmen of our country. The first Secretary was Thomas Jefferson. His successors have been, Edmund Randolph, of Virginia; Timothy Pickering, of Massachusetts; John Marshall, of Virginia; James Madison, of Virginia; Robert Smith, of Maryland;

James Monroe, of Virginia; John Quincy Adams, of Massachusetts; Henry Clay, of Kentucky; Martin Van Buren, of New York; Edward Livingston, of Louisiana; Louis McLane, of Delaware; John Forsyth, of Georgia; Daniel Webster, of Massachusetts; Hugh S. Legaré, of South Carolina; Abel P. Upshur, of Virginia; John Nelson, of Maryland; John C. Calhoun, of South Carolina; James Buchanan, of Pennsylvania; John M. Clayton, of Delaware; Edward Everett, of Massachusetts; William L. Marcy, of New York; Louis Cass, of Michigan; Jeremiah S. Black, of Pennsylvania; and William H. Seward, of New York. Surely no branch of the Government can boast a more brilliant record.

SECRETARY SEWARD,

the present incumbent of the State Department, has played a prominent part in the history of the United States for many years. He is a native of Orange County, N. Y., and is nearly sixty-eight years old. He was admitted to the bar at the age of twenty-one, and the next year settled in Auburn, N. Y., and comenced the practice of his profession. Seven years later, he was elected to the Senate of his native State, where he boldly avowed himself the champion of reform. He advocated the abolition of imprisonment for debt, the encouragement of various internal improvements, and the enlargement of the right of suffrage. In 1833, he made a visit to Europe, in company with his father, and, while there, wrote a series of letters to an Albany journal, which were afterwards reprinted in book form. He was a candidate for Governor of his State in 1834, but was defeated by William L. Marcy. He was elected to that office by a handsome majority in 1838. His administration is memorable, among other things, for the contest he produced between the Protestant and Roman Catholic citizens of New York, by his scheme for placing education under the control of the State. He resumed the practice of his profession at Auburn in 1843, declining to be a candidate for reëlection. He had an extensive practice, chiefly in the Federal Courts, and was one of the counsel in the famous "McCormick Reaper case." In March, 1849, he was elected to the Senate of the United States, and was reëlected in 1855. In 1861, he was appointed Secretary of State by President Lincoln, which position he now holds.

His political career began with his early manhood, and has been very active. He was one of the original Republicans, the great champion of personal freedom, when it was as much as a man's social position was worth to advocate such ideas, and did more than any other man to create and build up the party which triumphed in 1860. As a matter of justice, he was entitled to the nomination by the Chicago Convention in 1860, but he was thrown out by the Greeley men, whom he had mortally offended, and who threw their weight in the Convention for Mr. Lincoln. Mr. Seward acquiesced in the decision of his party, and exerted himself in behalf of the ticket. Mr. Lincoln appreciated his services highly. Said he: "Before sunset of election day, in 1860, I was pretty sure, from the despatches I received, that I was elected. The very first thing that I settled in my mind, after reaching this conclusion, was, that these two great leaders of the party (Seward and Chase) should occupy the two first places in my Cabinet."

Mr. Seward was a warm friend of Mr. Lincoln, whose opinion of him may be judged from the following remark of the President: "Seward is an able man, and the country, as well as myself, can trust him." "No knife," said Mr. Seward, "was ever sharp enough to divide us upon any question of public policy, though we frequently arrived at the same conclusion through different processes of thought."

Just before the assassination of Mr. Lincoln, Mr. Seward was thrown from his carriage, and terribly injured. While he lay helpless upon his sick-bed in consequence of this accident, he was attacked by one of Booth's confederates, and stabbed repeatedly, and so desperately, that at first his life was despaired of. He recovered, however, but still bears the marks of his fearful injuries.

"The knowledge of the terrible calamity which had befallen the nation was rightly withheld from Mr. Seward at the time, his physician fearing that the shock would be too great for him to bear. The Sunday following, he had his bed wheeled around so that he could see the tops of the trees in the park opposite his residence, just putting on their spring foliage, when his eyes caught sight of the Stars and Stripes at half-mast on the War Department, on which he gazed awhile, then, turning to his attendant, said· The President is dead!' The confused attendant stammered, as he tried to say Nay; but the Secretary could not be deceived. 'If he had been alive, he would have been the first to call on me,' he continued; 'but he has not been here, nor has he sent to know how I am; and there is the flag at half-mast. The statesman's inductive reason had discerned the truth, and in silence the great tears coursed down his gashed cheeks, as it sank into his heart."

XI.

THE TREASURY DEPARTMENT.

THE law organizing the Treasury Department was passed by Congress in August, 1789. By the terms of this act a Secretary, Assistant Secretary, Comptroller, Treasurer, and Solicitor were ordered to be appointed.

The head of the Department is

THE SECRETARY OF THE TREASURY,

who is a member of the President's Cabinet, and chosen for his financial ability. The first Secretary was Alexander Hamilton. His successors have been Oliver Wolcott, of Connecticut; S. Dexter, of Massachusetts; Albert Gallatin, of Pennsylvania; George W. Campbell, of Tennessee; Alexander J. Dallas, of Pennsylvania; William H. Crawford, of Georgia; Richard Rush, of Pennsylvania; Samuel D. Ingham, of Pennsylvania; Louis McLane, of Delaware; William J. Duane, of Pennsylvania; Roger B. Taney, of Maryland; Levi Woodbury, of New Hampshire; Thomas Ewing, of Ohio; Walter Forward, of Pennsylvania; George M. Bibb, of Kentucky; Robert J. Walker, of Mississippi; William M. Meredith, of Pennsylvania; Thomas Corwin, of Ohio; James Guthrie, of Kentucky; Howell Cobb, of Georgia; Philip Francis Thomas, of

UNITED STATES TREASURY.

Maryland; Salmon P. Chase, of Ohio; William Pitt Fessenden, of Maine; and Hugh McCulloch, of Indiana, the present incumbent.

The Secretary of the Treasury has the general charge of the finances of the United States. He recommends to Congress such measures as in his judgment are necessary, and superintends the execution of the laws of Congress relating to his Department. He has very great discretionary powers, and is possessed of immense patronage. He also superintends the execution of the laws concerning the commerce and navigation of the United States, the survey of the coast, lighthouse department, the marine hospitals of the United States, and the construction of certain public buildings for Custom Houses and other purposes.

His subordinates are two Assistant Secretaries, a Commissioner of the Revenue, Superintendent of the Treasury Building, two Comptrollers, a Commissioner of Customs, six Auditors, a Treasurer, a Register, a Solicitor, a Chief of the Currency Bureau, a Commissioner of the Internal Revenue, a Superintendent of the Coast Survey, and a Director of the Bureau of Statistics. There are over two thousand and fifty clerks in the Department, besides chiefs of division and higher officials, and employees of a lower grade.

THE FIRST COMPTROLLER

prescribes the mode of keeping and rendering accounts for the civil and diplomatic service, and the public lands, and revises and certifies the balances arising thereon.

THE SECOND COMPTROLLER

keeps and renders the accounts of the Army and Navy and the Indian departments of the public service, and revises and certifies the balances arising thereon.

THE COMMISSIONER OF THE CUSTOMS

prescribes the mode of keeping and rendering the accounts of the customs revenue and disbursements, and for the building and repairing of custom houses, *etc.*, and revises and certifies the balances arising thereon.

THE FIRST AUDITOR

examines and adjusts the accounts of the customs and revenue disbursements, appropriations and expenditures on account of the civil list and under private acts of Congress. The customs and revenue balances are reported by him to the Commissioner of the Customs, and the others to the First Comptroller, for their decisions thereon.

THE SECOND AUDITOR

examines and adjusts all accounts connected with the pay, clothing, and recruiting of the army; and for armories, arsenals, and ordnance; and those relating to the Indian Department. All balances are reported by him to the Second Comptroller, for his decision thereon.

THE THIRD AUDITOR

examines and adjusts all accounts for the subsistence of the army, for fortifications, the Military Academy, military roads, and the Quartermaster's department, as well as for pensions, claims arising from military services previous to 1816, and for horses and other property lost in the military service. He reports his balances to the Second Comptroller for his decision thereon.

THE FOURTH AUDITOR

examines and adjusts the accounts connected with the Navy Department, and reports his balances to the Second Comptroller for the final decision of that official.

THE FIFTH AUDITOR

examines and adjusts all accounts for diplomatic and kindred services performed by order of the State Department. His balances are referred to the First Comptroller for decision.

THE SIXTH AUDITOR

has charge of the accounts of the Post Office Department. He receives and audits all claims for services rendered the Post Office Department. His decisions are final, unless the claimant appeals within twelve months to the First Comptroller. He is charged with the collection of all debts due the Post Office Department, and all fines and forfeitures imposed upon the postmasters and mail contractors for neglect of duty; he oversees the prosecution of suits and legal proceedings, both civil and criminal, and sees that all lawful steps are taken to enforce the payment of moneys due the Department; sends out instructions to the Marshals, attorneys and clerks of the United States in such cases; receives returns from each term of the United States Courts of the condition and progress of such suits and legal proceedings; has charge of all lands and other property assigned to the United States in payment of debts due the Post Office Department; and has power to sell and dispose of the same for the benefit of the United States.

THE TREASURER

receives and keeps the public funds of the United States, in his own office and that of the depositories created by the Act of August 6th, 1846, and pays out the same upon warrants drawn by the Secretary of the Treasury, countersigned by the First Comptroller, and upon warrants drawn by the Post Master General, countersigned by the Sixth Auditor, and recorded by the Register. He also holds public moneys advanced by warrant to disbursing officers, and pays out the same upon their cheques.

THE REGISTER

keeps the accounts of the receipts and expenditures of the public funds; he receives the returns and makes out the official statement of commerce and navigation of the United States. He is the custodian of all the vouchers and accounts decided by the First Comptroller and the Commissioner of Customs, which are placed in his keeping by those officials.

THE SOLICITOR

is charged with the prosecution of all civil suits begun by the United States (with the exception of those originating in the Post Office Department), and issues instructions to the Marshals, attorneys, and clerks of the United States, concerning them and their results. A report is made to him at each term from the United States Courts, showing the progress and condition of such suits. He is in charge of all lands and other property assigned to the United States in payment of debts (except those connected with the Post Office Department), and has power to sell and dispose of the same for the benefit of the United States.

THE CHIEF OF THE CURRENCY BUREAU

has charge of all the operations connected with the manufacture and distribution of the national and fractional currency authorized by acts of Congress. His bureau has come to be one of the most important branches of the Treasury, and will be noticed more in detail farther on.

THE COMMISSIONER OF THE INTERNAL REVENUE

prescribes the manner of collecting the various taxes imposed by the Government, for revenue. All returns are made to him by his subordinates. The moneys received from the people are paid to him by the collectors, and by him handed to the Treasurer of the United States. In these days of heavy taxes this is a most interesting branch of the Treasury, the workings of which are each year brought home to every citizen.

THE LIGHT-HOUSE BOARD

is composed of officers of the Army and Navy, the Superintendent of the Coast Survey, and the Secretary of the Smithsonian Institution. The Secretary of the Treasury is *ex-officio* President of this Board. The Senior Naval member is usually chosen the chairman, and presides over its deliberations. The Board directs the building and repairing of light-houses, light vessels, buoys and beacons, and contracts for the supplies necessary to maintain such establishments.

SECRETARY McCULLOCH.

Hugh McCulloch, the present incumbent of the office, is a native of Maine. He is about fifty-eight years old, and was educated at Bowdoin College. He removed to Indiana soon after coming of age, and in 1835, began business as a banker. In 1855 he was President of the State Bank of Indiana, which position he held until May, 1863, when he was appointed by the President, at the request of Secretary Chase, Comptroller of the Currency.

Carpenter, in his "Six Months at the White House," relates the following incident, upon the authority of the Rev. John Pierpont. It happened soon after Mr. McCulloch's arrival in Washington to assume his new duties.

"The desk at which Dr. Pierpont was occupied was in a room with those of a large number of other clerks, among whom the tall figure and silvery beard of the poet-preacher were very conspicuous. One day, just after Mr. McCulloch had entered upon his duties in Washington, it was announced at the entrance of this room that the new Comptroller had called to see 'Dr. Pierpont.' The clerks looked up from their books, and at one another, inquiringly, as Mr. McCulloch took a seat by the poet's desk. 'I perceive, Dr. Pierpont,' said he, 'that you do not remember me?' The venerable preacher looked at him a moment, and replied that he did not think he had ever seen him before. 'Oh yes, you have,' returned the Comptroller; 'I was a member of —— Class, in Cambridge, in 1833 and '34, and used to hear you preach. Upon leaving the Law School, purposing to take up my residence at the West, I called upon you and requested one or two letters of introduction to parties in Cincinnati. You gave me two letters, one to a Mr. S—, and the other to a Mr. G—, of that city. Those letters, my dear sir, were the stepping-stones to my fortune. I have not seen you since; but learning that you were in Washington, I told my wife, upon leaving home to take the position offered me here, that the first call I made in Washington should be upon the Rev. John Pierpont.' As the Comptroller concluded, Dr. Pierpont put on his spectacles, and looked at him a moment in silence. He at length said: 'Why, Mr. McCulloch, you are the most extraordinary man I ever saw in my life.' 'How so?' was the reply. 'Why, you have remembered a favor for thirty years!'"

HOW MR. McCULLOCH CAME TO BE SECRETARY.

Mr. McCulloch gave great satisfaction and won much credit by the manner in which he conducted the affairs of his department.

Carpenter relates the following, as happening while Mr. Lincoln was casting about to find a fitting successor to Mr. Chase:

"In the solitude of the state dining-room, I resumed my work, as usual, that morning; but my mind had been too distracted overnight for success. Participating in the general solicitude, I also had been intently revolving the question of a successor to Mr. Chase. Unaccustomed to political currents, and rejecting all considerations of *this* character in a candidate, my thought fastened upon Comptroller McCulloch, as the man for the crisis. His name, at that time, singular as it may seem, had not been suggested by any one, so far as I knew,—certainly no newspaper had advocated his merits or claims. I was at length impelled, by the force of the convictions which engaged my mind, to lay down my palette and brushes, and go up-stairs and state them to the President.

"Improving the first opportunity, when we were left alone, I said, half playfully, 'Mr. President, would you like the opinion of a painter as to who would make a good Secretary of the Treasury?' He looked at me a moment, and said: 'Yes, I think I would. What is your advice?' Said I, 'Nominate Hugh McCulloch.' 'Why,' said he, 'what do you know of McCulloch? 'Mr. President,' I rejoined, 'you know painters are thought generally to have very little knowledge of financial matters. I admit that this is true, so far as *I* am concerned ; but I do claim to know something of *men*, from the study of character as expressed in *faces*. Now, in my humble judgment, McCulloch is the most suitable man in the community for the position. First; his ability and integrity are unquestionable. Second; as Comptroller of the Currency, he is fully acquainted with the past, present, and proposed future policy of Secretary Chase, and the entire " machinery " of the Department. Third; he is a practical financier. Having made finance the study of his life, it is obvious he is already educated to the position: whereas, a man taken from the political arena would have every thing to learn, and then even, his judgment would be distrusted.' Upon this Mr. Lincoln said, with emphasis,—'I believe McCulloch is a very good man!' I think he repeated this once or twice. My errand accomplished, I returned to my labor."

Mr. Fessenden succeeded Judge Chase, but held the office only a few months, resigning it at the close of Mr. Lincoln's first term.

Mr. Lincoln then appointed Hugh McCulloch Secretary of the Treasury, and it is more than probable that the interview above related, having turned his mind to a consideration of Mr. McCulloch's merits, was in reality the cause of the appointment.

THE TREASURY BUILDING

is located on Pennsylvania Avenue, at the corner of

Fifteenth street West, fronting G Street. The old building was commenced in 1836, and was constructed of inferior brown sandstone, painted in imitation of granite. In 1855, the extension was begun. It is now nearly completed. This extension has more than doubled the size of the original edifice, and has made the whole building one of the handsomest and most imposing in the country. The old building extended along Fifteenth Street, and was ornamented with an unbroken Ionic colonnade, 342 feet long, which, though showy, was inconvenient, as it excluded the light from the rooms.

The plan of the extension flanks the old building at each end with massive granite masonry, and makes beautiful terminations of the north and south fronts, which serve to relieve the dreary monotony of the long colonnade, besides providing a large new building at each end. "There are two inner quadrangles formed by the old rear building, extending back from the eastern entrance. These courts are each 130 feet square. The walls of the extension are composed of pilasters, resting on a base which rises some twelve feet above the ground on the southern or lower side. Between the pilasters or antæ are belt courses, beautifully moulded, and the facings of the doors and windows are fine bold mouldings in keeping. In the centre of the southern, western, and northern fronts are magnificent porticos. The west front has also the projecting pediments at the ends, corresponding with those on the east side, and each supported by square antæ at the angles, with two columns between. The whole building is of the Grecian or Ionic order, and is surmounted by a massive balustrade. The new structure is of the best and most beautiful granite in the world, brought from Dix Island, on the coast of Maine. The antæ and columns are monoliths. The large, solid antæ weigh nearly an hundred thousand pounds, and the columns some seventy-five thousand. The facility with which the immense masses are hewn out of the quarries, swung on board vessels, brought to the Capital, and raised to the positions which the architect in his studio designed them to occupy, conveys a high idea of American art and enterprise. The Treasury Building, as extended, is 465 feet long, exclusive of the porticos, by 266 feet wide."

The courts are ornamented with handsome fountains. A very beautiful one adorns the space in front of the western portico at the entrance to the President's park, and another is now being constructed before the north front. The entrances are through massive gateways. The yard on the north and west sides is lower than the street, and broad flights of steps lead to it. A handsome granite balustrade extends along the north wall.

The interior arrangements are unusually fine. The architecture ranks next to that of the Capitol in its magnificence, and is peculiarly American in its details. Unlike most of the public buildings, the offices are large, airy, and handsome, presenting the appearance of splendid saloons, and affording a greater degree of comfort to the occupants than the narrow, cell-like apartments of the old Treasury.

The extension is nearly completed. The wing designed for the accommodation of the Internal Revenue Department will be ready for use sometime during the present year. The new cash room will be one of the most magnificent halls in the world, and will cost over forty thousand dollars for marble work alone. The walls and ceiling will be beautifully panelled with rare specimens of Italian marble, and all the arrangements of the apartment will be on the most splendid and tasteful scale.

FOLDING ROOM OF THE CURRENCY BUREAU.

XII.

THE CURRENCY.

PREVIOUS to the Rebellion the circulating medium of the country consisted only of gold, silver, and copper coins, issued by the General Government. Besides these, the banks of the various States issued large quantities of notes, redeemable on demand in the legal currency of the Union. These notes were generally worth their full value in the States in which the banks issuing them were located, but in other States they were received only at a discount, the rate of which varied according to circumstances.

In those days, the metal currency of the Government was sufficient for the business wants of the country, and as it was known that the majority of the banks were well supplied with it, very few persons were unwilling to receive the bank notes at their full value. At the beginning of the war, however, the metal currency commenced to grow scarce, as is usual in all such cases. Private enterprises and securities were viewed with suspicion, as nothing was regarded as certain in the unsettled condition of the country, and those who had gold and silver money withdrew it from the market and laid it away, in order to provide against future troubles. This created a stringency in the money market, which was severely felt by all classes of the community. The trouble was made greater by the fact that the Government was demanding heavy supplies of all kinds, to be delivered almost immedi ately, and that there was not ready money enough in the country to carry on the work required. In order to remedy this, the issue of paper money by the Government was resolved upon. The necessary acts were passed by Congress, and approved by the President, and the notes were issued by the Treasury Department. At first the "Demand Notes," or *Greenbacks,* as they are most commonly called, were issued. Then followed the Postal Currency, then the National Currency, or notes of the National Banks, and lastly the Fractional Currency. The volume of paper money in circulation increased steadily after the first issue. At present it is the main dependence of the country, gold and silver having passed almost entirely out of circulation, and become articles of commerce.

HOW PAPER MONEY IS MADE.

It is not our purpose, however, to relate the history of our national finances, but to glance briefly at the manner in which the notes and bonds of the Government are prepared and issued for circulation. The gold, silver, and nickel coins, being made at the Mint in Philadelphia, and at its branches, have no place in this description.

PREPARING THE PLATE.

The first step in making paper money is to determine upon an appropriate design for the note or bond. This is usually selected by the Secretary of the Treasury The designs for the fractional notes are drawn up in the Treasury; but the Greenbacks, the National Bank notes, and the bonds, were designed by the *American Bank Note Company*, and the *National Bank Note Company*, of New York. The former designed the Treasury notes or Greenbacks, and the latter the National currency.

The design being selected, the plate is prepared by one of the companies mentioned, in its own establishment. Every care is taken to prevent an improper use being made of any part of the work or of the materials used. The great end is to make a note which shall defy the skill of counterfeiters.

The drawing selected for the new note is much larger in size than the note, and is prepared with the greatest care by the best artists. It is photographed upon a steel plate of the exact size required for the note, by which process its proportions are uniformly reduced. The outlines are then faintly cut in the steel, and the plate is sent to the engraver to fill up. This is a very slow process. A part of it is done by hand, but the delicate and intricate tracery work, which will defy any but the very best counterfeiters to imitate, is done by machinery, the machine, of course, being directed by a skilled workman. The greatest care is taken by the engravers to have their work as perfect as possible. Every line is cut separately, and frequently half a dozen different persons are employed upon a single plate. One man excels in landscape, another in portraits, another in animal figures, and to each one is assigned the part he can perform best. From two to four months' constant and careful work is spent on one of these plates before it is ready for use.

TRANSFERRING.

The plate which comes thus from the hands of the engraver is not used to print from, but is retained by the company as a mould from which others are made. It is called a "die," and the process by which copies are taken from it is termed transferring.

The original "die" is engraved on soft steel, and after being completed is placed in a crucible filled with animal carbon, and hermetically sealed. The crucible is then placed in a furnace, and subjected to an intense but regulated heat, which volatilizes the carbon and causes it to combine with the steel, thus rendering that metal as hard as it can be made. The "die" is then taken to the transfer press, which is a powerful machine, capable of exerting a pressure of thirty-five tons, by the mere exertion of the workman's foot. The "die" is placed on the press, and a roller of soft steel passed over it, the powerful press forcing the soft metal into each line of the hardened "die." This process is repeated as often as necessary, the press working with mathematical exactness. A raised impression of the original die is thus made upon the roller, which in its turn is subjected to the action of volatilized carbon and hardened. These rollers, or secondary "dies" are carefully preserved in the vaults of the company, and guarded with every possible precaution. When a note plate for printing is wanted, they are passed by the press over a plate of soft steel, and a sunken impression is made. This last plate is then hardened in its turn, and used for printing.

PRINTING THE NOTES.

In the Treasury notes and National Currency notes, two plates are used, whenever either side of the note is printed in two colors. In the Treasury notes, the face is printed in black and green, and the back in green. In the National Bank notes the face is printed in black, and the back in green and black, the picture in the centre being in black, and the border in green. A separate impression by a separate plate is necessary for each of these colors. This adds greatly to the cost of the notes, but is a cheap process in the end, as it is a sure protection against counterfeits.

It is acknowledged that a perfect fac-simile of the notes of the Government cannot be made by hand. An exact copy of every line, every shade, every letter, can, however, be obtained by photography, which science a few years ago seemed to break down every protection against spurious money. The old bank notes, printed in plain black and white, were imitated so successfully that the banks were obliged to resort to the use of colored notes. A photograph does not reproduce colors, its effects being simply in black and white, and for a while the counterfeiters were puzzled. Their ingenuity triumphed, however. They found a process by which the colored inks used could be removed without disturbing the black ink of the note, and they removed these colored inks, photographed the rest of the note, and reprinted the colored parts in imitation of the originals.

The American Bank Note Company, of New York, in order to prevent this practice, purchased the patent of a new chemical green ink, which had just been invented. This ink has almost put a stop to counterfeiting. It is of such a nature that it cannot be removed from the paper without the paper being destroyed by the means used, or the black ink combined with it on the same note being removed at the same time. The ink has been tested by the most eminent chemists in the land, who have been unable to discover any means of overcoming the obstacles presented by it to the arts of the counterfeiters. There are some few counterfeits in circulation, but unless prepared in a manner to be hereafter described, they may be easily detected.

The paper for the notes and bonds is selected with great care, its quality and finish being important features in a genuine note or bond. It is kept in a place of security, and is, or ought to be, issued with certain restrictions which insure its being used only for legitimate purposes. In the establishments of the Bank Note Companies of New York, not a sheet can leave the paper wareroom without being accounted for, but the Treasury officials are said to be more careless.

The greater part of a Treasury note is printed from the steel plate, but a portion of the colored work is done like ordinary printing, with a hand-press. The plate is kept warm by means of a brazier containing fire, in order to keep the ink in a proper state. The ink is passed all over the plate with a roller, and is then wiped off with a cloth, which leaves it only in the lines or diagram cut in the plate. It is then laid under a winch press, and an impression taken. The presses are required to be of the most accurate description, as the least difference in the position of the plates when two or more colors are used, would ruin the note. The numbers are printed by an ingenious little machine, and the signatures of the Treasurer and Register of the Treasury are engraved on the plate. The National Bank officials sign their notes by hand.

Thus, the reader will see that the best materials, the best skill, and the greatest care are employed in the preparation of the notes and bonds of the Government. The great object is to prevent counterfeiting.

The Greenbacks and National Bank notes are printed by the American and National Bank-note Companies, but the bonds, interest-bearing notes, and fractional currency notes are printed at the Treasury, where, also, the plates of the fractional notes are engraved.

CARELESS PRINTING OF THE CURRENCY.

The Currency-Printing Bureau of the Treasury Department is in charge of Mr. S. M. Clark, who was pronounced unfit for his position by a minority report presented in Congress in 1864, and signed by Messrs. James Brooks, John T. Stuart, W. G. Steele, and John L. Dawson. The following extract from the report of that committee, will show the frightful irregularities which existed in the Treasury in 1864:

"Your Committee were amazed to find, upon examination, that, in April last, when this Committee was created, the recognized issue of the fractional currency was under twenty millions! They cannot account for this discrepancy of reality and estimate. Upon the discovery, however, of the great discrepancy, they directed their attention to the mode and manner of printing this fractional currency, which to them is utterly unsatisfactory. The white paper upon which it is printed, has been very loosely purchased and received, and very loosely handled. It came into the hands of one lady in the Bureau of Printing, and instead of being turned out to the public in a far different direction, returned all of it to her hands, and she passed it over to Mr. Clark. Whatever system of checks and balances Mr. Clark may have for his own guidance, there is no check over him. He keeps no ledgers, balances no books for an accountant to see and understand at a glance. The eye is wearied, and the mind fatigued by innumerable figures of his, but no clear, close ledger, such as every merchant or corporation has, shows continuously his day's work, or the summary of that work, to be detected by a single glance of his eye. The whole arrangement of this, the most important of the Government, is loose, slovenly, unsatisfactory, and susceptible of a considerable amount of fraud. A plate printer of his, James Lamb, selected at random from the fractional currency workmen, testifies: 'There was no security to prevent the fractional currency from being taken or abstracted,' when he was at work on the hydrostatic presses; and adds, 'I could have taken off ten sheets a day, from October to December.' Mr. Lamb was very sharply cross-questioned, but adhered to this testimony to the end. Nor has there been shown to your Committee any satisfactory disposition that had been made of the numerous spoiled sheets of the fractional currency, sheets of the fifty cent sort, say, upon which two or three parts may be damaged, while the remaining parts are good. Indeed, the whole 'spoiled-sheet' management of Treasury notes and of bonds, especially the *coupons*, seems to us to be in a very unsatisfactory, if not dangerous state.

"We are fortified in these views by a report of January 2, 1864, to the Secretary of the Treasury, * * * signed by Mr. Field, the Assistant Secretary; Mr. Taylor, the First Comptroller of the Treasury; and Mr. Chittenden, the Register of the Treasury, and subsequently countersigned, February, 19, 1864, by a Senator from Rhode Island, Hon. Mr. Sprague. These gentlemen, in this report, offer many valuable suggestions to the Secretary of the Treasury, which is *not* done as advised. They desired that some distinctive mark should be placed upon each sheet; which is *not* done. They detail the mode and manner by which Mr. Clark should be held responsible for every sheet put in his possession; which is *not* done. They recommend a system of checks upon requisitions for paper; to which no attention has been paid. They deem it desirable that daily returns should be made to the Secretary as to each and every sheet; which is *not* done. They find, as this

Committee found, that through the hands of Mr Clark alone passes all paper into, and out of, the several divisions, and they recommend another counting division; to which no attention has been paid. They recommend, and think the existing laws demand, that the imprint of the red seal should be affixed in the office of the Secretary himself, under his especial direction, by an officer directly responsible to him—an imprint now done by Mr. Gray, an appointee and employee of Mr. Clark alone. Six distinct and very important recommendations are offered by these gentlemen holding high offices in the Treasury, to no one of which has any attention been paid.

"The inattention to these recommendations and the neglect of these precautions are greatly to be deplored—for, without them, an unscrupulous man may rob the Treasury of thousands and thousands of dollars. Apart from the perils of fraud, the existing system tempts and leads to carelessness and theft. Mr. John Oliphant, who has charge of the loan branch in the Treasurer's office, exhibited to the Committee a $1,000 ten-forty bond erroneously printed, which, with all others of the like kind, Congress, since this discovery, has been obliged to legalize by statute. The number or amount of these in circulation, he did not know. Mr. Clark, it would seem, discovered this error some time before it was made known to the loan branch in the Treasurer's office. The peril of error in the printing of large bonds is obvious without comment, and again demonstrates the necessity for separation of work, and of check and counter-check. The testimony of Mr. John G Clark, a teller in the banking-house of Riggs & Co., also discloses the fact that an interest-bearing note of twenty dollars (if not other notes) had been issued without any date of issue upon it, or any series of numbers. Taken to the Treasury Department by the teller, Mr. Clark, the remark there was, 'It was evidently stolen. It must have been stolen from the Bureau over which Mr. Clark presides.' Four or five of these notes were reported to be missing from the Bureau. Clark explained that the twenty dollar note, and three or four others, had been stolen by a scrubbing woman employed by him, and that the sheet upon which it had been printed, had been put into the vault as mutilated money. There would seem to be no need of emigrating to the *placers* of California, when scrubbing-women can thus pick up twenty dollar notes. Mr. John G. Clark further testified, that, in April, four thousand dollars of interest-bearing notes were paid him, dated, in advance, the 12th and 16th of May. The Treasurer told him they had got out *by accident*. 'They were intended for San Francisco, but *by accident* they got out here.' These are but accidental illustrations of a perilous printing of the public money.

"The testimony of Mr. Chittenden, the Register of the Treasury, is, as to this business of printing money, very significant and very important. Henderson and Clark, it seems, there again turn up as companions—'intimate associates.' Mr. Henderson advanced in his style of living very much—far beyond what heads of departments were able to afford. He was understood to keep two or three horses, to have bought a fine house, and to have furnished it elegantly. 'I heard yesterday (May 3) he was in Clark's division, though not employed there'—and there, in a money bureau, after being removed for gross frauds in his duties as requisition or warrant clerk—*there*, where not even a Member of Congress can go, without a written order from the Secretary himself!"

The investigation created no little excitement at the time, in consequence of the gross irregularities discovered; but it was hushed up by the majority in the Committee and in the House, for fear it would damage the prospects of the Republican party, the Presidential election of 1864 being close at hand. The report which we have quoted above, declared, "*Your Committee are therefore constrained to say, that they have not been permitted, in spirit or in fact, to examine into but a very small portion of the allegations made by the newspaper press, or by Mr. Brooks, or by General Blair, on the floor of the House.*"

MAKING MONEY.

The plates which are engraved in the Treasury Department, are prepared by a process similar to that already described. The printing is done in a similar manner. The small notes contain a profusion of bronze-work, which is placed on the paper preparatory to printing. This is done by first using mordant —which attaches the bronze to the paper—upon the

PRESS ROOM—CU

ENCY BUREAU.

sheet, by an ordinary Hoe cylinder press, in the same manner as paper is printed. The bronzing was formerly done by hand, but machines are now used for that purpose. Two women or girls are required for each machine, and can bronze from seven thousand to eight thousand sheets per day.

The notes and bonds, after beng printed and numbered, are carefully counted in a separate apartment, and are made up into packages of a prescribed size and value. These are then taken to the vaults, which are in charge of the Assistant Treasurer, and placed in his keeping, to be issued at such times and in such quantities as the Secretary of the Treasury may order.

Nearly all the operations connected with the currency manufacture are conducted by females, large numbers of whom are employed in its various branches

XIII.

COUNTERFEITING.

In spite of the efforts of the Government to suppress counterfeiting, and to place its notes beyond the reach of such unlawful skill, all kinds of money issued by the Treasury have been successfully imitated, and doubtless will continue to be imitated. The operations of the counterfeiters are but rarely carried on in Washington, but as they sometimes commence them there, it seems to us proper to present here a brief description of the "business."

WHO MAKE THE COUNTERFEITS.

It is said that the security of the notes of the Bank of England lies in their simplicity. The lines on these notes are so few and plain, that a genuine note can be distinguished from a counterfeit at a glance. The postal currency issued by our Government during the early part of the Rebellion to supply the demand for small change, had a similar safeguard. These notes contained nothing but the vignette, or head, copied from the postage stamps, and a few ornamental lines by way of security. The work was so simple that it was difficult to imitate successfully, and consequently but few counterfeits of this class were attempted.

The other notes of the Government, however, being more elaborate, afford a better opportunity to the counterfeiter, since they enable him to produce an imitation, the general effect of which will deceive many good judges. Counterfeiting requires skill, since a badly executed note will be quickly detected. The plates used for printing bogus notes are prepared in a manner similar to that we have described in connection with the genuine notes, and the workman is generally a skilful engraver. The majority of this class are said to be foreigners, who, having learned their trade in Europe, come here for the express purpose of counterfeiting. Englishmen, Germans, and Italians are principally engaged in it. Sometimes a man who has been discharged from one of the large engraving establishments for dissipation, or other faults, becomes a counterfeiter; and it is said that one engraver employed in the Treasury Department at Washington, devoted his leisure time to preparing currency plates for some "outside parties." The transaction was discovered, however, the parties arrested, and the plates turned over to the Treasury Department. Jerry Cowsden, who was arrested in New York a few years ago, is said to have been an unusually talented engraver.

HOW THE BUSINESS IS CARRIED ON.

Counterfeiting Government notes and securities is said to be carried on principally in the neighborhood of New York. Some of the establishments broken up by the detectives have been fitted up with all the necessary machinery and conveniences for engraving, and others have had merely a limited stock of tools. Sometimes as much as six or eight thousand dollars capital is invested in these establishments.

Here the plates are engraved, and the notes printed. The paper for printing them ought to be hard to get, but the counterfeiters seem to have no difficulty in procuring a sufficient supply. The engravers are in the employ of the "dealer," who pays them but little more than the same work would bring in a legitimate establishment. As soon as the notes are printed, they are turned over to the dealer, who has his headquarters generally in New York, with extensive connections in all parts of the country. The bogus issue is made up in small packages, and sent to those ordering it by mail or by express, an experienced dealer being nearly always able to tell with considerable exactness what amount he can dispose of. He receives about $35 in good money for $100 worth of bogus notes. His agents then dispose of it to those who expect to receive the full value of the note for about $45, or $50 on the hundred. The profit, all things considered, is but slight to the manufacturer, or dealer, or agent, the heaviest sum being realized by those who receive the full value of the note. The movements of the agents are generally agreed upon beforehand, and the bogus issue is put in circulation simultaneously in various part of the country. If the imitation is good, a very large amount is put in circulation before it is detected.

The heaviest operations are carried on in the small or fractional notes, those of larger denominations being generally more carefully scrutinized by persons receiving them, and being thus more liable to detection. It is said that a very large proportion of the small notes in circulation in the Western States consists of counterfeits. In the East they are circulated more carefully, but still in large quantities. Keepers of low-class grocery stores, bar-keepers, butchers, stage-drivers, canal men, and travelling pedlars purchase them, and "shove" them off upon their customers with considerable success.

The fractional notes pay the counterfeiter best. The National Bank Notes come next. They are difficult to imitate, but some very successful counterfeits of this class have been set afloat. Their circulation is so general in all parts of the country that few persons examine them closely, or look to see the character of the picture on the back, which is distinctive in each denomination. The fives of this issue can, without very much trouble, be altered to fifties, which is often done. Indeed, the operations of the counterfeiters with this class of notes are exerted chiefly to alter their denominations. There are few counterfeits, if any, of the whole note now in circulation, and the altered note may be detected by examining the picture on the back, and seeing if it is that which properly belongs on a bill of that denomination.

The *Greenbacks* or *Legal Tenders* are the most difficult of all to imitate. Counterfeits of this class, however, have been issued. The genuine notes being novel in character, and having many distinctive features, are easily recognized, and it is almost impossible to alter the denomination. The green ink cannot be removed without injuring the note, and thus prevents them from being photographed.

Still, as we have said, there have been counterfeits of this kind. The fifty and one hundred dollar notes have been imitated successfully. A one hundred dollar counterfeit was executed in St. Louis a few years ago, and with such skill that ten thousand dollars worth of the bogus bills were put in circulation before the counterfeiter was caught and the plate secured.

Notes and bonds are not unfrequently presented at the Treasury for examination, and are found to have been printed from the original plates, but without the authority of the Department. Many of our readers are doubtless familiar with the occurrences of this kink which have happened since the close of the war. The question arises, How did these plates pass into the hands of these parties? The Government detectives have taken from counterfeiters fac-simile impressions taken from the plates used in the Treasury. Every year new developments of this kind are made. More and more abundant proofs of dishonesty in the officials employed in the Money Bureau are furnished, but it seems impossible under the present administration to put a stop to them.

HOW TREASURY PLATES ARE OBTAINED.

The following report of an investigation made before Commissioner Osborne, of New York City, will throw some light upon the practice of printing counterfeit notes with Treasury plates:

"The evidence given before Commissioner Osborne in the recent case of counterfeiting goes to show, if it is to be relied upon, that one Holmes, and a confederate named Treat, concocted a plan with Eli and Edwin Langdon, father and son, who were printers in the Treasury Department. Holmes was to furnish the Langdons, through the agency of Treat, with lead plates, known technically as 'leads.' The Langdons were to take impressions from the genuine plates in the Department on these leads, and return them to Holmes.

"Edwin Langdon, the son, had a woman who lived with him as his wife, and they passed for husband and wife in Washington. The woman was employed in the Department to lay sheets on the press, and was known there by the name of Minnie Morton.

"The witness testifies that these leads were given to Holmes by Langdon. Minnie testifies that she knew the plates were being counterfeited by her so-called husband, and Langdon, the father, also testified that he knew of it.

"At the close of the prosecution one of the counsel stated that the Solicitor of the Treasury had agreed not to allow the counterfeit plates to be put in evidence against Holmes, and the case was adjourned to give Mr. Chatfield an opportunity to prove his assertions. Holmes also asserts that it was positively promised by Mr. Jordan that if he would give up the plates, and not have any thing more to do with counterfeiting, he would not be prosecuted.

"If these assertions are true, and Mr. Chatfield gives his son as authority, a most singular *dénouement* will be given to the affair. None of these counterfeiters will be punished. Holmes will be let go by one Government official; Eli Langdon, Treat, and the two women have been allowed to turn State's evidence; Edwin Langdon is dead, and no one remains to be punished."

When it is remembered that not one single counterfeit has ever been printed from a copy of a genuine plate made by any of the great Bank Note Companies of the Union, in consequence of the rigid and watchful system upon which their operations are conducted, the reader will not be slow to believe that these irregularities (to use no stronger term) in the Treasury are caused by a laxity in the management of the Money Bureau, which is most criminal.

Counterfeiting is punishable with imprisonment in the penitentiary. It is very hard to lay hands on the operators, however. Months are frequently passed by the Detectives in following suspected parties. The counterfeiters are generally on the alert, and are adepts at foiling the efforts of the officers of the law. When captured their effects are turned over to the Government and they themselves held for trial.

XIV.

THE WAR DEPARTMENT.

THE building used by the Department of War is situated on Pennsylvania Avenue, west of the President's House. It is a plain, old-fashioned edifice of brick, painted in lead color. It is in contemplation to tear down this building, and erect one more suited to the military renown of the country.

Previous to the late war, the old building was amply sufficient for the wants of the army, but the military service has been so largely increased since 1860, that several buildings in the immediate vicinity of the Department are also required for the accommodation of the various bureaux.

The War Department was organized by Act of Congress in August, 1789. It has been remodelled and reconstructed several times since then, and has now become one of the largest and most important establishments in the Government. It is in charge of a "Secretary of the Department of War," who is a member of the President's Cabinet. His subordinates are the General Commanding the Army, the Adjutant General, the Quartermaster General, Paymaster General, Commissary General, Surgeon General, Chief of Engineers, and Chief of Ordnance.

THE SECRETARY OF WAR

has the general supervision of the military affairs of the country, subject to the direction of the President. He has also a general superintendence of the whole Department, and all orders are issued in his name and by his authority. His orders and decisions can be revoked only by the President.

The first Secretary of War was Henry Knox, of Massachusetts, the gallant soldier of the Revolution. His successors have been, Timothy Pickering, of Massachusetts; James McHenry, of Maryland; S. Dexter, of Massachusetts; Roger Griswold, of Connecticut; Henry Dearborn, of Massachusetts; William Eustis, of Massachusetts; John Armstrong, of New York; James Monroe, of Virginia; William H. Crawford, of Georgia; Isaac Shelby, of Kentucky; John C. Calhoun, of South Carolina; James Barbour, of Virginia; Peter B. Porter, of New York; John H. Eaton, of Tennessee; Lewis Cass, of Ohio; Joel R. Poinsett, of South Carolina; John Bell, of Tennessee; John C. Spencer, of New York; William Wilkins, of Pennsylvania; William L. Marcy, of New York; George W. Crawford, of Georgia; Charles M. Conrad, of Louisiana; Jefferson Davis, of Mississippi; John B. Floyd, of Virginia; Joseph Holt, of Kentucky; Simon Cameron, of Pennsylvania; Edwin M. Stanton, of Ohio; Ulysses S. Grant (acting), of Illinois; and John M. Schofield, the present incumbent.

THE ADJUTANT GENERAL

is the medium of communication to the Army of all

general and special orders of the Secretary of War relating to matters of military detail. The rolls of the Army and the records of service are kept by him and all commissions are made out in his office.

THE QUARTERMASTER-GENERAL

is in charge of all matters pertaining to barracks and quarters for the troops, transportation, camp and garrison equipage, clothing, fuel, forage, and the incidental expenses of the military service of the United States.

THE COMMISSARY-GENERAL

has charge of all matters connected with the subsistence of the army. The splendid manner in which our armies were subsisted during the four years of the Rebellion is the best evidence that can be offered of the excellence and efficiency of this branch of the service.

THE PAYMASTER-GENERAL

has charge of the funds appropriated for the purpose of paying the officers and men of the army. He keeps the accounts of this branch of the service, and all the pay-rolls, returns, and like documents are filed in his office.

THE SURGEON-GENERAL

is charged with the control of the medical service of the army. He prescribes rules for the government of the various hospitals, sick camps, etc., and receives all returns and issues all orders connected with the same.

THE CHIEF OF ENGINEERS

is the immediate head of the engineer establishment of the army. He has two bureaux under his control, his own, and that of the *Topographical Engineers.* His own bureau has charge of all matters relating to the construction of fortifications, and to the Military Academy. The Bureau of Topographical Engineers has charge of all matters relating to river and harbor improvements, and the survey of the lakes, the construction of military roads, and of military surveys in general.

THE CHIEF OF ORDNANCE

has charge of all matters relating to the manufacture, purchase, storage, and issue of all ordnance, arms, and munitions of war. He also controls the management of the arsenals and armories of the United States.

THE JUDGE-ADVOCATE GENERAL

is the law officer of the Department, and is in charge of the *Bureau of Military Justice.* He supervises all proceedings connected with courts-martial, courts of inquiry, and other military courts.

THE UNITED STATES ARMY.

The military establishment of the United States consists of about 50,000 enlisted men, on duty in various parts of the Union. It is commanded by a General, whose headquarters are in Washington, and who is the subordinate of the President of the United States, who is the Constitutional Commander-in-Chief of the Army and Navy. The other officers are:

1 Lieutenant-General.
5 Major-Generals.
10 Brigadier-Generals.

1 Chief of Staff to the General, 1 Adjutant-General, 1 Judge-Advocate-General, 1 Quartermaster-General, 1 Commissary-General, 1 Surgeon-General, 1 Paymaster-General, 1 Chief of Engineers, 1 Chief of Ordnance,	Brigadier-Generals.

87 Colonels.
99 Lieutenant-Colonels,
327 Majors.
835 Captains.
857 1st Lieutenants.
583 2d Lieutenants.
6 Chaplains.

THE HEADQUARTERS OF THE ARMY

are located in a small red brick building on 17th street West, south of Pennsylvania Avenue, and diagonally opposite the War Department. The building was originally a private residence, and has a decidedly unmilitary appearance. There is no display, no show about it. Every thing is modest and simple, and it is the last place a stranger would take to be the headquarters of the great soldier who won peace and union for the country.

XV.

THE NAVY DEPARTMENT.

During the Revolution and for some years afterward, the affairs of the Navy were managed by a bureau of the War Department. On the 13th of April, 1798, Congress enacted a law "to establish an Executive Department, to be denominated the Department of the Navy." It was not until after the close of the war of 1812–15, during which the Navy fought its way, against heavy obstacles, into favor with the public, that the Government began to bestow upon the service the fostering care it merited at its hands.

The building used by the Department is situated immediately in the rear of the War Department, and fronts on 17th Street West. It is a miserably rickety old building, and, together with the War Department, forms the most unsightly object in the neighborhood. It is said to be the intention of the Government to replace it with a handsome and appropriate structure. It contains many interesting trophies, such as colors taken from the enemy in battle, &c.

The Department is in charge of a Secretary of the Navy, who is a member of the President's Cabinet. His subordinates are an Assistant-Secretary, and the Chiefs of the Bureaux of Yards and Docks, Navigation, Construction and Repairs, Steam Engineering, Equipment and Recruiting, Ordnance, Provisions and Clothing, and Medicine and Surgery.

THE SECRETARY OF THE NAVY

has the general charge of every thing connected with the Navy, and the execution of all the laws relating thereto is confided to him. All instructions to officers in command of squadrons or vessels, all orders of officers, commissions of officers both in the Navy and in the Marine Corps, appointments of commissioned and warrant officers, and orders concerning the enlistment and discharge of seamen are issued by him. The orders and instructions from the different bureaux are issued by his authority, as are those of the Commandant of the Marine Corps.

The first Secretary of the Navy (who was also Secretary of War,) was General Henry Knox. His successors have been; Timothy Pickering, of Mass.; James McHenry, of Md.; George Cabot, of Mass.; Benjamin Stoddert, of Md.; Robert Smith, of Md.; Jacob Crowninshield, of Mass.; Paul Hamilton, of S. C.; William Jones, of Penn.; Benjamin W. Crowninshield, of Mass.; Smith Thompson, of N. Y.; Samuel L. Southard, of N. J.; John Branch, of N. C.; Levi Woodbury, of N. H.; Mahlon Dickerson, of N. J.; James K. Paulding, of N. Y.; George E. Badger, of N. C.; Abel P. Upshur, of Va.; Thomas W. Gilmer, of Va.; John Y. Mason, of Va.; George Bancroft, of Mass.; William B. Preston, of Va.; William A. Graham, of N. C.; John P. Kennedy, of Md.; James C.

Dobbin, of N. C.; Isaac Toucey, of Conn.; and Gideon Welles, of Connecticut, the present incumbent.

SECRETARY WELLES.

Gideon Welles is a native of Connecticut, and is over sixty years old. Martin Van Buren made him Post Master of Hartford, in 1840, and upon the accession of President Polk to power he was appointed to a post in the Navy Department, which he filled with decided ability. He could not sanction the repeal of the Missouri Compromise, and consequently left the Democratic party and joined the Republicans, in whose ranks he played a conspicuous part during the Kansas-Nebraska troubles. In 1860, he was a member of the Chicago Convention, and was one of Committee appointed to visit Springfield, and inform Mr. Lincoln of his nomination. In March, 1861, he was appointed Secretary of the Navy, which position he still holds.

Mr. Welles has been much abused, and unjustly censured for his conduct of his department; but it would seem that the brilliant record made by the service over which he presided during the Rebellion, is the best vindication he could desire.

THE BUREAU OF YARDS AND DOCKS

has charge of all the navy yards, docks, wharves, buildings, machinery in navy yards, and every thing connected with them, and the Naval Asylum. The Chief of the bureau is usually an officer of the Navy, of the grade of Captain.

THE BUREAU OF NAVIGATION

is in charge of all matters pertaining to the business of navigation. It oversees the preparation of charts, sailing directions, and issues them to the ships of the Government; and also provides chronometers, barometers, &c., and such books as are furnished by the Government to vessels of war. "The United States Naval Observatory and Hydrographical Office," at Georgetown, and the Naval Academy at Annapolis are under the general supervision of the chief of this bureau, who is generally a Captain in the Navy.

THE BUREAU OF CONSTRUCTION AND REPAIRS

is presided over by a Captain in the Navy, and has charge of the construction and repair of all vessels of war of the United States, and of the purchase of materials for such work. The plans for all new vessels are submitted to, and decided upon, by this bureau, under the authority of the Secretary.

THE BUREAU OF STEAM ENGINEERING

was formerly a part of that just mentioned, but since the almost universal employment of steam vessels of war, has risen into such prominence that a separate existence has become necessary for it. It is in charge of the Engineer-in-Chief of the Navy, to whom all plans for steam machinery are submitted for examination. He reports upon them to the Secretary, and decides upon them by authority of that official.

THE BUREAU OF EQUIPMENT AND RECRUITING

was, also, until a few years ago, a part of the Bureau

of Construction and Repairs. It is in charge of a Captain in the Navy, and superintends the enlistment of seamen and petty officers, the manning of vessels with efficient crews, the equipment of all ships put in commission, with sails, anchors, water tanks, and all other stores and supplies except provisions and ordnance stores.

THE BUREAU OF ORDNANCE

is in charge of a Captain in the Navy, and is one of the most important in the Department. It has charge of all ordnance and ordnance stores, the manufacture or the purchase of cannon, guns, powder, shot, shells, and like articles, and of the equipment of vessels of war with ordnance and ordnance stores of all kinds. All plans for improved arms or ammunition are submitted to, examined by, and decided upon by it, under the authority of the Secretary. The chief of the bureau is generally an officer of experience and ability.

THE BUREAU OF PROVISIONS AND CLOTHING

has charge of the collection and issuing of all the provisions and clothing for the use of the Navy, and of all contracts for furnishing such stores. Its duties are similar to those of the Commissary-General's and Quartermaster-General's department in the Army.

THE BUREAU OF MEDICINE AND SURGERY

is in charge of the Chief Surgeon of the Navy. It has authority over every thing relating to medicines and medical stores, the treatment of the sick and wounded, and the management of naval hospitals.

THE UNITED STATES NAVY.

The naval establishment of the United States consists of 206 vessels, carrying 1,743 guns. Of these 35 are first-rates, carrying 662 guns. Each vessel is of at least 2,400 tons; the second-rates, of from 1,200 to 2,400 tons, are 37 in number, and carry 483 guns; the third-rates, of from 600 to 1,200 tons, number 76 vessels, and carry 414 guns; the fourth-rates, under 600 tons, are 38 in number, and carry 184 guns. Of the above force, 52 are iron-clads, carry 129 guns; 95 are screw steamers, carrying 938 guns; 28 are paddle-wheel steamers, carrying 199 guns; and 31 are sailing vessels, carrying 477 guns.

The *active list* of the service is as follows:

1 admiral, 1 vice-admiral, 10 rear-admirals, 25 commodores, 49 captains, 89 commanders, 139 lieutenant-commanders, 45 lieutenants, 30 masters, 52 ensigns, 157 midshipmen, 67 surgeons, 37 passed assistant-surgeons, 36 assistant-surgeons, 79 paymasters, 56 passed assistant-paymasters, 52 chief-engineers, 90 first assistant-engineers, 137 second assistant-engineers, 24 third assistant-engineers, 19 chaplains, 11 professors, 7 naval constructors, 5 assistant naval constructors, 52 boatswains, 57 gunners, 39 carpenters, 31 sailmakers. In the Naval Academy, there are 348 midshipmen undergoing instruction, 16 third assistant-engineers, and 1 cadet engineer.

The *retired list* is as follows:

18 rear admirals, 60 commodores, 31 captains, 17 commanders, 3 lieutenant-commanders, 6 masters, 1 midshipman, 24 surgeons, 3 passed assistant-surgeons,

3 assistant-surgeons, 14 paymasters, 14 assistant-engineers, 8 chaplains, 2 professors, 6 boatswains, 6 gunners, 6 carpenters, 5 sailmakers.

THE MARINE CORPS

consists of a force of picked soldiers, detachments of whom are assigned to vessels of war for the purpose of preserving order and doing guard duty, and assisting in action. They have their own officers, and while forming a part of the naval establishment, are yet distinct from it. The corps is commanded by a commandant, who has the rank of Brigadier-General.

XVI.

THE NAVY YARD.

OWING to the difficult navigation of the Potomac River, the Washington Navy Yard has never been as important, as a building station, as those located on the coast. Still, it is one of the most interesting features of the city, and is richly worth visiting. It is situated on the "Anacostia," or Eastern Branch of the Potomac, at the termination Eighth Street East, and may be reached by means of the cars of the Washington and Georgetown Street Railway.

It was established in 1800 for the purpose of constructing several vessels of war, which were ordered to be built here, and covers an area of twenty acres, which is surrounded by a high brick wall. The main entrance is at the foot of Eighth Street, through a handsome gateway, designed by the late Benjamin H. Latrobe, Esq. Near the gateway are several comfortable residences designed for the officers (and their families) on duty at the yard. Quarters for the marines and other enlisted men are also provided within the enclosure.

THE GROUNDS

are beautifully laid off, handsomely shaded, and are kept in the most perfect order. They are ornamented with a fine display of cannon and shot and shell. Many trophies won by our navy during former wars, and during the Rebellion, are to be seen here. The beautiful column erected to the memory of the heroic officers and men who fell at the siege of Tripoli, occupies a conspicuous place.

THE MACHINE SHOPS

are extensive, and most interesting. They are kept busy at all times, for this is one of the principal establishments of the Government for constructing the equipments of vessels. The articles turned out here have stood the severest tests, and are acknowledged to be among the best in the service. The anchors and cables made here are particularly good.

Two heavy "Nasmyth," or Steam Hammers, weighing 3,600, and 2,240 pounds, are used for forging anchors. The forges attached to them are worked by a fan blower, which is turned by the steam engine in the machinist's department. A "Kirk," or Direct Steam Hammer, in connection with a blast forge, is used for working up the scrap iron of the various Navy Yards and war vessels into bolts and blooms.

The massive chain cables turned out from this Yard, are made in another shop, which is provided with a Hydrostatic press for testing their strength. Nearly one hundred men are employed in forging these cables.

A separate department is provided for the manu facture of galleys, cabooses, copper powder-tanks, and the various articles of brass-work needed in a ship of war.

The large iron-foundry is kept constantly at work, casting heavy articles of iron used for machinery. Steam cylinders, shafts, and such articles, are made here.

The ordnance department manufactures light brass ordnance, boat howitzers, shot, shells, percussion caps, musket and pistol balls, and improved projectiles of various kinds. The percussion-cap and bullet-making machines are very interesting, as are many of the others in use.

In the boiler-making department, the immense boilers used in the largest class ships of war are made in the most skilful manner. The boilers made here are of the very best description, and are thoroughly and severely tested before being received into the service.

The "machine shop" is fitted up with every description of apparatus used in making marine steam engines and machinery of other kinds. It is one of the most complete establishments in the Yard.

The "rolling mill" is provided with a two hundred horse-power engine, and a full equipment of machinery. Here are manufactured all the bolts, sheathing, braziers' and boiler copper used in the Navy, and here the scrap-iron is worked into bolts and bars.

The pyrotechnical laboratory is on the western side of the Yard. It employs a large force of operatives. Ammunition of all kinds, rockets, torpedoes, &c., are prepared here.

Two ship-houses stand at the water's edge, one of which is provided with a marine railway for hauling up steamers for repair.

The frigate Minnesota was built at this Yard, and also several other lighter vessels. During the late war, several vessels of different classes were built here, and the various departments connected with the Yard were taxed to their utmost capacity to supply the demand upon them.

XVII.

THE DEPARTMENT OF THE INTERIOR.

The Department of the Interior is comparatively new, though it is now one of the most important in the Government. It was organized in 1849, and placed in charge of certain portions of the public service which had been previously connected with the Treasury and State Departments. Its quarters are at present in the Patent Office, to which it has no legal claim, and it is presided over by a Secretary, who is a member of the President's Cabinet. His subordinates are the Commissioners of the Public Lands, Patents, Indian Affairs, Pensions, and the Census.

THE SECRETARY OF THE INTERIOR

is charged with the general supervision of matters relating to the public lands, the pensions granted by the Government, the management of the Indian tribes, the granting of patents, the management of the Agricultural Bureau, of the lead and other mines of the United States, the affairs of the Penitentiary of the District of Columbia, the overland routes to the Pacific, including the Great Pacific Railway, and the taking of the Census, and also the direction of the acts of the Commissioner of Public Buildings. The

Insane Hospital for the District of Columbia and the Army and Navy is also under his control.

The first Secretary of the Interior was Thomas Ewing, of Ohio, appointed by President Taylor. His successors have been Alexander H. H. Stuart, of Virginia; Robert McClelland, of Michigan; Jacob Thompson, of Mississippi; J. P. Usher; and O. H. Browning, of Illinois, the present incumbent.

THE COMMISSIONER OF THE GENERAL LAND OFFICE

has charge of the survey, management, and sale of the public lands of the United States. He issues the titles therefor, whether derived from confirmations of grants made by former governments, by sales, donations of grants for schools, military bounties, and public improvements, and likewise the revision of Virginia military bounty-land claims, and the issuing of scrip in lieu thereof. The Land-Office audits its own accounts. It is also charged with laying off the land grants made to the various railroad schemes by Congress, which is a heavy undertaking in itself. The mines belonging to the Government are also in charge of this office.

THE COMMISSIONER OF PENSIONS

examines and adjudicates all claims arising under the various and numerous laws passed by Congress, granting bounty lands or pensions for military and naval services rendered the United States at various times. The Rebellion greatly increased the pension list, but few persons have been found ready to refuse a fair sum to the families of those who died for the Union.

THE COMMISSIONER OF INDIAN AFFAIRS

has charge of all the matters relating to the Indian tribes on the frontier. The Government has at sundry times purchased the lands of various tribes residing east of the Mississippi River, and has settled the Indians upon reservations in the extreme West. For some of these lands a perpetual annuity was guaranteed the tribes, for others an annuity for a certain specified time, and for others still a temporary annuity payable during the pleasure of the President or Congress. The total sum thus pledged these tribes, amounts to nearly twenty-one and a half millions. It is funded at five per cent., the interest alone being paid to the tribes. This interest amounts to over two hundred thousand dollars. It is paid in various ways—in money, in provisions, and in clothing. The Commissioner has charge of all these dealings with the savages, and, of late, serious charges have been brought against his Bureau and agents, by officers of the army, and others. These gentlemen assert that the agents employed by the Indian Bureau are thoroughly corrupt; that they swindle the savages out of a very large proportion of the money due them, and then urge them on to the commission of acts of hostility against the whites, in order to avert an inquiry into their own misdeeds. It is charged that there is a vast "Indian Ring" in active existence, with its headquarters in Washington, and its ramifications all along the frontier, whose only object is to swindle the poor savages for the purpose of enriching its members. It is also boldly asserted that the employees of the Indian Bureau form a considerable part of this "Ring," and many persons well informed in the matter, deliberately charge the "Ring" and its agents with the responsibility of the recent and present Indian hostilities. So serious, indeed, have these charges become, that a movement is on foot to place the tribes under the protection of the War Department, as the only means of getting rid of the "Ring."

THE CENSUS BUREAU

is now a permanent branch of the Interior Department. Its organization is not yet completed. Heretofore it has been the custom to disband its force immediately after each census is taken. It is supposed that in a few years, at the longest, the Bureau will be permanently organized as the Bureau of Statistics. The following table is interesting in this connection:

DATE.	COST OF CENSUS.	POPULATION.
1790	$44,337.28	3,929,827
1800	66,109.04	5,305,925
1810	178,444.67	7,239,814
1820	208,525.99	9,638,131
1830	378,545.13	12,866,020
1840	833,370.95	17,069,453
1850	1,318,027.53	23,191,876
1860	1,642,000.00	31,429,891

XVIII.

THE PATENT OFFICE.

The Patent Office is properly a bureau of the Department of the Interior, but it is in all its proportions and features so vast and imposing that we have decided to devote a separate chapter to it.

It is in charge of a Commissioner of Patents, who is appointed by the President, by and with the advice and consent of the Senate. It is entrusted with the duty of granting letters-patent securing a profitable reward to any person inventing articles beneficial to civilization. It was formerly a part of the Treasury Department, and is one of the best known branches of the Government. Patents are not monopolies, as some persons suppose, but are protections granted to individuals, as a reward for, and an incentive to discoveries and inventions of all kinds pertaining to the useful arts. The bureau is allowed to charge for these letters of protection only the cost of investigating and registering the invention. It is a self-supporting institution, its receipts being largely in excess of its expenditures, so that it is confidently expected that it will be able, before many years have elapsed, to pay for its splendid building entirely out of its own earnings. From July, 1836, to December, 1860, it issued 31,004 patents, a fact which attests its industry, and the fertility of the American inventive genius. During the Rebellion many more patents were issued, so that the whole number cannot now be much less than forty thousand.

A large library of great value is attached to the Patent Office, containing many "volumes of the highest scientific value; under judicious arrangement, a collection already rich and ample is forming, of every work of interest to the inventors, and that new, increasing, important class of professional men—the attorneys in patent cases. Upon its shelves may be found a complete set of the reports of the British Patent Commissioners, of which there are only six copies in the United States. The reports of French patents are also complete, and those of various other countries are being obtained as rapidly as possible. A system of exchanges has been established, which employs three agents abroad; and, in addition to various and arduous duties, the librarian annually despatches several hundred copies of the reports."

Persons having business with the bureau will always do well to avail themselves of the services of some experienced and responsible attorney, of whom there are many in Washington and elsewhere. This will save endless trouble and annoyance, and much expense, for with all its excellences, the Patent Office is thoroughly under the dominion of red tape.

THE BUILDING

in which the bureau is quartered occupies two whole squares, and fronts south on F Street, north on G

PATENT OFFICE.

Street, east on 7th Street West, and west on 9th Street West. The length of the building, from Seventh to Ninth Streets, is 410 feet, and the width, from F Street to G Street, is 275 feet. It is built up along the four sides, with a large interior quadrangle about 265 by 135 feet in size. It is constructed in the plainest Doric style, of massive crystallized marble, and though devoid of exterior ornament is one of the most magnificent buildings in the city. It is grand in its simplicity, and its architectural details are pure and tasteful. It is ornamented with massive porticoes, one on each front, which add much to its appearance. The eastern portico is much admired. That on the south front is an exact copy of the portico of the Pantheon at Rome.

The interior is divided into three stories. The ground and second floors are arranged in offices for the accommodation of the business of the Interior Department, but the third floor is occupied by an immense saloon extending entirely around the quadrangle. This is used as

THE MODEL-ROOM,

but partakes, as far as the south hall is concerned, of the character of a museum. The models and other articles are arranged in glass cases on each side of the room, ample space being left in the centre for promenading. There are two rows of cases, one above the other—the upper row being placed in a handsome light gallery of iron, reached by tasteful iron stairways, and extending entirely around the east, north, and west halls. The halls themselves are paved with handsome tiles. The ceiling is supported by a double row of imposing pillars, which also act as supports to the galleries, and both the walls and ceiling are finished in marble panels and frescoes. A more beautiful saloon is not to be found in America.

THE SOUTH HALL.

You enter from the beautiful south portico, pass through the marble hall, and up the broad stairs to the door of the saloon. Entering it, you find a large register, with pens and ink, at the right of the door, in which you are expected to record your name and the date of your visit.

The first case on the right of the entrance contains

BENJAMIN FRANKLIN'S PRESS,

at which he worked when a journeyman printer in London. It is old and worm-eaten, and is only held together by means of bolts and iron plates, and bears but little resemblance to the mighty machines by which the printing of to-day is done. But a greater mind than that which invented the steam-press, toiled at this clumsy old frame. It calls up the whole history of the philosopher, and quietly teaches a powerful and wise lesson, as it stands there in its glass case, safe from the defiling hands of relic-hunters.

The next case is devoted to models of water-closets which though useful and instructive, are not calculated to deepen the patriotic impressions aroused by Franklin's press. Then come models of "fire-escapes," some of which are curiosities in their way, and well worth studying. The impression left by the majority, however, is that if they constitute one's only hope of escape in case of fire, an old-fashioned headlong leap from a window may just as well be attempted at once.

Near by are the models of those inventive geniuses who have attempted to extinguish conflagrations by discharging a patent cartridge into the burning mass. The guns from which these cartridges are thrown are most remarkable in design.

Then follow tobacco-cutting machines of various kinds, all sorts of skates, billiard-table models, ice-cutters, billiard registers, improved fire-arms, and toys of different designs, among which is a most ingenious model of a walking horse.

Having reached the end of this row of cases, we cross over to the south side of the hall. The first cases contain models of cattle and sheep stalls, vermin and rat traps, and are followed by a handsome display of articles in gutta percha, manufactured by the Goodyear Company. They are well worth examining carefully.

In the bottom of one of these cases is an old mariner's compass of the year 1604, presented by Ex-Governor Wise, of Virginia, then U. S. Minister to Brazil, in the name of Lieut. Sheppard, U. S. N. The ticket attached to the compass is written in the bold, running hand of the famous ex-rebel statesman. Near by is a razor which belonged to the celebrated navigator, Captain Cook. It was recovered from the natives of the island upon which he was murdered, and is hardly such an instrument as any of those who behold it would care to use. A piece of the first Atlantic cable lies just below it.

THE TREATIES.

Several of the cases following contain the original treaties of the United States with Foreign Powers. They are written upon heavy sheets of vellum, in wretchedly bad hands, and have a worn and faded appearance. All, save the treaties with England and the Eastern nations, are written in French, and are all furnished with a multiplicity of red and green seals. The first is the treaty with Austria, and bears the weak, hesitating signature of Francis I. The signature of Alexander I., attached to the first Russian treaty, has more character in it. The treaty of peace with England in 1814, which ended our second war with that Power, bears the signature of George IV., which is so characteristic of the individual, that one almost seems to see the contemptible monarch's face on the parchment. The treaty of 1803, with the Republic of France, is signed "*Bonaparte*," in a nervous, hasty hand. There is no hesitation about the signature; it is not a clerkly hand, but it is vigorous and decisive. Bernadotte's smooth and flowing hand, treacherous and plausible in appearance, and a true index of his character, adorns the first treaty with Sweden. The original treaty with Turkey is a most curious document. It consists of a number of long slips of parchment, covered with columns of Turkish characters. Near by it hangs a bag, in which it was conveyed to this country. The bag is its legal covering or case, and is provided with a huge ball of red wax by way of a seal. Next to it is the first treaty of alliance with France—the famous treaty of 1778—which gave the aid of the French king to the cause of the suffering and struggling States of the New Republic. It is signed by the ill-fated Louis XVI. The "Louis" is written in a round, scholarly hand, but the lines are delicate, as if the pen did not press the paper with the firmness of a true king. The French treaty of 1822 bears the autograph of Louis XVIII., and that of 1831, the signature of Louis Philippe. Don Pedro I., Emperor of Brazil, has affixed his hand to the Brazilian treaty, and the name of Ferdinand (the last, and least) graces that with Spain. These old parchments are very interesting, and one may well spend an hour or two in examining them.

In the glass cases with the treaties are several handsome Oriental articles—a Persian carpet, and horse-cover, presented to President Van Buren by the Imam of Muscat, and two magnificent rifles, presented to President Jefferson by the Emperor of Morocco. These rifles are finished in the highest style of Eastern art, and are really very beautiful. In the same cases are collections of medals, some of European sovereigns, and others of American celebrities. Among them is a copy of the medal awarded by Congress to the captors of Major Andre. Near these are several splendid Eastern sabres, presented by the great Ali Pacha, the Bey of Egypt, to Captain Perry and the officers of the U. S. Ship of War Concord, at Alexandria (Egypt) in 1832.

The next cases at once absorb our attention, for they contain

THE WASHINGTON RELICS,

which are amongst the greatest treasures of the nation. They consist of the camp-equipage, and other articles used by General Washington during the Revolution. They are just as he left them at the close of the war, and were given to the Government for safe keeping after his death. Here are the tents which constituted the headquarters in the field of the great soldier. They are wrapped tightly around the poles, just as they were tied when they were struck for the last time, when victory had crowned his country's arms, and the long war was over. Every cord, every button and tent-pin is in its place, for he was careful of little things. His blankets, and the bed-curtain worked for him by his wife, and his window-curtains, are all in an excellent state of preservation. His chairs are in perfect order, not a round being broken; and the little square mirror in his dressing-case is not even cracked. The washstand and table are also well kept. His knife-case is filled with plain horn-handle knives and forks, which were deemed "good enough for him;" and his mess-chest is a curiosity. It is a plain wooden trunk, covered with leather, with a common lock, the hasp of which is broken. It is divided by small partitions of thin wood, and the compartments are provided with bottles, still stained with the liquids they once held, tin plates, common knives and forks, and other articles pertaining to such an establishment. In these days of luxury, an ordinary sergeant would not be satisfied with so simple and plain an establishment; but our forefathers doubtless considered it well suited to their great commander. His cooking utensils, bellows, andirons, and iron money-chest, all of which went with him from Boston to Yorktown, are in the same case, from the top of which hangs the suit of clothes worn by him upon the occasion of the resignation of his commission as Commander-in-Chief at Annapolis, in 1783. A hall-lantern, and several articles from Mount Vernon, a "travelling secretary," Washington's sword and cane, and a surveyor's compass, presented by him to Captain Samuel Duvall, the surveyor of Frederick County, Md., are in the same case, as are also a number of articles taken from Arlington House, and belonging formerly to the Washington family.

A coat worn by Andrew Jackson at the battle of New Orleans, and the war-saddle of the Baron De Kalb, a bayonet used by one of Braddock's soldiers, and found on the fatal field upon which that commander met his death-wound, together with the panels from the State-coach of President Washington, complete the collection.

The original draft of

THE DECLARATION OF INDEPENDENCE,

with the signatures of the Continental Congress attached, is framed and placed near the Washington case. It is old and yellow, and the ink is fading from the paper. Looking at it, you can hardly realize that this was indeed the first bold proclamation of those great principles which changed the destiny of the world. Near it hangs

WASHINGTON'S COMMISSION

as Commander-in-Chief of the American Army, bearing the bold, massive signature of John Hancock, President of the Continental Congress.

ABRAHAM LINCOLN'S MODEL.

In the same case is a plain model, roughly executed, representing the framework of the hull of a Western steamboat. Beneath the keel is a false bottom, provided with bellows and air-bags. The ticket upon it bears this memorandum: "*Model for Sinking and raising boats by bellows below.* A. LINCOLN. *May* 30, 1849."

By means of this arrangement, Mr. Lincoln hoped to solve the difficulty of passing boats over sand-bars in the Western rivers. The success of his scheme would have made him independently wealthy; but it failed, and, twelve years later, he became President of the United States. During the interval, however, the model lay forgotten in the Patent Office; but, after his inauguration, Mr. Lincoln got one of the employ ees to find it for him. After his death, it was placed in the Washington case.

The opposite case contains another memento of

him—the nat worn by him on the night of his assassination.

Passing by a couple of cases filled with machinery for making shoes, we see a number of handsome silk robes, and Japanese articles of various kinds, presented to Presidents Buchanan and Lincoln by the Tycoon of Japan.

The remainder of the hall is devoted to models of machines for making leather harness and trunks, models of gas and kerosene oil apparatuses, liquor distilleries, machines for making confectionery, and for trying out lard and fat. Also methods of curing fish and meat, and embalming the dead. A great medley. A splendid model of a steel revolving tower, for harbor defence, stands near the door, and is one of the most conspicuous ornaments of the room.

THE OTHER HALLS

are devoted exclusively to models of patented machinery, and other inventions. The cases above and below are well filled; models of bridges span the spaces between the upper cases, and those of the larger machines are laid on the floor of the hall. Here is every thing the mind can think of. Models of improved arms, clocks, telegraphs, burglar and fire alarms, musical instruments, light-houses, street cars, lamps, stoves, ranges, furnaces, peat and fuel machines, brick and tile machines, sewing machines, power looms, paper-making machinery, knitting machines, machines for making cloth, hats, spool-cotton, for working up hemp, harbor cleaners, patent hooks-and-eyes, buttons, umbrella and cane handles, fluting machines, trusses, medical instruments of gutta percha, corsets, ambulances and other military establishments; arrangements for excluding the dust and smoke from railroad cars, railroad and steamboat machinery, agricultural and domestic machinery of all kinds, and hundreds of other inventions, line both sides of the three immense halls. One might spend a year in examining them, and learn something new every day. For every article one can think of, there are at least half a dozen models, and there are many inventions to be seen of which nine people out of ten have never dreamed before. The number increases every year. As the country grows greater, new wants are felt. They are sure to be supplied, and the model-room of the Patent Office keeps a faithful record of the history of our civilization.

XIX.

THE BUREAU OF AGRICULTURE.

THE Bureau of Agriculture was formerly a branch of the Patent Office, but is now separate and distinct from it. It is located in an elegant building near the Smithsonian Institution, and is in charge of the Commissioner of Agriculture. We take the following description of it from a Washington letter recently published.

THE NEW BUREAU.

"The old Agricultural Department, tucked away as it was in the vaulted cellars of the Patent Office, had a life, which, to the public, was much like the white sprouts of the potatoes scattered in some of its underground storerooms. The new Department is quite a different institution, and has a vigorous growth in the upper air. The grounds and the building will soon be among the most attractive places to visit in the Capital. In many respects they are so now.

"The new building stands upon a portion of the Smithsonian reservation. The grounds about it comprise about twenty acres, and have been laid out with much taste. The building is of pressed brick, is four stories high, and is surmounted with a French roof.

It is one hundred and sixty-six feet, by sixty. The basement is well lighted, and contains, besides furnace and stove rooms, a laboratory and folding rooms. Upon the first floors are the offices, the library, and a second laboratory for the lighter work. The rooms of the Commissioner, three in number, are finished with the patent wood-paper, lately coming into use. The paper was cut for the purpose from the most beautiful woods the country affords, and the panels, inlaid with rare varieties, are by far the richest, and more beautiful than any panel-work in the Capitol.

"The halls are laid with imported tiles, and the walls and ceilings are tastefully preserved. Upon the second floor is the main hall, fitted up with massive walnut cases, made air-tight, for the specimens which compose the museum. This will soon be the most complete, interesting, and valuable collection pertaining to agriculture to be found anywhere. Visitors will remember the great California plank, which stood in one of the underground halls of the Patent Office, and was partially discernible on a bright day. It has been manufactured into a large and elegant table, and stands in the museum. It is seven feet by twelve, and looks like a billiard table with the cloth and outer guard removed, and then highly polished. The legs and frame are made of a fine species of cedar, found in Florida. The top of the table, composed of this single plank, is without a knot or seam, and looks as rich as mahogany. Through communications with our consuls in all parts of the world, official arrangements have been entered into, to send appropriate specimens to this museum. Many are now on the way to this country.

"On this same floor are rooms in which work connected with preparing specimens is done, and also the Statistical Bureau of the Department, under the charge of Mr. E. W. Dodge. This Bureau has regular correspondents in every school district of the country, and the whole subject of receiving and recording the conditions of the various crops is now so perfect under the methods pursued by Mr. Dodge, that the monthly reports are in great demand in commercial circles, as affording the best attainable data from which to prejudge the character of our harvests. The seed rooms are fitted up in the most convenient manner for sorting, packing, and mailing the various kinds. Hereafter, nothing is to be purchased by contract for this branch of the department. The varieties used, will be selected with care from the catalogues of the best foreign and domestic dealers, and, hereafter, nothing will be sent out to the country unless it is really valuable. Heretofore, transactions in this branch have brought a good deal of ridicule upon those who were responsible for the varieties furnished. Some of the stories were exaggerations, though much of the severe criticism evoked was merited. A peck of sunflower seeds, properly distributed in packages, with French names, as imported and rare, would go far toward shaking the public faith; and a few papers of sorghum seed, sent out in response to requests for rare house-plants, would naturally create a suspicion of carelessness.

"But, under the new regimé, these mistakes will not occur. Contractors will not in future have an opportunity of mowing prairie flowers by the acre, threshing out the seeds, and selling them here under all the Latin names known to botany.

"The fourth floor, which is immediately under the roof, extends over the whole building, and resembles in all respects a great grain warehouse. An elevating platform connects it with the basement, and gives an easy method of raising the supplies of seed-grain, which are kept in this thoroughly dry and well ventilated space. Invoices have been received of seven thousand bushels of choice spring wheat from Odessa, eight hundred bushels of oats from Scotland, England, and Odessa, and four hundred bushels of spring barley from Odessa. This will soon be ready for distribution.

"A very large variety of flower seeds, seeds of shrubs and shade-trees, and such varieties of foreign fruits and vegetables as it is thought may be raised in some portions of the Union, will be on hand before many months. The communications through the State Department with all our consuls, have, in most cases, been answered, and active measures have been taken by most to contribute to the supplies named. A system of international exchanges has also been introduced, which promises most valuable returns. Through the Smithsonian Institute, the department has been put in communication with the leading foreign societies interested in agriculture, and many of them are now exchanging both reports and specimens with us. In many cases, the consuls of foreign nations are coöperating with our own. An English society at the Cape of Good Hope is now making a complete collection of grasses, fruit-trees, and flowers from all that section. A like collection is in preparation by the British Consul at Melbourne, in Australia. One of the associates of Ross Browne, our Minister to China, has full instructions to gather from different portions of China whatever he regards as valuable. One of our consuls in Japan is busily engaged upon a collection, as are also consuls in South America and the West Indies.

"Particular attention is being given to the fibrous grasses which are widely used in the manufacture of lasting and beautiful cloths in China and some other sections. Specimens of such grass, and portions of the material made, in all stages of manufacture, are now on exhibition in the museum. A tract of several acres has been set apart, near the building, which is to be covered with such useful varieties of these fibrous grasses as can be obtained.

"The shade-trees of the whole country will be represented in these grounds, so far as it is possible to make them grow. There are one thousand four hundred native varieties already planted, and it is expected that nearly as many more will be added, besides a large number of foreign trees.

"The display of flowers in these grounds will soon exceed any thing to be found in the country. They are massed together in sections according to the season in which they are most brilliant, either in leaves or flowers.

"In short, under the new order of things brought about by Commissioner Capron, the Agricultural Department has changed from one which excited a general smile when mentioned, to one which is not only a credit to the Government, but of vast importance to its material interests.

"Not the least satisfactory part of it all is, that it will be carried on at small expense. The system of exchanges, and making collections through the consular service, brings nearly every thing that is needed at very little cost. The material sent out in return, though of the best the country affords, requires only a small outlay of money.

"There is no deficiency of any moment in the appropriation for the various branches, although the opposite opinion is quite general. Of the one hundred thousand dollars appropriated for the new building, two hundred dollars remained unexpended when it was completed. In return, the Government has a beautiful and substantial structure, which is an ornament to the grounds, and admirably adapted to the desired uses, and at a cost of only twenty-two cents a cubic foot of space, where buildings in the same style in various portions of the country have cost from fifty-one to fifty-five cents per cubic foot."

XX.

THE POST-OFFICE DEPARTMENT.

THE postal service of the country is the oldest branch of the Government. Our forefathers were deeply impressed with the importance of providing prompt and reliable means of communication between the various parts of the country, and as early as the year 1792, a proposition was introduced into the Assembly of Virginia, to establish the office of "Postmaster General of Virginia and other parts of America." The proposition became a law, but was never carried into effect. In 1710, during the reign of Queen Anne, the British Parliament established a General Post-Office for all Her Majesty's dominons. By this act, the Postmaster-General was permitted to have "*one chief letter office in New York, and other chief* letter offices at some convenient place or places in each of Her Majesty's provinces or Colonies in America." When the Colonies threw off their allegiance to the Crown, especial care was given to preserving the postal facilities of the country. When the present Constitution was adopted, the right was secured to Congress "to establish post offices and post roads." In 1789, Congress established the office of Postmaster-General, and defined his duties. Other laws have since been passed, regulating the increased powers and duties of the Department, which is now, next to the Treasury, the most extensive in the country.

THE POSTMASTER-GENERAL

is a member of the President's Cabinet, and is in charge of all the postal affairs of the United States. The business of the various branches of the Department is conducted in his name and by his authority. He has a general supervision of the whole Department, and issues all orders concerning the service rendered the Government through his subordinates.

The first Postmaster-General was Samuel Osgood, of Massachusetts. His successors have been Timothy Pickering, of Massachusetts; Joseph Habershaw, of Georgia; Gideon Granger, of Connecticut; Return J. Meigs, of Ohio; John McLean, of Ohio; William T. Barry, of Kentucky; * Amos Kendall, of Kentucky; John M. Niles, of Connecticut; Francis Granger, of New York; Charles A. Wickliffe, of Kentucky; Cave Johnson, of Tennessee; Jacob Collamer, of Vermont; Nathan K. Hall, of New York; Samuel D. Hubbard, of Connecticut; James Campbell, of Pennsylvania; Aaron V. Brown, of Tennessee; Joseph Holt, of Kentucky; Montgomery Blair, of Maryland; William Dennison, of Ohio; and Alexander W. Randall, of Wisconsin, the present incumbent.

The subordinates of the Postmaster-General are,

* Mr. Barry was appointed by General Jackson in March, 1829. Previous to this, the Postmaster-General was looked upon as the head of a Bureau; but President Jackson invited Mr. Barry to a seat in his Cabinet, since which time the Postmaster-General has continued to sit in the Cabinet.

UNITED STATES GENERAL POST OFFICE.

three Assistant Postmaster-Generals, and the Chiefs of the Appointment, Contract, Finance, and Inspection offices. The following description of the organization of the Department is taken from *Lanman's Dictionary of Congress.*

THE APPOINTMENT OFFICE

is in charge of the First Assistant Postmaster-General. "To this office are assigned all questions which relate to the establishment and discontinuance of post-offices, changes of sites and names, appointment and removal of postmasters, and route and local agents, as, also, the giving of instructions to postmasters. Postmasters are furnished with marking and rating stamps and letter balances by this Bureau, which is charged also with providing blanks and stationery for the use of the Department, and with the superintendence of the several agencies established for supplying postmasters with blanks. To this Bureau is likewise assigned the supervision of the ocean mail steamship lines, and of the foreign and international postal arrangements."

THE CONTRACT OFFICE

is in charge of the Second Assistant Postmaster-General. "To this office is assigned the business of arranging the mail service of the United States, and placing the same under contract, embracing all correspondence and proceedings respecting the frequency of trips, mode of conveyance, and times of departures and arrivals on all the routes; the course of the mail between the different sections of the country, the points of mail distribution, and the regulations for the government of the domestic mail service of the United States. It prepares the advertisements for mail proposals, receives the bids, and takes charge of the annual and occasional mail lettings, and the adjustment and execution of the contracts. All applications for the establishment or alteration of mail arrangements, and the appointment of mail messengers, should be sent to this office. All claims should be submitted to it for transportation service not under contract, as the recognition of said service is first to be obtained through the Contract Office as a necessary authority for the proper credits at the Auditor's office. From this office all postmasters at the ends of routes receive the statement of mail arrangements prescribed for the respective routes. It reports weekly to the Auditor all contracts executed, and all orders affecting accounts for mail transportation; prepares the statistical exhibits of the mail service, and the reports of the mail lettings, giving a statement of each bid; also, of the contracts made, the new service originated, the curtailments ordered, and the additional allowances granted within the year."

THE FINANCE OFFICE

is in charge of the Third Assistant Postmaster-General. "To this office is assigned the supervision and management of the financial business of the Department, not devolved by law upon the Auditor, embracing accounts with the draft offices and other depositories of the Department, the issuing of warrants and drafts in payment of balances, reported by the Auditor to be due to mail contractors and other persons, the supervision of the accounts of offices under orders to deposit their quarterly balances at designated points, and the superintendence of the rendition by postmasters of their quarterly returns of postages. It has charge of the dead-letter office, of the issuing of postage stamps and stamped envelopes for the prepayment of postage, and of the accounts connected therewith.

"To the Third Assistant Postmaster-General all postmasters should direct their quarterly returns of postage; those at draft offices their letters reporting quarterly the net proceeds of their offices; and those at depositing offices their certificates of deposit; to him should also be directed the weekly and monthly returns of the depositories of the Department, as well as applications and receipts for postage stamps and stamped envelopes, and for dead letters."

THE INSPECTION OFFICE

is in charge of a Chief Clerk. "To this office is assigned the duty of receiving and examining the registers of the arrival and departures of the mails, certificates of the service of route agents, and reports of mail failures; noting the delinquencies of contractors, and preparing cases thereon for the action of the Postmaster-General; furnishing blanks for mail registers and reports of mail failures; providing and sending out mail bags and mail locks and keys, and doing all other things which may be necessary to secure a faithful and exact performance of all mail contracts.

"All cases of mail depredation, of violations of law by private expresses, or by the forging and illegal use of postage stamps, are under the supervision of this office, and should be reported to it.

"All communications respecting lost money-letters, mail depredations, or other violations of law, or mail locks and keys, should be directed 'Chief Clerk, Post Office Department.'

"All registers of the arrivals and departures of the mails, certificates of the service of route agents, reports of mail failures, applications for blank registers, and all complaints against contractors for irregular or imperfect service, should be directed 'Inspection Office, Post Office Department.'

THE DEAD-LETTER OFFICE

is one of the most interesting branches of the Department. To this office are sent all letters held for postage, or unclaimed by the parties to whom they are addressed. The following interesting summary of the work done by it during the past year, is condensed from the annual report of the Postmaster General:

"The whole number of dead letters of all classes received during the year which ended 30th June last, by actual count, was 4,162,144, showing a decrease of 144,364 letters from the number *estimated* to have been received during the previous year. Of these letters, 3,995,066 were domestic letters; 167,078 were foreign, and were returned unopened to countries where they originated. The domestic letters received may be stated as follows: Ordinary dead letters, 3,029,461; drop and hotel letters, 522,677; unmailable, 363,898; fictitious addresses, 9,190; registered letters, 3,282; returned from foreign countries, 66,558. In the examination of domestic dead letters for disposition, 1,736,867 were found to be either not susceptible of being returned or of no importance, circulars, &c., and were destroyed; about 333,000 more were destroyed after an effort to return them—making about 51 per cent. destroyed. The remainder were classified and returned to the owners as far as practicable. The whole number sent from the office was 2,258,199, of which about 84 per cent. were delivered to owners, and 16 per cent. were returned to the Department; 18,340 letters contained $95,169 52, in sums of $1 and upward, of which 16,061 letters, containing $86,638 66, were delivered to owners, and 2,124, containing $7,-86236, were filed or held for disposition; 14,082 contained $3,436 68 in sums of less than $1, of which 12,513, containing $3,120 70, were delivered to owners; 17,750 contained drafts, deeds, and other papers of value, representing the value of $3,609,271 80, of these 16,809 were restored to the owners, and 821 were returned and filed; 13,964 contained books, jewelry, and other articles of property, of the estimated value of $8,500; of these 11,489 were forwarded for delivery, and 9,911 were delivered to their owners; 125,221 contained photographs, postage stamps, and articles of small value, of which 114,666 were delivered to owners; 2,068,842 without inclosures. Thus, of the ordinary dead letters forwarded from this office, about 84 per cent. were delivered, and of the valuable dead letters (classed as money and minor) about 89 per cent. were delivered. The decrease of money letters received (about 3,000) is probably owing to the growing use of money orders for the transmission of small sums. Prominent among the causes of the non-delivery of letters is the unmailable character of many of them, ascertained during the past year to be 363,898 letters, showing a decrease of 79,888 the previous year. Of these 290,448 were detained for non-payment of postage, 58,387 returned for misdirection or want of proper address, 13,470 were addressed to places for which no mail service had been established, and 1,593 had no address whatever. There were also returned 23,425 letters addressed to persons stopping temporarily at hotels, departures or non-arrivals preventing delivery, and 9,190 letters found to be addressed to fictitious names. These are mostly cases where the causes of the non-delivery appear from the letters themselves, and no effort was made to deliver them. The number of dead letters returned during the year to foreign countries was 184,183, and the number received from foreign countries was 66,558. It further appears that out of 4,666,673 letters mailed to the United States through British, French, and German mails, 126,866—or 2 93-100 per cent.—were returned to Europe as dead letters; and out of 5,401,986 letters forwarded from this country through those mails, 30,-970—or 57 per cent.—were returned as dead letters, showing an extraordinary discrepancy between the proportion of dead letters received from Europe and the proportion returned from the United States to European countries. This difference is doubtless largely owing to causes existing in this country which do not operate in the same proportion in Europe. The geographical extent of the United States and Territories, as yet largely unsettled, the constant arrival of emigrants in search of new homes in remote regions, and the continual changing of places of abode in a sparsely settled country, all operate to increase the difficulty in the delivery of foreign letters. There were received at this office during the fiscal year, 5,459 applications for letters, of which 1,151 were answered satisfactorily, the letters applied for being found. About one-third of these applications were for ordinary letters without inclosures, no record of them being kept, and search for them being useless. The amount of money taken from all dead letters undelivered since last report, and deposited in the United States Treasury, was $27,967 71. The amount realized from sales of waste paper and deposited, was $1,280 42.

"Statement of letters received and disposed of during the fiscal year ending June 30, 1868: Domestic letters received, 3,029,461; domestic drop-letters received, 499,252; unmailable letters received, 363,898; hotel letters received, 23,425; fictitious letters received, 9,190; registered letters received, 3,282; domestic letters returned from foreign counties, 66,558. Total domestic letters received, 3,995,066; foreign letters received, 167,078. Whole number of letters received, 4,162,144. Domestic letters for disposition, 3,995,066.

Letters sent out by return letter division, 2,210,620; letters sent out by money letter division, 18,340; letters sent out by minor letter division, 17,750; letters sent out by property letter division, 11,489. Number of original letters destroyed, 1,737,867; number of return letters destroyed, 333,286—whole number destroyed, 2,070,153. Of domestic letters for disposition 51 per cent. destroyed. Whole number of letters sent out, 2,258,199. Return letters received and destroyed, 333,286; articles of small value, photographs, &c., filed, 12,400; money letters filed, 2,124; minor letters filed, 821; property letters filed, 2,578. Total delivered to owners, 1,906,990. Of domestic letters for disposition 56 per cent. were sent out. Of letters sent out 84 per cent. are delivered; of letters sent out 16 per cent. are returned.

Request Letters.—Number returned to writers by postmasters, as reported by 410 offices, 60,690; number returned from dead-letter office, 12,803. Total, 73,493.

Return Letter Division.—Letters returned to writers, 2,210,620; "return" letters received and destroyed, 333,286. Total delivered to writers, 1,877,334. Money letters containing sums less than $1, 14,082, inclosing $3,436 68; number delivered to writers, 12,513, inclosing $3,120 70; number returned and filed, 1,569, inclosing $315 98; letters containing articles of small value, photographs, &c., sent out, 125,221; number returned and filed, 10,555; number delivered to writers, 114,666.

Money Letter Division.—Received for disposition,

17,589 letters, containing $86,263 02; registered for disposition, 751 letters, containing $8,933 50; total received, 18,340 letters, containing $86,638 66; filed and held for disposition, 2,124 letters, containing $7,-862 36; lost, 31 letters, containing $143 50; outstanding, 124 letters, containing $552. Of money letters 87 per cent. were delivered to owners.

Minor Letter Division.—Received and sent out 17,-750 letters, nominal value $3,609,271 80; delivered to owners 16,809 letters; filed and for disposition 821 letters; outstanding 120 letters. Of minor letters 20 per cent. were delivered to owners.

Property Division.—Received 13,964 letters and packages, probable value $8,500; letters and packages sent out, 11,489; letters and packages delivered, 9,911; letters and packages unclaimed, 1,578; letters and packages filed and destroyed, 2,475; number of packages of jewelry, 1,130; miscellaneous articles, books, &c., 5,439; number of unmailable letters received and disposed of, 387,323; held for postage, 290,448; misdirected, 58,387; no mail service, 13,473; blank, 1,590; hotel, 23,425.

Letters sent to this office are carefully examined, and if they are of value to the writer, are returned to him. Letters with a request printed or written on the envelope, to return to the writer in a given number of days if not called for, are not advertised, but are sent to the Dead Letter Office, and immediately returned to the writer.

THE POST-OFFICE BUILDING

covers an entire block, almost directly opposite the Patent Office, and is bounded by E and F Streets North, and Seventh and Eighth Streets West. It is 300 feet long, from North to South, and 204 feet wide, from East to West. It is built of white marble, in the Corinthian style of architecture, and is the best representation of the Italian palatial ever erected upon this continent. It is rectangular in form, with a spacious interior court-yard, 95 by 194 feet in size. On the Seventh Street side there is a vestibule, which constitutes the grand entrance into the building. The ceiling is composed of exquisitely ornamented marble panels, supported by four marble columns; and the walls, niches, and floor, are of marble, the floor being richly tesselated. On Eighth Street there is an entrance for mail wagons, handsomely ornamented. The City post-office is in the F Street side of the building, and is tastefully arranged.

XXI.

OFFICIALS.

There are nearly sixty thousand public offices within the gift of the Government, and of the occupants of these, about 6,000 are on duty in Washington. Nearly all of the latter are strangers to the city. They come from all parts of the Union, and are generally appointed, without regard to merit, for the purpose of rewarding or securing political services. They are strangers to the city, and hold their appointments by so frail a tenure that they never become fully domesticated. They are in Washington, but not of it.

The above estimate of the number of Government employees, includes every individual whose name is on the rolls, who is on duty in Washington, from the grade of Assistant-Secretary of a Department down to the watchmen and laborers employed in the various offices. They are of both sexes, all ages and conditions, and of various degrees of competency.

AN INSIDE VIEW OF THE DEPARTMENTS.

At the beginning of each new administration, especially when its political character is changed, there is an overhauling of the civil list of the Government. Over fifty thousand positions of various kinds are to be filled, and for each position there are scores of applicants. The claims of each one are pressed with vigor by Members of Congress, or influential public men from the various States, and the President and heads of Departments are greatly embarrassed with such importunities.

It is astonishing to see the amount of ingenuity, energy, and patience exerted by persons to secure offices to which they are utterly unsuited, and in which they can earn but a meagre support. The same qualities exhibited in any other pursuit would secure independence, if not wealth, but thousands every year prefer depending upon the Government. These Government employees are made up of all sorts of people. Poets, preachers, lawyers, doctors, artists, authors, merchants, mechanics, and loafers are represented in the various departments. You may know them as a general rule, by their affectation of superiority to the townspeople, their general seedy appearance, and their imitations of the airs and style of "the first men in the Government." They form a "colony" distinct in themselves from the Washingtonians proper, with whom they rarely deign to associate unless they are invited to partake of their hospitality, when it is amazing to see how quick they are to accept the invitations. The majority of them are unmarried, or persons whose families are at their own homes. Living is high in Washington, and few of the salaries given are sufficient for the support of a family.

The rush for office, as we have said, is immense. Mr. Lincoln had an especial horror of office-seekers. "As the day of his re-inauguration approached, he said to Senator Clark, of New Hampshire, 'Can't you and others start a public sentiment in favor of making no changes except for good and sufficient cause? It seems as if the bare thought of going through again what I did the first year here, would *crush* me. * * * To remove a man is very easy, but when I go to fill his place, there are *twenty* applicants, and of these I must make *nineteen* enemies.'"

The business of the Departments commences at nine in the morning, and closes at three in the afternoon. The balance of the twenty-four hours the clerks are at liberty to employ as they please. Some are men of family, others have nothing to occupy their time. Some spend their leisure in lounging about the city or the hotels, or in visiting their friends, and others are employed as newspaper correspondents for the journals in the States. Their spare moments hang horribly upon them, and they are eager for any means of driving off the "blues," a disease peculiar to Washington.

The majority of them live at private boarding-houses, or in private families, where the comforts are more mythical than real. A very large part of their pay goes for board, so that after clothing themselves they have very little money left. This, however, they spend freely, and have little or nothing saved at the end of their official careers.

Their duties are very monotonous, consisting of the same set routine every day, and the holidays are few and very far between.

The appointments in the Executive Departments

and their various branches are nominally made by the President, but in reality the choice is made by the officers immediately in charge of the Departments, their recommendations being usually acted upon by the President. Changes are constantly made, and the struggle for place goes on from year's end to year's end. As appointments are not made upon the merits of the applicants, their capacity forms no ground for retaining them in office. Each one holds his place, it would seem, by the favor of the head of his bureau, and as a means of retaining that place, he exerts himself to secure the favor of that head. The higher officials take good care that it shall be known among their subordinates that they hold their official lives in their hands. Consequently, there is a feeling of uncertainty on all sides, from the Secretary down, as no one knows at what moment he may lose his place. Men fawn upon and flatter their superiors in the most sickening manner. They exert themselves, not to discharge their duties well and faithfully, but to please their superiors by humoring and pandering to their whims and caprices. Naturally enough, such a life takes all the manhood out of a man, and transforms him into an object of contempt.

SALARIES.

The salaries paid by the Government to its employees are small. A Secretary at the head of a Department receives $8,000. Assistant-Secretaries, $3,500. The Chief Clerks of the Departments receive $2,200; the heads of the Bureaus from $3,500 to $2,000; and the salaries of the other clerks range from

$1,800 to $600. These amounts are not sufficient to enable those to whom they are paid to live with any degree of comfort, and many of the employees of the Departments are unable, even by the most rigid economy, to "make both ends meet."

BLACK-MAILING.

Small as these salaries are, those who have earned them are not allowed to enjoy them. The party to which they belong claims a share in the "Government plunder," and clerks must pay the toll demanded of them upon pain of losing their places. Whenever money is needed for political purposes, the leaders of the party in power, whether Republican or Democratic, levy an assessment upon each Federal officeholder, the sum being regulated by the amount of his salary. The great officers of the Government are exempted from this tax, which falls heavily upon the humbler members of the civil service. A circular is sent to each individual, informing him that he is expected to contribute a certain sum, which is named, for the purpose of paying the contingent expenses of the party. He is *requested* to send the amount to a stated place within a given time. No order could be more peremptory than this politely worded request. Woe to the clerk who dares to disregard it! It matters not how much be may need the amount, which is always heavy for him; he must pay it, or he will be discharged, and some one put in his place who will be more amenable to party discipline. His children may be sick, or in want of comforts, his wife may need the money for the household expenses, but no matter, it must go to the party. True, he has earned it, but it is not his. It is the party's, and if his wife or child were dying for want of the comforts that money would bring them, he would have to pay it to the bloodhounds demanding it of him, or lose his place under the Government. Of course, the reason that would be assigned for his discharge would not be his refusal to pay this money. Oh, no! the political black-mailers understand their work better than this. They would accuse him of incompetency, neglect of duty, or something of the kind, or the Chief of his bureau would, without assigning any reason, politely tell him that his services were no longer required, and set him adrift. And not once a year only do these black-mailers make their demands. The poor clerks are liable to them at any moment, whenever the party needs money, and out of a salary of one thousand dollars, may be forced to "*give*" the party one hundred dollars.

The worst feature of all is, that it is said that much of the money thus extorted goes into the pockets of private individuals. It is well known that all of it, if really used by the party demanding it, is expended for the purpose of perpetuating those systems of bribery and corruption which have disgraced our land in the eyes of the civilized world.

ARE PUBLIC OFFICES FOR SALE?

You hear it stated on all sides that clerkships and other appointments under the Government may be purchased, either for so much money paid down on the spot, or for a share in the compensation of the office. Various persons are charged with being guilty of selling these offices, and names that ought to be above suspicion are dragged through the mire in connection with such charges. How much is truth and how much is error, it is hard to tell. Charges are abundant, but proofs are scarce. All such stories may be true, or all may be false ; but it is certain that there are very many persons both in Washington and elsewhere who profess to believe them, and to have good grounds for such belief. Similar charges are frequently set afloat by the newspaper press. A Congressional investigation might set the matter at rest.

A WARNING TO OFFICE-SEEKERS.

To the thousands of persons who display such eagerness to secure appointments under the Government, we would say, "Turn your attention to some honest pursuit, and let Government clerkships alone." To nine men out of ten such offices are utterly unprofitable. The salaries are small, the tenure by which they are held is uncertain, and they are generally more vexatious than profitable. A Government clerk has at least twenty rivals constantly working against him, each one hoping to have him discharged and be appointed in his stead. All sorts of stories are told to his prejudice, many of which are devoid of truth, and he is haunted with a fear of being discharged, which poisons all his pleasures. He has no independence while in office, no true manhood. If his opinions differ from those of the Chief of his bureau or department, he dare not express them, for his chief tolerates no such liberty on the part of his subordinates. He must openly avow his implicit faith in all his superiors, on pain of dismissal, and must cringe and fawn upon them, even when they rob him—in the name of their party—of his earnings. And, at last, at the end of four years, if not sooner, he must give way to some new man, and seek some other mode of employment. His clerkship has, by this time, unfitted him for business pursuits, or mechanical labor. It has engendered ideas and habits which are so many obstacles to his success in other employments. To young men of ambition a Government clerkship of any kind is a positive curse, and is generally the ruination of a promising career.

GOING HOME TO VOTE.

During political struggles in the States, of more than usual importance, the clerks and employees in the departments are expected to play their part in the States to which they belong. This they can only do by going home to vote. They are notified that all who desire to avail themselves of the "privilege," will be allowed a sufficient time to go to their legal homes and deposit their votes. In times of great political contests this is expected of them, and a failure on their part to comply with this expectation is sure to bring down upon them the wrath of the leaders of their party, which wrath is fatal to their official existences. These journeys home are very expensive to both the clerk and the country. His part of the public service is at a "stand-still" during his absence, and he is paid his full salary for work he does not perform. In this the country loses. His loss lies in the heavy expense to which his journey subjects him, and for which he receives no compensation.

PROPOSED REFORMS IN THE CIVIL SERVICE.

Under the present system of political appointments, two-thirds of the men holding office under the Government are incapable of discharging their official duties. As a natural consequence, the service rendered the Government is such as would not be tolerated in any first-class establishment. The country resounds with complaints upon this subject, and it is a wonder that our people are so patient in submitting to the evil. A reform is demanded—one that will ensure the employment of none but competent officials. The people are taxed heavily to pay for their Government, and they have the right to demand that it shall be administered at least intelligently.

A movement in that direction has at length been set on foot, and the Hon. T. A. Jenckes, of Rhode Island, has introduced a bill in Congress, the meritorious features of which are thus explained by him in a recent speech:

"We ought to put in the offices by which the Government is administered the best men fit for the places, that can be obtained for the money we pay. To that abstract proposition all agree. But how shall we get at these men? Not by continuing the present system surely, for it is full of inherent defects. All that is known of the men who apply for office by the heads of departments who appoint them to office is the recommendations they bring. These are often false, and the result is, many are incompetent to perform the duties of the office they hold. The proposed measure meets this difficulty. It does not undertake to break up the organization by which the Government is carried on at the present time, by dismissing the officers who are now in place; it does not intend to produce any check or violence in the administration whatever. It proposes to place a commission of competent men at the doors to examine into the fitness of the person who applies for one of these minor places. Men are to be selected according to their fitness for the post they are to occupy. In order that this commission may not be broken down by political cliques, nor overborne by Members of Congress, it is propósed to create a new department, with the Vice-President at its head; the Department of Civil Service. This department will extend itself according to the need of its services throughout the country; and it will conduct the examination, and test the qualities of candidates for office. If this system shall be adopted we shall have the nearest approach to an independent administration of the affairs of the country. The Vice-President has hitherto been almost a useless appendage to this Government, with light duties and no responsibilities. By this mode he will occupy an important position, will have a place in the Cabinet, and the charge of a large number of men. If called upon to assume the duties of Presi dent, he will have the advantage of knowing the men in his service, and the position at the head of this department is one which it is eminently proper he should fill. Besides the Vice-President, it is proposed to have four commissioners, and with these five gentlemen shall rest the controlling power. These commissioners will have the authority to call upon men of learning and high character in different parts of the country, to aid them in conducting the examinations. This system has been found practicable and is now in operation in England, France, and Prussia. Having established the measure which provides that all persons admitted to office shall be competent, the next question is, who shall be admitted? In answer to that the speaker said, he would give the largest liberty; he would throw the doors open to all. Every citizen of the United States of the requisite age, with the proper degree of health and character to stand investigation, and with sufficient learning to perform the duties of the office which he seeks, shall be a candidate for admission. A blow would then be struck at the root of every thing which could be called patronage. Patronage is a plant of foreign growth in our republic, inherited and derived from alien and adverse organizations. It has gained a foothold here, but it should never be allowed to remain an instant after it can be safely extirpated. The proposed measure would tend to emancipate every servant of the republic from the servitude of office; every man who received a commission from the United States would know that he received it from the people; and he should hold it as long as he served the people well and efficiently. The measure does not propose to introduce a tenure of office; it does not propose to issue commissions for life, or during good behavior, which is almost equivalent to a commission for life. An officer should hold his commission during efficiency of service, and no longer. The people have a right to demand that for the money they pay they shall have the best ability to serve which that money will buy. It would remove another badge of servitude, which is, that a man may be disgraced by being removed at the will or caprice of his superior without just cause. This has done more to degrade office than any other thing associated with it. If this system is adopted the subordinates will discover and bring to notice the dereliction of duty in the superiors, and every man will be placed on trial. By this bill any one, or a class of officers, can be examined when so requested by the heads of the department; and idle, incompetent, and inefficient men will be weeded out, and their places supplied by those who have better qualifications; so that in the course of time we shall have men in the public service who regard it an honor to be there, and an honor also in the estimation of others. Under the present system, the worst men seek the public offices; especially is this the case in New York, and the Southern and some of the Western cities. The element of honor is more valuable and more binding than all the bonds which could be given. No bonds are required in the army and navy, the *esprit du corps* keeps them pure; the same spirit of honor should be infused in the civil service, and public officers will rise in the esteem of the nation. The necessity of some change is felt more and more every hour More than one hundred millions of dollars of the whiskey-tax alone never finds its way into the Treasury for want of competent and reliable officers. The element of honor is yet alive in this nation; nine years ago some thought the spirit of bravery had died out, but we have since found out it was not so. We are now threatened with great danger in the civil service, as the life of the nation was threatened in the time of war. We must now turn out the thieves, and put in faithful and honest men. Under the old law, the speaker said he knew a case in which a certain politician had the appointment of the warehousekeeper, the assistant assessor, and the assistant collector in a certain district; he furnished the grain for the distillery, and owned the whiskey which was manufactured. The amount of tax collected there was probably small. The proposed bill is not a copy of the systems of other nations. It is not the home English service system; it is precisely what the civil service commissioners of England asked for some years ago from Parliament. The proposed measure does not depend upon the competitive examination alone, hence there has been introduced into the bill a provision of the law of Prussia, and which, to a certain extent, is enforced in France, and also found in Great Britain, especially in the India service, viz.: the system of probation. Persons are appointed to offices for a certain length of time, and if they are found incapable of performing its duties, at the end of that time they are dropped. They must fulfil the expectations raised on their examination; they must be efficient as well as competent."

The merits of these reforms will not fail to commend themselves to the reader, who will echo our wish that Mr. Jenckes' bill may speedily become a law.

XXII.

FEMALE CLERKS.

STANDING in the doorway of the *National Theatre*, a few nights ago, watching the audience leave the building, we heard a young snob near us exclaim to his companion, "Let us go now, Tom! We've seen all the ladies! The rest of these women are only Treasury Clerks!"

The remark affected us unpleasantly, and we could not help asking ourself, "Are not the Treasury Clerks ladies?" The majority of them are, but it is a melancholy fact that many of them are either suspected of immoral practices, or looked down upon by the Washingtonians as beings of a lower order.

There are about 600 female clerks in the service of the Government, in Washington. They are employed in the Treasury, Interior, and Post Office Departments, the Treasury clerks being in the proportion of five to one. The highest salary paid is $900, the lowest $600, sums notoriously insufficient to support the women decently.

Some of these female clerks are the wives of men employed in the same, or in some other department; others are married, and support their families in this way; but the great majority are unmarried. There are both widows and young girls. Some are old and ugly, others are passable, not to say *passé*, and others still are young and pretty. They come from all parts of the country, but principally from New England, where the females are so largely in excess that all cannot find employment at home. They board, like the male clerks, at the various boarding houses of the city, and in private families. Their mere living expenses are heavy, and their slender salaries are scarcely sufficient to keep them decently. They are blackmailed and plundered for political purposes, like the men, and are liable to be removed from their places at any moment. Their positions are not to be envied, and ought to be shunned by women who can obtain honest employment elsewhere.

THE TREASURY COURTESANS.

The Minority Report presented in Congress in 1864, presents the following picture of the immoralities which prevailed in the Treasury Department at that time:

"These affidavits disclose a mass of immorality and profligacy, the more atrocious as these women were employees of Clark, hired and paid by him with the public money. These women seem to have been selected, in the Printing Bureau, for their youth and personal attractions. Neither the laws of God nor of man, the institution of the Sabbath, nor common decencies of life seem to have been respected by Clark in his conduct with these women. A Treasury Bureau —there, where is printed the money-representative, or expression of all the property and of all the industry of the country—there, where the wages of labor are more or less regulated, and upon the faith and good conduct of which depends, more or less, every man's prosperity—is converted into a place for debauchery and drinking, the very recital of which is impossible without violating decency. Letters go thence, arranging to clothe females in male attire to visit 'the Canterbury.' Assignations are made from thence."

Accompanying this report were affidavits, pronounced by Mr. Jordan, the Solicitor of the Treasury, to be, in his judgment, "true," which showed that several officers connected with the Printing Bureau, two of whom, at least, were married men, used their positions to seduce the women employed in the Bureau. The father of one of these girls made oath that the Superintendent of the Sixteenth Division of the Printing Bureau, deliberately told the said girl that if she would go with him to a certain hotel in that city, and submit to his wishes, he would raise her salary to seventy-five dollars per month.

These disclosures attracted considerable attention at the time, and, unfortunately, had the effect of causing every female employee of the Treasury to be suspected, and was, doubtless, the original cause of the suspicion attaching to their position to-day.

There are, no doubt, impure women in the employ of the Government, but there are also many who are good and true, and who would grace any walk of life. The good and the bad are mingled together. Outwardly, they are all ladies. The pure women, however, who are in a large majority, know their erring sisters, for such conduct cannot be hidden, and avoid them. The suspicion which rests upon these clerks, as a class, is most unjust and unfounded.

PERSECUTIONS OF FEMALE CLERKS.

You will hear it said in Washington that the acceptance of a Government clerkship by a woman is her first step in the road to ruin. If she is young and pretty, she is surrounded by men who seek her moral destruction—men oftentimes high in position, and who ought to shrink with horror from such devilish acts. She has need of all her purity, all her firmness, for those who would injure her, ply every art known to man. They surround her with flattery, with temptations of every description, and when these fail, threaten her with a dismissal from the place in which she earns her bread, if she does not yield. Nine times out of ten she is the child of poor parents, or her father may have died under the old flag, and she may be the only hope of a widowed mother for bread, and, to lose her place, would be to bring starvation upon her loved ones. Her persecutors weigh well all these things, and urge them upon her, until she is nearly driven mad, and—she yields.

Again, it is said that a woman's virtue is made the price of such an appointment, which price is paid to the party through whose influence the place is obtained; and it is asserted that public men provide for their mistresses by placing them in the Government offices.

Vice of this kind is secret in all its workings, and it is impossible to tell how many of these female clerks are pure women, or how many impure. As we have said, all are outwardly virtuous, and each would indignantly repel any charge brought against her. The black sheep are greatly in the minority, but are still believed to be numerous. Strong efforts are made by devils, in the form of men, to increase their number, and it is to be feared that these efforts will, in many cases, be successful.

XXIII.

THE SMITHSONIAN INSTITUTION.

The Smithsonian Institution stands on a part of the portion of the public grounds extending westward from the Capitol to the Potomac River, and called "*The Mall.*" The grounds extend from Seventh Street West to Twelfth Street West, and from the Canal (which forms the northern boundary) to B Street South. They are very extensive, comprising an area of fifty-two acres, and were laid out by the distinguished horticulturalist and landscape gardener, Andrew Jackson Downing, who died while engaged in this work. A handsome monument to his memory stands in the grounds. It consists of a massive vase resting on a pedestal, the whole being executed of the finest Italian marble.

THE BUILDING

stands near the centre of the park. The site is about twenty feet above the average level of Pennsylvania Avenue, and the centre of the building is exactly opposite Tenth Street West.

The structure is in the style of architecture belonging to the last half of the twelfth century, the latest variety of rounded style, as it is found immediately anterior to its merging into the early Gothic,

SMITHSONIAN INSTITUTION.

and is known as the Norman, the Lombard, or Romanesque. The semicircular arch, stilted, is employed throughout—in doors, windows, and other openings.

The main building is 205 feet long by 57 feet wide, and, to the top of the corbel course, 58 feet high. The east wing is 82 by 52 feet, and, to the top of its battlement, 42½ feet high. The west wing, including its projecting apsis, is 84 by 40 feet, and 38 feet high. Each of the wings is connected with the main building by a range, which, including its cloisters, is 60 feet long by 49 feet wide. This makes the length of the entire building, from east to west, 447 feet. Its greatest breadth is 160 feet.

The north front of the main building is ornamented with two central towers, the loftiest of which is 150 feet high. It has also a handsome covered carriage way, upon which opens the main entrance to the building. The south central tower is 37 feet square, 91 feet high, and massively constructed. A double campanile tower, 17 feet square, and 117 feet high, rises from the northeast corner of the main building; and the southwest corner has a lofty octagonal tower, in which is a spiral stairway, leading to the summit. There are four other smaller towers of lesser heights, making nine in all, the effect of which is very beautiful, and which once caused a wit to remark that it seemed to him as if a "collection of church steeples had gotten lost, and were consulting together as to the best means of getting home to their respective churches."

The entire edifice is constructed of a fine quality

of lilac gray freestone, found in the new red sandstone formation, where it crosses the Potomac, near the mouth of Seneca Creek, one of its tributaries, and about twenty-three miles above Washington. It is comparatively soft when first quarried, and is easily worked with the chisel and hammer; but exposure causes it to harden rapidly, and enables it to withstand the severest usage. It is one of the most beautiful building materials in use, and renders the "Smithsonian" one of the handsomest and most attractive edifices in the city.

THE INSTITUTION

was founded by James Smithson, an eminent Englishman, belonging to one of the best families of Great Britain. He died in 1828, and left the sum of $515,169 to the United States, for the purpose of founding the institution which bears his name. The United States accepted the trust confided to it, and, in 1846, Congress passed an act establishing the "Smithsonian Institution," and in May, 1847, the corner-stone was laid, with Masonic ceremonies, in the presence of President Polk and an immense concourse of strangers.

The object of James Smithson in founding this institution, was, in his own words, "to found at Washington, under the name of the Smithsonian Institution, an establishment FOR THE INCREASE AND DIFFUSION OF KNOWLEDGE AMONG MEN." In order that his wishes might be carried out to their fullest extent, the Board of Regents decided upon the following general plan.

upon which the operations of the Institution are conducted:

"*To Increase Knowledge.* It is proposed: 1. To stimulate men of talent to make original researches, by offering suitable rewards for memoirs containing new truths; and, 2. To appropriate annually a portion of the income for particular researches, under the direction of suitable persons.

"*To Diffuse Knowledge.* It is proposed: 1. To publish a series of periodical reports on the progress of the different branches of knowledge; and, 2. To publish, occasionally, separate treatises on subjects of general interest.

"*Details of Plan to Increase Knowledge.* I. By stimulating researches. 1. Facilities to be afforded for the production of original memoirs on all branches of knowledge. 2. The memoirs thus obtained to be published in a series of volumes, in a quarto form, and entitled Smithsonian Contributions to Knowledge. 3. No memoir, on subjects of physical science, to be accepted for publication, which does not furnish a positive addition to human knowledge, resting on original research; and all unverified speculations to be rejected. 4. Each memoir presented to the Institution to be submitted for examination to a commission of persons of reputation for learning in the branch to which the memoir pertains, and to be accepted for publication only in case the report of this commission is favorable. 5. The commission to be chosen by the officers of the Institution, and the name of the author, as far as practicable, concealed, unless a favorable decision be made. 6. The volumes of the memoirs to be exchang ed for the transactions of literary and scientific societies, and copies to be given to all the colleges, and principal libraries, in this country. One part of the remaining copies may be offered for sale; and the other carefully preserved, to form complete sets of the work, to supply the demand for new institutions. 7. An abstract, or popular account, of the contents of these memoirs to be given to the public through the annual report of the Regents to Congress. II. By appropriating a part of the income, annually, to special objects of research, under the direction of suitable persons. 1. The objects, and the amount appropriated, to be recommended by counsellors of the Institution. 2. Appropriations in different years to different objects; so that in course of time each branch of knowledge may receive a share. 3. The results obtained from these appropriations to be published, with the memoirs before mentioned, in the volumes of the Smithsonian Contributions to Knowledge. 4. Examples of objects for which appropriations may be made: (1.) System of extended meteorological observations for solving the problem of American storms. (2.) Explorations in descriptive natural history, and geological, magnetical, and topographical surveys, to collect materials for the formation of a Physical Atlas of the United States. (3.) Solution of experiment problems, such as a new determination of the weight of the earth, of the velocity of electricity and of light; chem ical analyses of soils and plants; collection and publi cation of scientific facts, accumulated in the offices of government. (4.) Institution of statistical inquiries with reference to physical, moral, and political subjects. (5.) Historical researches, and accurate surveys of places celebrated in American history. (6.) Ethnological researches, particularly with reference to the different races of men in North America; also, explorations and accurate surveys of the mounds and other remains of the ancient people of our country.

"*Details of the Plan for Diffusing Knowledge* I. By the publication of a series of reports, giving an account of the new discoveries in science, and of the changes made from year to year in all branches of knowledge not strictly professional. 1. These reports will diffuse a kind of knowledge generally interesting, but which, at present, is inaccessible to the public. Some reports may be published annually, others at longer intervals, as the income of the Institution or the changes in the branches of knowledge may indicate. 2. The reports are to be prepared by colaborators eminent in the different branches of knowledge. 3. Each colaborator to be furnished with the journals and publications, domestic and foreign, necessary to the compilation of his report; to be paid a certain sum for his labors, and to be named on the title-page of the report. 4. The reports to be published in separate parts, so that persons interested in a particular branch can procure the parts relating to it without purchasing the whole. 5. These reports may be presented to Congress for partial distribution, the remaining copies to be given to literary and scientific institutions, and sold to individuals for a moderate price. II. By the pr lication of separate treatises on subjects of general interest. 1. These treatises may occasionally consist of valuable memoirs translated from foreign languages, or of articles prepared under the direction of the Institution, or procured by offering premiums for the best exposition of a given subject. 2. The treatises should, in all cases, be submitted to a commission of competent judges previous to their publication.

"The only changes made in the policy above indicated have been the passage of resolutions, by the Regents, repealing the equal division of the income between the active operations and the museum and library, and further providing that the annual appropriations are to be apportioned specifically among the different objects and operations of the Institution, in such manner as may, in the judgment of the Regents, be necessary and proper for each, according to its intrinsic importance, and a compliance in good faith with the law."

THE GOVERNMENT

of the Institution is regulated by an Act of Congress, dated August 10, 1846, which provides that "the President and Vice-President of the United States, the Secretary of State, the Secretary of the Treasury, the Secretary of War, the Secretary of the Navy, the Postmaster-General, the Attorney-General, the Chief Justice, and the Commissioner of the Patent Office of the United States, and the Mayor of the City of Washington, during the time for which they shall hold their respective offices, and such other persons as they may elect as honorary members, be and they are hereby constituted an 'establishment,' by the name of the 'Smithsonian Institution,' for the increase and diffusion of knowledge among men."

The law also provides for a "Board of Regents," to be composed of the President of the United States, the Mayor of the City of Washington, three members of the United States Senate, and three of the House of Representatives, who shall serve during the time for which they hold their respective offices, and six other persons, other than members of Congress, two of whom shall be members of the National Institute, in the City of Washington, and resident in the said City. The other four shall be citizens of other States, no two of whom shall be chosen from the same State.

A general supervision is exercised by the "establishment" over the affairs of the Institution; but its business is carried on by the Board of Regents, who make annual reports of the same to Congress.

The Executive officer of the Institution is the Secretary, who is elected by the Board of Regents. He has charge of the building and all its contents, and the grounds, and is provided with as many assistants as are necessary to the discharge of his various duties.

Though the Institution is not a Government establishment, its property is guarded by the laws which protect the public buildings and grounds in the City.

The Library of the Institution, consisting of over forty thousand carefully selected volumes, was transferred in 1866 to the Library of Congress, in the Capitol, as has already been related.

THE FIRE OF 1865.

On the 24th of January, 1865, a fire occurred at the Institution which destroyed the upper part of the main building and the towers. It was extinguished before it reached the lower story, but destroyed the official, scientific, and miscellaneous correspondence, record books, and manuscripts in the Secretary's office, the large collection of apparatus, the personal effects of James Smithson, Stanley's gallery of Indian portraits, and a large amount of the property of the Institution, and of persons connected with it.

The loss was heavy, but the fire caused no interruption in the practical workings of the Institution. The library, museum, and laboratory were uninjured, and the burned portion has since been restored.

THE MUSEUM

is on the ground floor, and occupies the principal hall of the main building, and is beautifully fitted up. The hall is one of the most elegant in the city, and is surrounded by rows of glass cases, in two tiers, containing the specimens on exhibition. The upper tier is reached by means of light iron stairways and galleries. We take the following description of the hall and its contents from a pamphlet sold in the Institution to visitors:

"Under these provisions, the Institution has received and taken charge of such Government collections in mineralogy, geology, and natural history as have been made since its organization. The amount of these has been very great, as all the United States Geological, Boundary, and Railroad Surveys, with the various topographical, military, and naval explorations, have been, to a greater or less extent, ordered to make such collections as would illustrate the physical and natural history features of the regions traversed.

"Of the collections made by thirty Government expeditions, those of twenty-five are now deposited with the Smithsonian Institution, embracing more than five-sixths of the whole amount of materials collected. The principal expeditions thus furnishing collections are the United States Geological Surveys of Doctors Owen, Jackson, and Evans, and of Messrs. Foster and Whitney; the United States and Mexican Boundary Survey; the Pacific Railroad Survey; the Exploration of the Yellow Stone, by Lieutenant Warren; the Survey of Lieutenant Bryan; the United States Naval Astronomical Expedition; the North Pacific Behring Straits Expedition; the Japan Expedition, and the Paraguay Expedition.

"The Institution has also received, from other sources, collections of greater or less extent, from various portions of North America, tending to complete the Government series.

"The collections thus made, taken as a whole, constitute the largest and best series of the minerals, fossils, rocks, animals, and plants of the entire continent of North America, in the world. Many tons of geological and mineralogical specimens, illustrating the surveys throughout the West, are embraced therein. There is also a very large collection of minerals of the mining regions of Northern Mexico, and of New Mexico, made by a practical Mexican geologist, during a period of twenty-five years, and furnishing indications of many rich mining localities within our own borders, yet unknown to the American people.

"It includes, also, with scarcely an exception, all the vertebrate animals of North America, among them many specimens each of the Grizzly, Cinnamon, and Black Bears; the Panther, Jaguar, Ocelot, and several species of Lynx or Wildcat; the Elk, the Mexican, Virginian, White-tailed, Black-tailed, and Mule Deer; the Antelope, Rocky Mountain Goat and Sheep; several species of Wolves and Foxes, the Badger, Beaver, Porcupine, Prairie Dog, Gopher, and also about seven hundred species of American Birds, four hundred of Reptiles, and eight hundred of Fishes, embracing Salmon, Trout, Pike, Pickerel, White Fish, Muskalonge, Bass, Redfish, &c.

"The greater part of the Mammalia have been arranged in walnut drawers, made proof against dust and insects. The birds have been similarly treated, while the reptiles and fish have been classified, as, to some extent, have also been the shells, minerals, fossils, and plants.

"The Museum hall is quite large enough to contain all the collections hitherto made, as well as such others as may be assigned to it. No single room in the country is, perhaps, equal to it in capacity or adaptation to its purposes, as, by the arrangements now being perfected, and denoted in the illustration, it is capable of receiving twice as large a surface of cases as the old Patent Office Hall, and three times that of the Academy of Sciences of Philadelphia.

"Every article will be distinctly and accurately labelled by naturalists of the highest authority in each department, and the duplicates will be distributed to the principal museums in the world."

There are several fine specimens of meteorites in the museum, one of which is the largest specimen to be seen in this country, next to the Texas meteorite in Yale College.

THE SOUTH HALL

contains a number of articles of special interest. Among these is an ancient *sarcophagus*, brought by Commodore Elliott, in the frigate Constitution, in 1839, from Beirut, in Syria. It is believed to have held the mortal remains of the great Roman Emperor Alexander Severus, and was designed by Captain Elliott and his officers as a last resting-place for the body of Andrew Jackson, at his death; but "Old Hickory" declined the honor of being buried in another man's coffin, and the sarcophagus is now amongst the treasures of the "Smithsonian."

In the same hall is a plank from one of the "Big Trees" of California, and several Idols from Central America, presented by the Hon. E. G. Squier, late U. S. Minister to Nicaragua.

XXIV.

GAMBLERS.

WASHINGTON is the paradise of gamblers, and contains many handsome and elegantly-fitted-up establishments. It is said that at least one hundred of these "hells" were in full blast during the war. The number has been greatly reduced by the departure from Washington of the vast army of persons temporarily sojourning in that city for various purposes during the Rebellion.

The majority of these establishments are located on "Pennsylvania Avenue," or in the streets leading immediately from it. You may recognize them by the heavily-curtained windows through which the gaslight shines dimly, by the general air of silence and mystery which pervades the whole place, and by the brightly-lighted hall, over the door of which shines the number of the house in heavy gilt letters. Some of these houses are furnished magnificently, and provide their guests with suppers and wines of the most superb quality.

Every thing is done to draw custom. The best houses are fitted up in a style of magnificence which is princely. The floors are covered with the richest and most yielding carpets, so soft that the tramp of a thousand men would scarcely awaken an echo in the

A WASHINGTON GAMBLING HELL.

gorgeous apartments. The walls and ceilings are exquisitely frescoed and adorned with choice works of art. The furniture is costly and tasteful. Heavy close curtains of the most sumptuous materials cover the windows and exclude all noises from without and deaden all sounds within. Splendid chandeliers, with scores of gas jets shining through cut-glass globes, shed a brilliant glare through the rooms, and negro servants, exquisitely dressed, attend your every want with a grace and courtesy positively enchanting.

The proprietor, if you did not know his trade, you would take for one of the high officials of the Republic, so courtly are his manners, and so lofty his bearing. He is, as gamblers understand the term, a gentleman of the bluest blood, and would scorn to commit what he considered a mean act. He will treat you fairly, is glad to see you, and exerts himself to leave you with an impression which will induce you to repeat your visit.

The table and wines are free to all, and you can play or not, as you please. Few have the assurance, however, to partake of such magnificent hospitality without making some return, and generally lose a few dollars during the evening, by way of payment.

THE GAME.

In these first-class establishments "square games" alone are allowed, and the visitor is sure of being dealt fairly with. Faro is the principal game, and is played as follows: In front of the dealer is a table with a green cloth, upon which a number of cards are laid.

These cards are sometimes fastened down to the table, to prevent their being disarranged in the excitement of play. This is called the "lay out." A pack of cards, corresponding to those on the table, is then placed in a patent silver case, and the dealer shuffles them out one by one upon the "lay out." A player deposits his stake upon a card, the Jack of diamonds, for instance. If the dealer, in shuffling, throws the corresponding Jack from the pack in the box upon the Jack in the "lay out" upon the table, the player wins from the bank, which is owned by the proprietor of the house, an amount equal to his stake; but if a different card falls upon it he loses his stake.

In first-class houses, the shuffling is done fairly by the dealer, who is a proficient in his trade, and rarely loses. The bank relies upon his superior skill to keep its coffers full; and as a general rule, he wins, for *faro* is decided by skill as often as by chance.

There is generally but little money to be seen on the table. The sums risked are represented by ivory checks called counters, each of which has its value stamped upon it. They are purchased from the proprietor by persons wishing to play, and are promptly cashed upon presentation. This is done as a matter of safety. The law forbids gambling for *money*, and if, in case of a descent by the police, no money is visible, it is hard to make a case against the proprietor and his friends.

The gaming-room is usually in the rear of the building, so that it shall not be the first room entered by the police in case of a descent by them. The table is surrounded by players all through the evening Some lose only a few dollars. Others play heavily and lose or win thousands. There is very little conversation in the apartment. The players are too much interested in the game to talk. Men lay down their stakes in silence, and the cards are shuffled amidst an unbroken stillness. The bank wins or loses, the stakes are gathered up and replaced, but not a word is said. The dealer is calm, cool, and smiling, as are a few of the old players, but the majority are excited and nervous. As the fascination of the game grows upon them, they brace up their nerves with liquors, until they lose all semblance of reason, and play with a recklessness that is sure to ruin them. Hundreds, thousands of dollars change hands in a single night.

THE PLAYERS.

If you wish to see the "great men," as they are called, of the country, get some one who has the *entrée* to take you to the principal faro-bank of Washington upon almost any night during the winter, which is not devoted to a reception by one of the high officers of the Government. Here you will see not only "professional" gamblers, and visitors to the city, whom they have drawn thither, but also men high in position and authority in the land—Governors, Congressmen, Executive officers, officers of the Army and Navy, who shame the blue and gold of their country's livery by parading it in such a place, clerks, contractors, paymasters, and a host of such worthies. The proprietor of this house counts the magnates of the land among his intimate friends. Some of them are old players, and lose and win heavily here, their losses being the heavier in the end. The luckiest man we ever heard of in Washington, was a Congressman, who, a few years before the war, broke the bank in a single night, thereby winning over one hundred thousand dollars. During the memorable session of 1859–60, when the organization of the House of Representatives was delayed by the fight over John Sherman for Speaker, it is said that the proprietor of this bank held orders for a large share of the total pay and mileage of nearly every member of the House.

You see here men charged with the disbursement or collection of the public funds, and you are not surprised to hear soon after of discrepancies in their accounts. It would be interesting, to say the least, to know how much of the people's money goes into the pockets of the keepers of these "hells." Many good, trusting wives at home, would hardly be pleased to look in here and find their husbands.

Sad as is the assertion, it is nevertheless true, that the greatest men this country has ever produced, have been frequenters of these fashionable "hells." This has been so for fully half a century, and it seems hardly probable that the practice will be discontinued. The proprietor of the house we are discussing could tell you rare stories of our great men, living and dead, in and out of power, but he never talks of these things except in the society of his confidential friends.

There are four houses in Washington which deserve the name of "first-class establishments." These are conducted upon principles of the strictest integrity as the term is understood in the profession, and the proprietors are very careful as to whom they admit to their hospitalities. Visitors must be introduced or vouched for by some party known to be reliable. Members of Congress, or of the Government, and officers of the Army or Navy, are always welcome.

Thousands of dollars belonging to the Government were lost in these places during the late war, by commissaries, quartermasters, paymasters, and others in charge of the public funds. Many a man has entered these doors with the consciousness of and a reputation for honesty, and has left them a perjured thief. Some have averted the ruin which they have brought upon themselves, by suicide on the spot. All is not so fair and pleasant in the history of these gilded palaces of sin as the outward show would indicate. There are dark chapters, records of deep tragedies, deeper than any romancer ever dreamed of, and for which the courtly gentlemen who preside over these gateways to hell will be called upon to answer when the Great Books are opened.

SECOND-CLASS HOUSES.

Besides the establishments already described, there are many of a lower and viler character. Some are gaudily furnished, and some have female dealers to lure the unwary to their fate. They are managed and frequented by scoundrels, and every advantage is taken of a visitor. He is made drunk, forced to play, and swindled out of his last cent. The frequenters of these places are desperate men, and think nothing of taking human life. Visitors are expected to play, and are apt to be insulted or assaulted if they refuse to do so. The amount of villainy practised in these places increases as one descends the scale of their so-called respectability.

You never see in these places the men who frequent the first-class houses. The visitors are men who cannot get into better establishments, and strangers to the city. The proprietors keep their decoys about the hotels and the Capitol. They are well-dressed, rather flashy in fact, have an abundance of time on their hands, and are the most obliging men in Washington. They will introduce themselves to strangers, take any amount of trouble to show them the sights of the city, and end by taking them to the "hell" to which they are attached, where the poor victims are made drunk and fleeced of their last dollar. They rarely make a mistake in accosting strangers, for they are keen judges of human nature. They know a lobby-agent or an office-seeker at a glance, and as their time would be wasted upon such persons, pass them by and ply their arts upon those who are strangers and sight-seers. They are paid a commission upon the winnings from their victims, on which they live very handsomely.

Persons visiting Washington would do well to avoid these over-civil "gentlemen." Honest men are not apt to take up sudden fancies for strangers, and such demonstrations afford good presumptive evidence that your new acquaintance is plotting your ruin. Give him a wide berth. Decline his proffered civilities, and beware how and where you drink with him. If necessary, repulse him rudely, and decline instantly all his offers to show you the mysteries of a gambling house, for there is not a man connected with, or who "has the run" of any first-class establishment, who will volunteer or consent to introduce there a person who is a total stranger to him. He would just as soon think of taking him into his own family. If, therefore, any man, whom you do not *know* to be a gentleman, asks you to go to a gambling-house with him, refuse, or you will repent it. Of course, all these fellows represent the establishment they ask you to visit as the best in the city, but their very invitation is a proof of their falsehood. Keep away from all such places, fashionable and disreputable. Ruin awaits you in each one. Your only safety lies in a total avoidance of them.

A CONGRESSIONAL GAMBLER.

Don Piatt, whose Washington letters have won him such a brilliant reputation, draws the following sketch of a well-known gentleman in public life:

"Armed with a card, I sought one of the more famous of the four known to the better—I beg pardon—the upper class of the sporting fraternity. I found the number brightly gilt on the transom light, by the red glare of a chandelier, in the most frequented part of Pennsylvania Avenue. Entering the unlocked door, I passed along the handsomely carpeted hall, and ascending the stairs, found myself at a door closed and locked, and gave the bell-pull a jerk, that was responded to in a second by a pair of bright eyes peering at me through a small grating that I had not before observed. I put before these watchful eyes the magic bit of pasteboard I held, and immediately the door flew open and exhibited a well-dressed mulatto, who invited me to walk in; and, following this guide, I ascended more stairs, passed along another hall, and was ushered into a large, well-lit, handsomely furnished suite of rooms. On my right was a sideboard, glittering with decanters and goblets, on every side were paintings that come under the popular head of "old masters," and some under that of old mistresses; and at the further end of the last room, under a huge painting of a tiger, large as life, that looked like a hearth, very gorgeously framed, stood the fatal green table, where men wagered their money and lost their souls.

"There were few in the room, and those few were, singly or in groups, reading the papers, or conversing in a subdued tone, or sipping quietly from glasses of mixed drinks. The proprietor came forward in an easy, courteous manner, and bade me welcome. He was a man of sixty or sixty-five years of age, with a white head of hair so evenly and regularly combed out that it suggested a wig, and flowing whiskers, English cut, of the same snowy tint. A smile sat amiably in his gray eyes, and lingered about his forehead and nose, but faded out near the mouth, that was as poison-cold and rigid as that of an executioner. He had the firmly-fixed, old, stilted politeness of Virginia, that goes so well with the peculiar dialect that comes from the much-abused African—as, indeed, the manner does.

"I have given the interior in detail, for the description will serve for all of the four first-class establish ments. This is one of the oldest in Washington. Here you meet your Congressmen, your rich contractor your head of the "ring," and respectable navy and army officers. This was the favorite haunt of the late Thad. Stevens, now eulogized, lamented, and sainted—he who is so well canonized, and was so lately cannonaded.

"But, to return to our mutton: I made the knowledge of this wicked interior many years since, and I cannot give a better illustration of the fascinations of the den than by relating the manner of it. I was passing through the rotunda of the Capitol immediately after the adjournment, for the day, of Congress, when I encountered, as I shall call him, the Hon. Dick Dashall, M. C., from a border State.

"'For what are you heading, mine ancient?' he asked, locking his arm in mine.

"'Making for my daily indigestion, called a dinner,' I replied.

"'You don't mean to say that you have had a dinner since coming to Washington? That's all nonsense. But I say, pay for the hack, and I'll show you a dinner.'

"This sentence was uttered in the good fellow's most insinuating, confidential, and fascinating manner.

"'Dick,' I said solemnly, 'I know what that means, and I won't do it.'

"'Nonsense. I want only the princely meal. I promise not to gamble. I am in earnest; you may carry my purse—that is the most solemn assurance of earnestness that I can give. Now come.'

"I permitted myself to be persuaded, and we drove to the place I have described. It was the hour of dinner, and the guests were about taking their places at the glittering board. Dick was hailed with delight. One and all knew that he had, for weeks back, been on the reform, and they laughed merrily on seeing him in the old haunt again. The dinner was superb. The choicest wines threaded their glittering way through the rarest dishes, and for nearly two hours the gay crowds ate, drank, smoked and talked. It would startle many of your readers were I to give the names of the guests about that table.

"The dinner over, Dick lingered. I could not get him away. He wished to watch the playing for a few minutes. Then he demanded a V out of his purse to pay for the dinner.

"'But you promised me—'

"'Well, yes; but we can't sneak off like loafers, without paying for our dinner. Come, give me a V, and I swear I'll go then like a gentleman.'

"I reluctantly gave him the golden five. Unfortunately, it won. Again I urged him to go, but he persisted in his determination to pay for the dinner, and so continued playing. In despair, I at last abandoned my friend, carrying away his purse, believing that the best way to stop his gambling.

"At ten o'clock I went to his room, to find it deserted. I waited an hour without seeing him return. I went away, and came back, but found no Dick. At last, about midnight, I sought the hell I have described. The rooms were partially deserted, and at the table I found my friend with a pile of gold at his elbow.

"'Has he won all that?' I asked of his cousin, an old *habitué* of the place.

"'Devil a bit!' he replied; 'he has been checking out his pay and mileage, and for hours has been running up and down like a rotten bucket in a well.'

"I knew that remonstrance would be useless, and standing by, I watched the varying run of luck, sometimes favorable to the player, but generally against him. At last, long hours after my arrival, he seemed to take the down train without brakes, and lost all.

"The day was just breaking over the white dome of the Capitol, and the yet sleeping town, when we emerged from the hell, and turning to my friend, I said:

"'Well, Richard, what do you think of yourself along about this time?'

"'That I am, as I always have been, and will be forever and forever, a d—d fool.'"

XXV.

THE NATIONAL OBSERVATORY.

The National Observatory is situated upon an elevated site, southwest of the President's Mansion, near the Georgetown line, and commands a fine view of both cities and of the Potomac River as far down as Fort Washington and Mount Vernon. It is under the control of the Navy Department, and is in charge of a corps of Naval officers selected for their scientific abilities. It ranks high amongst the Observatories of the world, that of Russia only being superior to it. It is in charge of all the nautical books, maps, charts, and instruments belonging to the Navy.

The usual astronomical duties of such an establishment are performed here most skilfully, but as they would be interesting chiefly to men well versed in the sciences, no description of them will be attempted here.

THE CHRONOMETERS

belonging to the Government are kept in a room set apart for that purpose. These instruments are purchased by the Navy Department with the understanding that they are to be tested in the Observatory for one year. They are placed in the chronometer-room, and carefully wound and regulated. They are examined daily, and compared with the Great Astronomical Clock of the Observatory, and an accurate record of the movements of each one is kept in a book prepared for that purpose. The temperature of the room is also examined daily, and recorded. These minute records enable the officers of the Observatory to point out the exact fault of each imperfect chronometer. Thanks to this, the maker is enabled to remedy the defect, and the instrument is made perfect. At the end of the year, the instruments found to be unsatisfactory are returned to their makers, and those which pass the test are paid for. The returned instruments are usually overhauled by the makers, and the defects remedied. They are then sent back for a trial of another year, at the end of which time they rarely fail to pass.

There are usually from 60 to 100 chronometers on trial at the Observatory, and the apartment in which they are kept is one of the most interesting in the establishment.

The researches connected with the famous "Wind and Current Charts," begun and prosecuted so successfully by Lieut. Matthew F. Maury, whose services were unfortunately lost to the country by his participation in the Rebellion, are conducted here, and also those connected with "The Habits of the Whale," and other ocean phenomena.

THE EQUATORIAL,

which is the largest telescope in the Observatory, is mounted in the revolving dome which rises above the main building. It has a fourteen-feet refractor, and an object-glass nine inches in diameter. Its movements are most ingenious, being regulated by machinery and clock-work. Its powers are so great, that it renders stars visible at mid-day; and, if directed to a given star in the morning, its machinery will work so accurately that it will follow with perfect exactness the path of the star, which will be visible through it as long as the star is above the horizon.

The Meridian and Mural Circles are in one of the rooms below.

THE TRANSIT INSTRUMENT

is placed in the west wing of the building, under a slit twenty inches wide, extending across the roof, and down the wall of the apartment on each side, to within four or five feet of the floor. It was made by Ertel & Son, of Munich, and is a seven-foot achromatic, with a clear aperture of 5.3 inches. "The mounting consists of two granite piers, seven feet high, each formed of a solid block of that stone, let down below the floor and imbedded in a stone foundation eight feet deep, and completely isolated from the building. Midway between the piers, and running north and south, is the artificial horizon, composed of a slab of granite ten feet long, nineteen inches deep, and thirteen inches broad; it rests on the foundation, and is isolated from the floor, with the level of which the top of it is even, with a space all around it of half an inch; in the middle of this slab, and in the nadir of the telescope, there is a mortise, nine inches square and ten inches deep, in which the artificial horizon is placed to protect it from the wind during the adjustment for collimation, or the determination of the error of collimation of level, and the adjustment for stellar focus, verticality of wires, and the other uses of the collimating eye-piece."

THE GREAT ASTRONOMICAL CLOCK,

or "Electro-Chronograph," is placed in the same room with the Transit Instrument, and used in connection with it to denote sidereal time. It was invented by Professor John Locke, of Cincinnati, and is one of the most remarkable instruments in the world. By means of an electrical battery in the building, the movements of this clock can be repeated by telegraph in any city or town in the land to which the wires extend. With the wires connected with it, its ticks may be heard in any part of the country, and it will record the time so accurately, that an astronomer in Portland or New Orleans can tell with exactness the time of day by this clock.

It also regulates the time for the city. There is a flag-staff on top of the dome, upon which a large black ball is hoisted at ten minutes before noon every day. This is to warn persons desiring to know the exact time to examine their watches and clocks. Just as the clock records the hour of twelve, the ball drops, and thus informs the city that it is high noon.

The Observatory is open to visitors daily from 9 A. M., until 3 P. M. Its officers take pleasure in explaining its workings to those who desire to learn them.

XXVI.

SOCIETY.

Society in Washington is divided into many classes. First, there is the society proper of the city, into which are admitted the high dignitaries and their families, residing at the Capital during their official terms, and the members of the Diplomatic Corps and their families. Second, the heads of Bureaus, and the class which constitutes the second grade of society in most cities. Third, the clerks and their families. Fourth, the usual lower class. The lines between these various classes are drawn with the utmost rigor. There is but little intimacy between them, and nothing but promotion to a higher place under the Government can ensure a rise in society.

SOCIETY BEFORE THE WAR.

Don Piatt thus sketches the social condition of Washington, previous to the Rebellion:

"No place in the Union has suffered such a change, through the war, as Washington City. I cannot say that it is 'a sea change into something rich and strange.' It is certainly strange, and in rather better circumstances than was the old affair.

"There is a class of people here, more respectable than loyal, called the 'old families,' who lament sadly the 'good old times.' I remember those old times, more jolly than good, when Washington City was a Southern city, and the social atmosphere was heavy with the taint of Southern institutions; when it was considered here to be in the lowest stages of degradation to be an Abolitionist; when New England civilization was sneered at, as made up of strong-minded women and weak-minded men.

"It was a pleasant sort of life, if one would steer clear of the humanities and be a philosopher of the Southern make; that is, to have more egotism than charity. It was not a very cultivated condition. People did not talk books, and had no pretension to artistic taste or scientific attainments. We dealt largely in politics and little social chit-chat; and the women were fair and very attractive, from a certain ease of manner, tinged with confidential frankness, while the men had a certain stilted politeness, a little grotesque and amusing to outsiders, but nevertheless very pleasant.

"But the beauty of it all was that mere wealth had little or no influence. To be a member of a good family, or to have position officially, was all that was necessary. A rich man found himself here stranded like a whale on a sandy beach. He did not amount to any thing. He could not write a letter or influence a vote.

"Then the admiration felt and expressed for eloquent efforts was beautiful. Days before Henry Clay or Webster, or later, Pierre Soule, was to speak, the great fact was bruited abroad, and on the day of the speech the galleries were crowded by fair women and brave men, and for weeks after the town rang with praise.

"'A statesman, yes, sah, by ——, sah; hasn't his equal in the world, sah.'

"And the same enthusiasm broke out over the belle of the season. You heard uttered in bar-rooms and elsewhere the earnest assertion—

"'Know Miss Belinda? Magnificent girl, sah. It is acknowledged, sah, by the best judges that she is the most magnificent creature in all the South, sah. Yes, sah, by ——, sah.'

"Now all this is changed. The old Southern ways, tastes, and enthusiasm are driven into the keeping of the few old families, where they are cherished like relics of a sacred past. New England civilization has come in, with short-haired women and long-haired men. Wealth is omnipotent, and the humanities drive about in gorgeous carriages, and live among stunning upholstery. Washington is no longer a Southern city. It freezes and snows and storms, even like a Northern town. We laugh at the old families. We are bored by speeches, and measure our belle by the depth of her pocket. I must say, as an impartial observer, that the Southern aristocracy was a better article than this aristocracy of wealth. I hate both, but of the two, give me the first-named.

"The last little remnant of Southern aristocracy burst out under Buchanan. It was led by the Davises, Slidells, Brights, and the venerable C. How they used to dine, and receive, and flirt, and law-make, and gamble in those golden days of the 'old families.' The houses were not so capacious, the turn-outs were not stunning, the upholstery, save C.'s, was not immense. But it was all intensely genteel.

"The last social exhibition made before the evacuation of the city by the South, previous to the first Bull Run, was characteristic, and very amusing. Old C. had a handsome house, and gave receptions to exhibit his upholstery, which was, for the time, a wonder. The old gentleman had one fair daughter to inherit his upholstery and wealth, and this fair daughter won the willing heart of an attaché of the Spanish Legation, residing near the court of his Excellency, James the last, vulgarly called 'Old Pub. Func.' But the course of true love did not run smooth, for it had to run over the paternal C., and it was broken into foamy rapids by the indignant old progenitor, who believed the young Spaniard did not love his fair daughter so much as he did his purse. So he made the young attaché, so attached to his house, walk Spanish, and forbade his ever darkening the door or sitting down on the upholstery again.

"Fearful that his house might be invaded, for love laughs at locksmiths and irate old fathers, he advised with his circle, Davis, Slidell, Bright & Co., and was told to put a watch upon his premises.

"One day, not long after, while the prudent paternal was taking dinner with his Slidell, word came that the enemy had appeared. The old gentleman dropped his soup-spoon, and, not waiting to remove the napkin from his venerable chin, hurried away, followed by all the male attendants of the party Arriving at the house, the party found the miss performing a complicated piece of music with a nonchalant manner really beautiful. The search began and continued without result, and was about to be abandoned, when the keen-eyed Bright saw the heel of a boot protruding from under the grand piano. The heel was found attached to a boot, the boot to a leg, the leg to an attaché, the attaché attached to the fair maiden. The heel, the boot, the leg, and the body were, with loud outcries, curses, screams, and some unavailing resistance, simultaneously ejected from the front door. The Spaniard was for the last time made to walk Spanish, and so ended the little drama."

SOCIETY TO-DAY.

The war changed every thing, and the old aristocracy of the Capital were forced to give way to the sudden irruption of wealth which the jobs and contracts of the great struggle introduced. New York was the model which every one tried to imitate, and, of course, being without the advantages of the Great Metropolis, the imitation was a very feeble one. Fine houses, flashy and showy, sprang up on all sides; the saloons of the city glittered with jewels, and rustled with costly fabrics; and magnificent equipages whirled through the streets with a dash that made the "old citizens" fairly hold their breath. Former social position, good birth, good breeding, went for nothing. Money became the standard of social excellence, and could be offset only by official position.

It is the same to-day that it was during the war Wealth and official position carry every thing before them, and merit, unsupported by either, stands in the background.

Each class, as we have said, excludes from its intercourse the members of other classes. Wives of Senators and high officials visit only wives of other Senators and high officials. The better halves of heads of Bureaus or chiefs of division would never think of associating with the better halves of their husbands' subordinates; and so it goes, down to the servants. Bridget, living in the family of a Secretary, would scorn to associate with Bridget living in the family of the chief clerk of her employer. Strangers arriving in the city are recognized and treated according to their wealth. Your millionaire is welcomed into the "first circles," while your modest, rising merchant, or professional man, must find a lower level.

THE SOCIAL CODE.

The observances of society are most rigid. Each grade has its rights, privileges, and immunities assigned to it by certain fixed laws, which cannot be violated without subjecting the offender to the social ban. The following is the code:

The President's family are recognized as the head and front of the social fabric. As we have already stated the observances required of and by them, in the chapter relating to the White House, we shall not inflict upon the reader a repetition of it here.

The Vice-President is expected to pay a formal

visit to the President on the meeting of Congress, but he is entitled to the first visit from all other persons, which he may return by card, or in person.

The Judges of the Supreme Court call upon the President and Vice-President on the annual meeting of the Court in December, and on New Year's Day. They are entitled to the first call from all other persons.

Members of the Cabinet call upon the President on the 1st of January and the 4th of July. They are required to pay the first calls, either in person or by card, to the Vice-President, Judges of the Supreme Court, Senators, and the Speaker of the House of Representatives on the meeting of Congress. They are entitled to the first call from all other persons.

Senators call in person upon the President and Vice-President on the meeting of Congress, New Year's Day, and the 4th of July; if Congress is in session at the last named time. They also call first upon the Judges of the Supreme Court, and upon the Speaker of the House of Representatives, on the meeting of Congress. They are entitled to the first call from all other persons.

The Speaker of the House of Representatives calls upon the President on the meeting of Congress, on New Year's Day, and on the 4th of July, if Congress is in session. The first call is due *from* him to the Vice-President, and to the Judges of the Supreme Court, but *to* him from all others.

Members of the House of Representatives call in person upon the President on the meeting of Congress and on New Year's Day, and by card or in person on the 4th of July, if Congress is in session. They call first, by card or in person, upon the Vice-President, Judges of the Supreme Court, Speaker of the House, Senators, Cabinet officers, and Foreign Ministers, soon after the opening of the session.

Foreign Ministers call upon the President on the 1st of January. They call first, in person or by card, upon the Vice-President, Cabinet officers, Judges of the Supreme Court, and the Speaker of the House, on the first opportunity after presenting their credentials to the President. They also make an annual call of ceremony, by card or in person, on the above mentioned officials soon after the meeting of Congress. They are entitled to first calls from all other persons.

The Judges of the Court of Claims call in person upon the President on New Year's Day and the 4th of July. They pay first calls to Cabinet officers and Members of the Diplomatic Corps, and call annually, by card or in person, upon the Vice-President, Judges of the Supreme Court, Senators, Speaker and Members of the House, soon after the meeting of Congress.

The intercourse of the other officers of the Government is regulated by superiority of rank in the public service.

The intercourse of the families of officials is regulated by the rules which govern the officials themselves.

TITLES.

Every body in Washington has a title. If it does not legally belong to him, he appropriates it, and that answers the same purpose. At the hotel tables, in the hotel parlors and bar-rooms, at the receptions of the President and other dignitaries, everywhere, and on all occasions, the ear is wearied with the incessant repetitions of "Senator," "Judge," "Secretary," "Mr. Speaker," "Governor," "Marshal," "General," "Captain," "Colonel," "Major," "Lieutenant," "Admiral," "Commodore," "Doctor," "Bishop," "Professor," &c., &c. One positively longs to see some plain, honest individual who has no handle to his name. There are few such in Washington, however; for people coming here find it vastly useful to them to prefix the aforesaid handle. To say nothing of the Governors, Senators, Judges, and Secretaries, one meets in a single day military titles enough to supply the combined armies of the world—titles, in many instances, with as much in them as in that of the famous "Captain Jinks, of the Horse Marines."

The women carry it to excess. In high life the Mrs. Judges, Mrs. Secretaries, Mrs. Governors, Mrs. Senators are numerous. They are fully aware of the importance of their titles, and parade them upon all occasions. Indeed, they frequently make more use of them than do the husbands to whom they legitimately belong. The man may be content to continue plain John Smith, but his better half never fails to declare herself Mrs. *Senator*, or Mrs. *Secretary* Smith, and to assert her dignity and rights accordingly. You may have known her at home as plain Mrs. Smith, and have been then one of her "most intimate" friends, but you must remember, now, that she has stepped a peg higher, and gotten into the female branch of the Government, and you must regulate your conduct towards her according to this knowledge. Certainly it will not be her fault if you do not; for if you forget that there is a difference between Mrs. John Smith of the past, and Mrs. *Senator* Smith of the present, she will not forget to remind you of it.

In the good old days of the militia, now gone by forever, there was a certain unsophisticated "citizen" of one of the interior districts, who was raised to the grade of *Corporal* in his company. Very proud of the honor conferred upon him, he hastened home to inform his wife of it. The good woman shared his satisfaction intensely, and communicated the intelligence to the children, who were much delighted thereby. The eldest, after thinking the matter over for a few minutes, asked his mother:

"Mother, shall we play with the other children, now that we are corporals?"

"Nonsense, child," said the mother, reprovingly, "this matter doesn't affect you. *Your father and I are the only corporals.*"

Like this good woman, the wives of our great men claim their full share in the husband's title. If the man is *Mr.* President, the wife is *Mrs.* President. If he is *Mr.* Speaker, she is *Mrs.* Speaker.

AN INSIDE VIEW OF SOCIETY.

"If you would see the thorny road of a public man's wife," says a writer well versed in the mysteries of Washington society, "look at Mrs. Andrew Johnson. She taught her husband how to read. He went off immediately and bought a copy of the Constitution, and kept reading it until he was impeached under it. It made him every thing, from Alderman up, and now his house begins to wear that hospitable look that all houses have when we feel that moving day approaches. I dare say that Mrs. Johnson, pleased as she must have been in her ambition to see the father of her children ascending into history, would have been a happier lady had her husband adhered to his goose. She is an invalid, who has been seen by few during all these eminent years, but in her seclusion she must still read and feel most poignantly all the bitter taunts of speech and paragraph flung at her husband, while in his public absorptions she no doubt misses much of that endearment so sweet and grateful to the sick. Of her children, one daughter is a widow, the other the wife of a Senator, but not such a Senator as you conceive for your daughter's protector; while her son, who might in private life have been a fireside ornament, is unequal to his dazzling situation, and a source of disconsolation all the time. What happiness can there be, think you, in this mingling of so much honor and misery—to be unpitied because your rank is so enviable, while in your wife's and mother's heart you need more sympathy than the servant woman in your great pantry. A lady informs me of an interview held with Mrs. Johnson by her friend during the impeachment trial.

"'But for the humiliation and Mr. Johnson's feelings,' she said, 'I wish they would send us back to Tennessee—if it were possible, give us our poverty and peace again, so that we might learn how to live for our children and ourselves.'

"To a sympathetic remark, Mrs. Johnson said further:

"'I have not seen a happy moment since I came to this house. I get none of the society incident to it, and desire none. Every body is busy with public duties. My daughters dislike all these receptions and displays, and only consent to them at a sacrifice. If life were to go over again, I sometimes think I should never marry a public man.'

"The wives of Senators and Congressmen do not generally come to Washington during the session. The pay of a Member is only five thousand dollars a year and his mileage, and this will not suffice to keep up the establishments, for the Member must maintain his state among his constituents all the while. If the wife and family come here, they must relinquish their excellent home for the miserable imprisonment of a hotel, or the associations of a boarding-house; and the few who can afford parallel private establishments are run down with company, made conveniences of by constituents, and expected to rival each other's parties and routs. The children of such Congressmen must either separate from their parents, or accept the indifferent schools and associations of an indefinite and uncertain city, where carpet-bagging is the rule and birthright the exception, and the wife loses her neighbors, loses her private rights, is dragged into the newspapers, and seduced to ccmmand her husband's influence for adventurers and schemers. Heaven must be a place of insupportable scandal, if the rato increases straight on from high life in Washington, or anywhere at public court, indeed; for St. James' and the Tuileries are yet more newsy and uncharitable. Ir. this depot of schemers the good name of a beautiful woman is made the jest of every euchre-party, and bandied in faro-banks and committee-rooms. Criticism is busy with her dress, her person, and her graces. If she avoid society, it is imputed to her boorishness; if she be cheerful in it, she is said to be frivolous or heartless. What higher purposes can she subserve at the capital than at home among her husband's constituents? I think I hear your lady readers say: 'She can exert an influence.' Perhaps! but this town is freckled into reformers of every sort, and the sort of questions that woman lays to heart are invariably the follies of legislation. I never knew a woman to exert an 'influence' here, who did not become common, descend to lobbying, lose her credit, and increase the skepticism of men. Emotional subjects, such as ladies take to heart, are infinitesimal fractions of legislation, which is, in the main, dull, sturdy, statistical man's work, like the sawing and measuring of lumber. The surest way to be a nuisance here and cost the country dignity and money, is to be a 'gusher,' breaking out in sympathy with the struggling Cretans, resolving to break the yoke of Brigham Young's poor wives, sprinkling public documents with tears. Tne whole of that business, by common consent, has been referred to John A. Bingham, who has trained his voice for it.

"I do not write this in a spirit of reprehension of what is sympathetic, gentle, and womanly in public legislation. Nor am I expressing an opinion upon the woman's suffrage question—which I still believe, if ever successful, would turn public business into drivel, and make the Capitol gush. Doubtless Providence has higher intentions for woman than making her the mother of man—though a good deal of mechanism seems to have been wasted upon that exclusive department—and among these is of course the right to rule herself, quote the Declaration of Independence, and speak her mind and draw salary for it.

"Under that ambiguous term of 'society,' there are many ladies here who are presumed to lead it. Mrs. Sprague, Mrs. Chandler, and Mrs. Morgan are among them, all three taking rank from their wealth and establishments; the former also from her public graces and natural social accomplishments. I do not know that any of these ladies, if poor, would be distinguished as 'Queens of Society,' which is, I believe, the term used in fashion-books and annuals. Mrs. Sprague is a very slender and delicate lady, without the repose of the Vere de Veres, being rather a nervous and nail-biting beauty, capable of strong affection and jealousy, I should say, and upheld in her labors to please by the strong ambition she inherits from her father. I can imagine her, poor, holding the place of a public-school teacher—a position where I am warranted in supposing her, because of her father's life-long interest in Democratic education. Well! as a school-teacher, she would charm the directors, be quoted as a very interesting young girl, receive bouquets from the girls on New Year's day, and be asked a good many questions as to what dresses would be becoming, and whether blue eyes in a man were a sign of a deceitful nature. Finally, the youngest and richest directors would fall in love with her. Every body would have sympathy for her and congratulate her. She would step into society where she is so naturally, that afterward people would say: There is no queen about her at all. She is just the same girl she was when she taught school!

"To be a queen, you know, one must strut a little, swing a 'train'—or trail, which is it?—and look scornfully out of the front window upon peanut-boys and shoe-blacks. Mrs. Sprague is not a queen, I am warranted in saying. Mrs. Chandler is a little more 'on' that order, holding herself very straight and statuesque. Mrs. Morgan is merely a banker's wife, who rides beside her husband in a respectable brougham, looks as if born to the use of silver plate and Sevres china, and she gives you a feeling, when she looks at you, as if you would greatly like to have her for an aunt.

"I hope all this matter is legitimate; for my only object, as I said before, is to persuade ladies to stay at home and keep their 'influence' for their nephews.

"The greater your husband is, the poorer house he will live in, the less you will see of him, and the more he will be asked out to stag-dinners. Webster lived in a little two-story house here, next door to the Unitarian Church, that a tinner has bought since and raised a story. He could go a story better than the god-like Daniel! Clay died in the poisonous purlieus of the National Hotel, and Calhoun died in a cheap boarding-house. You must marry a mutton-headed Senator, like Squobbs, the nigger-driver, Appleking, the speculator in Osage beans, or Tallow, the yard-stick. Then your husband can go where he likes, but you will be the Senator. When Tom Benton died, there was a mortgage on his house a little bigger than the roof of it, and his prettiest daughter ran away with a barrack captain who parted his hair in the middle. If you want fame, you 'go' for it; but if you prefer position, follow the other end of the finger-board."

THE RECEPTIONS.

It is the custom for the wives of the higher officials residing in the city to hold receptions at stated times during the session of Congress, generally once a week. Don Piatt draws the following capital picture of these receptions, and their attendant customs:

"It is the etiquette in Washington, soon as you arrive, to empty your trunk, and hire a hack to drive around and call on people. It is not necessary to know them, or to be known. If you have a paper collar and a pair of kids, the official people are glad to see you. They advertise to this effect in the *Chronicle* and *Intelligencer*. True, these notices, like the coffin-maker's 'please to ring the bell,' immortalized by Coleman, implies something more than a compliance with the request. When the morning journal says that 'Mrs. B. will be pleased to see her friends on Wednesdays, between the hours of 12 and 4 P. M.,' it does not mean that every body friendly to Mrs. B., in the abstract, shall rush in, shake her hand, and drink her punch or coffee. It really means one known to fame, or known to Mrs. B. Now, were my learned friend, David Quinn, or the deep-read lawyer, Mr. Meyers, to arrive in Washington, it would be expected they would hack themselves and call on the female officials.

"But if you have any doubt as to your social status in this respect, call upon your immediate Representative in the House, and say that you want to be presented to all the officials' wives in Washington, and such other ladies as your immediate Representative may think of. If you order your Representative to turn summersaults, or to stand on his head, 'he's got to do it'—or die trying.

"My friend Scutim tells me all this. Scutim is a weakly young man whose ambition is immense. He seeks to be considered a fast man about town. People are to believe that Scutim has no principles to speak of; is a cold, unfeeling wretch, a heavy swell who has seen great depth of social wickedness, and is now *blasé*. The fact is, Scutim is not a fast man about town. It is all make-believe. He hasn't the constitution for that sort of thing. One glass of whiskey will upset him in a minute. His man tells me, privately, that Scutim reads a chapter in the

Bible, and says his prayers every night. Scutim would be filled with shame and confusion were that to get out on him.

"To see my friend in his tight pantaloons, bob-tailed coat, high-heeled boots that look as if a horse could trot under them, head and tail up, his plug hat set gracefully upon his blonde head, with whiskers *à la Anglais*, and little stick under his arm—to see him in this rig, slowly swinging along Pennsylvania Avenue, is to realize how a man appears when he reaches the last stages of modern civilization and English imbecility.

"This friend of mine procured a hack—a resplendent hack—a hack that looked as if we owned a dozen like it, all private carriages—and drove around among the official people, and some others Scutim had a right to introduce us to. I was glad to have this glass of fashion and mould of form with me, for I propose to profit by his criticisms, and transmit to your lady readers the precise get-up of the ladies receiving.

"'We will first go to Mr. Randall's,' cried Scutim. 'By Jove, you will see a lady—yes, sir, a lady—perfect in dress, beautiful in person, and fascinating in manner.'

"And so my friend continued, for quantity, until we drew up in front of the handsome residence. We found Scutim had not exaggerated. The fair woman is all that he described her, and something more. And he wrote down for me that she 'wore a pearl-colored satin dress, long train, trimmed with point lace.' And that Miss Upton, who assisted in the reception, had a frock of 'pink silk, trimmed with point lace.'

"This description is as dry and uninteresting as the technicalities of botany in describing a rose. The easy grace with which this lady received and entertained, beggars description. I find her photograph on my mind to-day as the *beau ideal* of an American woman.

"From the Postmaster-General's we drove to Mr. Secretary Browning's, and found the handsome house crowded, and 'the air redolent of Illinois and Kentucky,' if you know what that means—I am sure I don't. Scutim said so, and added that 'Mrs. Browning had on brocade silk, severe in its absence of trimming;' that 'Miss Browning wore a black silk, low in the neck, and trimmed with folds of green satin.' I found a Miss O'Bannon, of Covington, Kentucky, very charming, and she had good clothes on I'll be affidavited, but I forgot to ask Scutim what they were.

"We found the feminine part of the Treasury doing the polite, assisted by the Misses Bailey, daughters of Admiral Bailey, and wearing—Mrs. McCulloch, I mean—'a green moire antique, trimmed with folds of white satin, and set off by jewelry of amethyst and pearl.'

"I was struck with the interior of the residence of General Schofield, Secretary of War. It presented, unusually so, evidences of refinement and good taste —I have lost Scutim's dress-notes, and can't tell for the life of me what the lady had on. It was something exceedingly nice, I'll be bound—but it has gone glimmering.

"We finished our official calls at the Vice-President's-elect, Mr. Speaker Colfax. And my notes tell me that 'Mrs. C. wore a handsome green silk, high in the neck, and trimmed with white satin fringe, while Mrs. Matthews wore a wine-colored (don't see how Skiler could permit that), and Miss Carrie a pink-and white striped silk.'

"The great majority of these callers were ladies, gotten up regardless of expense or appearance. It was a continuous stream of rustling silks. No one remained over five minutes, and ninety-nine out of the hundred made some remark about the weather. The poor ladies receiving had to stand four weary hours and hear the weather complimented. Is it not possible for the ingenious American mind to invent some other phrase for conversation than this everlasting one of the weather? And one can't vary it. I said to a lady, 'We have a first-class article of sunshine to-day,' and Scutim rebuked me. He said it was believed I had taken too much punch. It is in society as it is in religion—all dull things are considered good.

"From the mass of cards left, the fair hostess selects a certain number to invite to her evening receptions, when there is more wine and less talk about the weather. And this is all an administration does for society in Washington."

RESIDENCES OF CELEBRITIES.

The residence of the President we have already described.

Mr. Ben Wade, the acting Vice-President, boards

at the Washington House, where he maintains a cozy establishment.

Mr. Colfax, the present Speaker of the House and the incoming Vice-President, resides at No. 7 Lafayette Square, 16½ Street, almost opposite the White House. It is a plain, stuccoed house, painted white, with green blinds. A high flight of stairs leads up to the door from the street, and the building looks simple and modest in the midst of its handsome neighbors. Yet it has an interesting history attached to it. It is quite an old house, and has sheltered many a man whose name is inseparably bound up with the history of the country. A few years before the war it was the residence of Daniel E. Sickles, then a Member of Congress from the city of New York. It was in this house that the intrigue between Mrs. Sickles and Philip Barton Key was begun. From the upper chambers, which look out upon the handsome park, the guilty wife watched for the signals of her lover; and it was just across the enclosure, at the foot of those noble old trees which shade 15½ Street, that the victim lay, helpless, pleading with his murderer for his life; a plea which was answered only by the swift bullet of the assassin.

Secretary Seward lives in a large, plain red brick house on 15½ Street, fronting Lafayette Square, and it was almost before his door that Key was murdered. Since the attempt upon his own life, the Secretary has kept a sentinel on guard before his door, night and day.

H Street North contains a number of the celebrities.

It forms the northern boundary of Lafayette Square, and is one of the handsomest portions of the city. Mr. McCulloch, Secretary of the Treasury, resides at No. 306 on this street; General Schofield, Secretary of War, at No. 320; Mr. Welles, Secretary of the Navy, at No. 312; Attorney-General Evarts at No. 356; Senator Chandler at No. 357; Senator Harlan at No. 304; Senator Pomeroy at No. 318; and Senator Sumner at the corner of H Street and Vermont Avenue.

Secretary Browning resides at 339 I Street; and Mr. Randall, the Postmaster-General, at the corner of 12th and K Streets.

Senator Morgan's handsome house is one of the ornaments of I Street, and is situated on the corner of 15th Street. Senator Sprague has a fine mansion on the northwest corner of Sixth Street West and E Street.

XXVII.

THE OLD CAPITOL.

OPPOSITE the northeast angle of the Capitol Park, you will see a row of handsome dwelling-houses ornamented with Mansard roofs. They are the property of Mr. Brown, the Sergeant-at-Arms of the Senate, and, until a short time ago, constituted a single building, known as the *Old Capitol.* It was erected about the year 1812, and in December, 1815, passed into the hands of the Government. The Capitol having been destroyed by the British in August, 1814, Congress moved into this building immediately after it was leased by the Government, and held its sessions in it until the completion of the Capitol in 1825. From this circumstance it gained the name of the *Old Capitol.*

It was a dingy red-brick edifice of the old English style, and very much like one of the primitive Quaker buildings one sees in the city of Philadelphia. It had a gloomy, forbidding appearance, and resembled somewhat the old Carroll Mansion, which stands a little to the left of it. It was used for various purposes after being abandoned by Congress in 1825, and fell very much out of repair. At the commencement of the war it was converted into a prison for the detention and punishment of state and military prisoners.

Prisons are never pleasant, and the Old Capitol was not one of the pleasantest. It was the writer's fortune once or twice to enter it to minister to the wants of a friend who had been captured by Sheridan in one of his raids, and who was "stopping" at the Old Capitol on his way to Fort Delaware, and he can testify that a gloomier, more terrible-looking prison did not exist in the land. The effect of a confinement here must have been very depressing, and it is no wonder that many fierce sons of Dixie were glad enough, after a few weeks' experience of it, to take the oath and get out.

The prison was in charge of Colonel Wood, who was the Superintendent. He was a man of great firmness and decision of character, and somewhat stern in his manner, but, judging from our own observation of him, we believe he was, although strict to the letter in the discharge of his duty, kind and humane in his treatment of prisoners. They naturally regarded him as a cruel tyrant, and have not spared him in their accounts of the prison; but we found him both willing and anxious to do all he could to lighten the captivity of the gentleman in whom we were interested, and as we were both strangers to him, we cannot suppose that he extended any unusual favor to us.

Yet, whether the discipline was cruel or humane, it was a great pity that the building was put to such uses during the war. It had become historical by reason of the many great deeds that had occurred within its walls, and it was unfortunate that its proud history should be stained with a four-years' prison record. Doubtless there were many persons confined there who richly deserved their punishment, but (now that one may say these things without fear of injuring the cause of the country by retailing the faults of the Government) there can be no doubt that the old prison held many an innocent victim of political hostility and official malice. Many a good man, whose most earnest prayers were for the success of the Union arms, was immured within these walls in consequence of having offended some high official. We all know that there were many grave faults committed by the Administration during the Rebellion, not the least of which was its readiness to disregard the liberty and personal rights of the citizens of the Union. Stanton was an able and true man, and a good Secretary, but he was a despot also, and too hasty to arrest men upon very slight proof; and Mr. Seward was too fond of tinkling his "little bell." Ex-Chief Detective Baker sent, perhaps, the majority of prisoners to this institution. He had reduced blackmailing and intimidation to a science, and those who would not comply with his unlawful demands were moderately sure of a residence in this place. These arbitrary acts are a blot upon the country, which ought never to have been cast upon it.

Now that the old building has disappeared, however, and been changed so that its longest inmate would not know it, let us hope that the darker pages of its history will be forgotten, or remembered only as a warning to cherish and guard well those sacred principles of personal freedom, which are the very foundation of our glorious system of government.

XXVIII.

HOTELS AND BOARDING HOUSES.

In addition to the regular population of the city, there are about six or seven thousand officials in the employ of the Government temporarily sojourning in Washington for the period of their official service, the majority of whom are not able to undertake the expense of keeping up their own establishments. Besides these, every winter brings hosts of Congressmen, contractors, lobbyists, agents of all kinds, and thousands of visitors who have no idea of remaining in the city longer than their business will oblige them to do so. All these must be provided with temporary accommodations, and, as a consequence, the hotels are filled, and thousands are obliged to seek lodgings and meals elsewhere.

THE HOTELS

of the city are *Willard's*, the *National*, the *Metropolitan* (formerly Brown's), the *United States*, the *Clarendon*, and the *St. Charles Hotel*, and the *Ebbit*, the *Kirkwood*, the *Washington*, and the *Avenue Houses*. These are the principal public houses, but there are also a score or more parading the word "*Hotel*" on their fronts in large letters, which must be seen to be appreciated.

The hotels are managed upon a plan similar to that of the majority of the first-class houses of the land, and their rates of board are the same as those charged by the best New York hotels. They claim to be equal in comfort and style to any in the land, but a very brief experience will convince any unprejudiced person that they are vastly inferior to the best hotels of our large cities. With every advantage in the way of good markets, the table they set is poor; the attendance is indifferent; the rooms are small, common, and often dirty; and the furniture old-fashioned, *and often well occupied.*

Many of the higher officials and Members of Congress board at the hotels. The clerks are not able to afford such "magnificence," and you never see them here, unless it may be in the bar-room. At the breakfast-table of any of the principal houses you may see a goodly row of legislative faces, some of which do not show over well for the work of the past night. The conversation is generally political. Nobody thinks or talks of any thing else.

During the greater part of the day the hotels have a silent, deserted air, but early in the morning and after the close of the daily sessions of Congress and the labors of the Departments, they fill up rapidly. The halls, sitting-rooms, and parlors are crowded to excess with a noisy, boisterous crowd, all talking at the same time, and producing a very Babel of sounds. The air is hazy with tobacco smoke, and the floors are slippery with tobacco juice. Governors, Senators, Members of the House, clerks, contractors, lobbyists, members of the rings, citizens, and loafers are mingled in fine democratic confusion, and the only peaceful man in the place is the inevitable card writer, who is working steadily and silently at his little table in the glare of his St. Germain lamp.

Up-stairs, the scene is changed. The parlors and halls on the first floor are brilliantly lighted. Richly dressed and sometimes beautiful women, the wives and daughters of the men below, hold their court here. They are here for the season with their husbands, fathers, or other relatives, and the long evenings, when there are no receptions on hand, hang heavily over them. They resort to a thousand-and-one ways of dissipating the blues. A favorite mode of doing this, is to get up a "hop" in the hotel parlors, which is sure to draw enough of the other sex to make it a success.

These fair dames are great politicians, and never let slip an opportunity to advance the cause of the official or Member to whose family they belong. They catch the infection as soon as they reach the Capital, and the disease lasts until they leave it.

BOARDING-HOUSES.

A stroll through the streets of Washington is very apt to induce the belief that the city contains very few really *private* residences, for almost every house has affixed to it a sign or a written card announcing that boarders are taken there. These houses may be divided into two classes: regular boarding-houses, and private houses into which boarders are received.

Full board ranges in price from $5 to $25 per week. Rooms only, are rented for from $3 to $10 per week. Many of the Department officials, and some of the Members of Congress, merely rent their rooms, and take their meals at restaurants, of which there are all kinds in the city.

Boarding-house life is not pleasant anywhere. In Washington it is simply abominable. The fare is worse than that provided at the majority of such places in the country, and the rooms are scantily furnished and uncomfortable, if not dirty. Even in the best houses there is a careless, slipshod way of doing things, which is exceedingly unpleasant to persons accustomed to the neat and orderly system of the white-labor States. Negro servants are the general rule here, and the few white ones in the city are decidedly the most indifferent of their class.

In the private families you are "made to feel at home," and treated to all the confidences and scenes incidental to all households. The landlady patronizes you in the most motherly way, and the children regard you as a brother, and take the most brotherly liberties with yourself and your property. The "young ladies" are devoted to you, and expect you to take them around, and spend your spare cash on them in the most liberal manner. Altogether, you wish you were not made so much at home, and become decidedly averse to being treated as a member of the family.

In the regular boarding house you find yourself the subject of the gossip of all the other inmates, and your peace of mind, if you are at all sensitive, is destroyed by the scandal which is soon set afloat about you. You meet with sundry women, boarding in the same establishment, who have no visible protectors, and often no visible means of support, and sometimes in the effort to be civil to them, you compromise yourself in a manner you little dream of at the outset.

Your accommodations are not such as you could desire. Indeed, you pay the highest possible price for the greatest possible discomfort, and if you venture to remonstrate at all, however mildly, you are told by your irate landlady that you are too hard to please. The first men in the land, she will tell you, have boarded with her, and have never complained of her accommodations. You will find her eloquent on this subject, and you will be glad to hold your tongue in future. Change your quarters, and you will fare no better. Mrs. A and Mrs. B have the same system. Both consider boarders their legitimate prey, and both make as much out of them as possible.

In all seriousness, boarding in Washington is very unpleasant. The houses are mostly old and uncomfortable, the table is poorly provided, and the attendance is miserable. Besides this, there are a thousand-and-one discomforts which one can learn only by experience, and which cause him to hail with unfeigned pleasure the day which sends him away from the city

XXIX.

THE CONGRESSIONAL CEMETERY.

THIS beautiful cemetery covers an area of nearly twenty acres, and is located upon the high ground immediately overlooking the "Anacostia," or Eastern branch of the Potomac. It is the property of one of the Episcopal churches of the city, by which it is kept in order.

It is called the "Congressional Cemetery," because when a Member of Congress dies during the term for which he was elected, his memory is perpetuated by the erection of a plain cenotaph in these grounds. There are at present about one hundred and fifty of these memorial stones in the cemetery—one for each member who has died during his term of office, since the Capitol was located at Washington.

There is also a vault for the reception of the remains of public men, which are placed here until they can be removed. The bodies of General Taylor and Mr. Calhoun rested here for a few days after their decease. It is a very plain structure, and is situated near the centre of the grounds.

There are a number of interesting monuments to be seen. The following are some of the inscriptions:

"Sacred to the memory of PHILIP PENDLETON BARBOUR, associate-justice of the Supreme Court of the United States, who was born in Orange County, Virginia, on the 25th of May 1783, intermarried with Frances Todd Johnson, on the 4th of October 1804, and died at Washington city on the 24th of February 1841."

"This monument is erected by order of his majesty Frederick William III., King of Prussia, to the memory of his resident minister in the United States, the Chevalier FREDERICK GREHUM, who departed this life on the 1st of December, 1823, in the 53rd year of his age."

"Sacred to the memory of Gen. JACOB BROWN. He was born in Bucks co., Pennsylvania, on the 9th of May 1775, and died at the city of Washington, commanding general of the army, on the 24th of February, 1828.

"Let him who e'er in after days
Shall view this monument of praise,
For honor heave the patriot sigh,
And for his country learn to die."

"JOSEPH LOVELL, late surgeon-general of the army of the United States, born in Boston, Massachusetts, Dec. 22, 1788; died in the city of Washington, October 17, 1836."

"PUSH-MA-TA-HA, a Choctaw chief lies here. This monument to his memory is erected by his brother chiefs, who were associated with him in a delegation from their nation, in the year 1824, to the general government of the United States. He died in Washington, on the 24th of December, 1824, of the croup, in the 60th year of his age. Push-ma-ta-ha was a warrior of great distinction. He was wise in council, eloquent in an extraordinary degree, and on all occasions, and under all circumstances, *the white man's friend.* Among his last words were

CONGRESSIONAL CEMETERY.

the following: '*When I am gone let the big guns be fired over me.*'"

"Here lie the remains of TOBIAS LEAR. He was early distinguished as the private secretary and familiar friend of the illustrious Washington; and after having served his country with dignity, zeal, and fidelity, in many honorable stations, died accountant of the war department, 11th October, 1816, aged 54. His desolate *widow* and mourning *son* have erected this monument, to mark the place of his abode in the city of silence."

"The tomb of ELBRIDGE GERRY, Vice President of the United States, who died suddenly in this city, on his way to the capitol as president of the Senate, November 23d, 1814, aged 70; thus fulfilling his own memorable injunction, 'it is the duty of every citizen, though he may have but one day to live, to devote that day to the good of his country.'"

"To the memory of GEORGE CLINTON. He was born in the state of New York, on the 26th July, 1739, and died at the city of Washington on the 20th of April, 1811, in the 73d year of his age. He was a soldier and statesman of the revolution. Eminent in council, distinguished in war, he filled with unexampled usefulness, purity, and ability, among many other high offices, those of governor of his native state, and Vice President of the United States. While he lived, his virtue, wisdom, and valor, were the pride, the ornament, and security of his country · and when he died, he left an illustrious example of a well spent life, worthy of all imitation."

Besides the above are the graves of William Wirt, Major-General McComb, who immediately preceded General Scott in the chief command of the army,

General Gibson, General Archibald Henderson, Commodore Isaac Chauncey, Abel P. Upshur, of Virginia, formerly Secretary of State, and Ex-Mayors Towers and Maury, of Washington City.

XXX.

PLACES OF AMUSEMENT.

There are two theatres in Washington, the *National Theatre*, and *Wall's Opera House*. *Ford's Theatre* was formerly the principal temple of the drama in the city, and was a handsome and well conducted establishment, but the Government very properly closed it after the terrible tragedy which occurred in it in 1865, and the theatres we have mentioned constitute the sole dependence of the Washingtonians for histrionic amusements.

Both of these places are old-fashioned, flashy, and dirty. They would rank as second-class establishments in other cities, and contrast strangely with the audiences they sometimes contain. Performances are given during the winter only, and the establishments are managed on the "Star" system. Generally a very fair business is done during the season, for the city is full of strangers and others with a plenty of spare time, who gladly avail themselves of the amusement thus offered them.

The acting is scarcely above the average, except when some travelling company visits the city. Actors who could not earn a decent living in our larger cities flourish in Washington, and furnish food for the dramatic criticisms of the "grave and reverend seigniors" of the Government.

Once or twice during the winter a brief opera season is inaugurated, and is well supported. The Washingtonians are dear lovers of good music, and profess to be keen critics of such performances. Certain it is, that they come out in goodly numbers to hear singers seeking their patronage, but we have heard them applaud lustily and even *encore* performances which a really cultivated audience would receive with a forbearing silence, to say the least.

Besides the theatres, there are one or two fine halls in the city, used for concerts, lectures, and exhibitions, which are well patronized during the winter season, the majority of the audiences being made up of strangers.

THE CANTERBURIES.

Canterburies and concert halls abound also. They are as low and disgusting as such places in our large cities usually are, and are quite as well patronized. They are great favorites with the Department Clerks, who constitute the "great men" of such places, and, alas that it should be so, you may generally see high officials in these polluted halls. The performances are simply disgusting, oftentimes brutal. The company is flashy, and largely made up of thieves and street walkers. The police have several times made descents upon these places, and arrested both proprietors and guests, but the evil continues. Men are drugged by the confederates of the keepers of these places, robbed, and maltreated, and sometimes murdered. Decency, law, and humanity are nightly outraged here, but the authorities continue to tolerate the places. During the war they flourished to a fearful extent, and many unsophisticated "boys in blue" from the rural districts were lured into them, drugged, and robbed. The military authorities tried to suppress them, but it is said that the officer charged with the duty of doing so was bribed by the keepers, and being of easy virtue himself, licensed and protected those which paid him for so doing, but remorselessly closed all that refused to submit to his black-mailing system.

XXXI.

FORD'S THEATRE.

On 10th Street West, between E and F Streets North, there is a plain stuccoed building, which a few years ago was suddenly thrown into painful prominence in the history of the country. At the time of its erection it was hoped that it would become the best and most popular theatre in the city, but no one dreamed that it would ever be the scene of such a terrible tragedy as that which occurred within its walls. It was built and conducted by John T. Ford, Esq., a well known and popular manager, from whom it derived its name.

On the night of the 14th of April, 1865, President Lincoln was assassinated by John Wilkes Booth, while witnessing a performance in this theatre. He was conveyed from the box in which he was shot, to a dwelling-house on the opposite side of the street, where he died at twenty-two minutes past seven o'clock the next morning.

The theatre was immediately closed by the Government, as it was felt that the place was henceforth too sacred to be put to its former uses. The action of the Government was endorsed by the entire country, and, in accordance with the national wishes, Congress purchased the building from Mr. Ford, and remodelled it for the use of the Government. It has been rendered fire-proof, and the interior has been thrown into a large square hall, with a gallery running around the upper part. It was formerly used as a receptacle for the captured archives of the Rebel Government, but is now

THE ARMY MEDICAL MUSEUM

of the United States. Its contents are exceedingly interesting to professional men, who will be amply repaid for a visit to it.

The following description of the theatre, as it was arranged at the time of the assassination, is interesting:

"Ford's theatre, now converted into a museum of war relics, is situated on Tenth Street, just above E Street; a large edifice, built of brick, and plain in appearance. The four upper boxes were *the* boxes of the theatre, and very elegant and spacious.

"The box which the President occupied, and which was known as 'The President's Box,' consisted of the two upper boxes on the right-hand side of the house as you face the stage, thrown into one. It was fitted up with great elegance and taste. The curtains were of fine lace and buff satin, the paper dark and figured, the carpet Turkey, the seats velvet, and the exterior ornamentations were lit up with a chaste chandelier suspended from the outside. A winding staircase led up to the lobbies which conducted to the box, and unless the arrangements were stringent, no decently-dressed person would find much difficulty, probably, in entering, after being opened for the ingress of the party. The house would probably hold between two and three thousand people.

"There were two alleys at Ford's Theatre. One led from the stage along the east side of the theatre, between the theatre and a refreshment saloon, and so out to Tenth Street. The alley was neatly paved, and boarded and papered on both sides. The entry to it from the stage was through a glass door, and the exit from it on to Tenth Street through a wooden one.

"The other passage-way led from the back of the theatre to a small alley which communicated with Ninth and other streets, and conducted to a livery-stable locality. It was in this alley that the horse of the murderer was kept waiting.

"The Tenth Street door would have been too public, and escape, even temporary, a matter of impossibility. But the escape by the alley leading back from the stage was comparatively safe.

"There were two doors there, one used for the egress and ingress of the actors, and the other devoted to the accommodation of scenery and machinery. It was through the smaller one that the assassin made his exit."

XXXII.

THE SOCIAL EVIL.

It is commonly supposed throughout the country that Washington City is the most immoral place in the land. That there is a frightful amount of immorality prevalent in the city is true, but it is not fair to charge it to the *citizens*. The residents proper of the Capital will compare favorably with those of any other city in the land of similar size and population. They are neither better nor worse, and it is unjust to regard them as the most vicious of the nation.

There is, in addition to the citizens proper, an average floating population during the sessions of Congress, of from ten to twenty-five thousand persons. During the war the floating population was fully one hundred thousand. These persons represent all classes of society, and have a vast amount of leisure time on their hands. As they are thrown together with a comparative freedom from restraint, and in considerable numbers, the usual consequences of such promiscuous intercourse follow. Intrigues are formed and carried on, and a vast amount of immorality stares an observer in the face, all of which is laid to the charge of Washington. Undoubtedly the Washingtonians are guilty of a fair share of it, but the sum total would not be so great were not the city so much over run with idlers from other parts of the country.

HOUSES OF ILL-FAME

are numerous, and are scattered all through the city. With rare exceptions, however, they have not yet ventured to intrude into respectable neighborhoods. The inhabitants, with all their faults, are more sensitive upon this point than those of the majority of our large cities.

A few of these houses are superbly furnished, and are conducted in the most magnificent style. The women are either young, or in the prime of life, and are frequently beautiful and accomplished. They come from all parts of the country, and rarely remain in the city after the adjournment of Congress. New York, Boston, Philadelphia, Chicago, and New Orleans furnish the greater portion of them. To the credit of Washington, be it said, the city furnishes very few. These women well know that crowds of strangers collect in the Federal City every winter, and that they will have an abundant means of making money during the season. This brings them here in great numbers, but when Congress adjourns they seek some more profitable part of the country. They rarely return more than two seasons in succession, for their fearful life soon breaks down their beauty, and robs them of their attractions. Then they go down to those awful depths of sin and suffering from which death offers them the only means of escape. They cannot avoid their fate, try as they may. Let a woman once enter upon such a life, and she is sure to die in a few years in want and squalor, however splendid ly she may begin her career.

THE GUESTS.

It must not be supposed that the persons who visit these places are, like the women they seek, avowedly the most abandoned of the community. On the contrary, the majority of the "patrons" of the better class houses are men of nominal respectability, men high in public life, officers of the army and navy, Governors of States, lawyers, doctors, and the very best class of the city population. Many of them are husbands and fathers, whose wives and families, at home, hundreds of miles away, are in blissful ignorance of their conduct. Some come here under the influence of liquor, others in "cool blood," and with a full knowledge of the enormity of their conduct. They come openly, too, and exchange greetings with each other in these dens of infamy with the coolness and assurance of "old hands;" and then they go away and talk eloquently about morality and virtue, and cry down, oh most lustily, the poor creatures in whose company they passed the previous night, and whose degradation they have deepened as far as lay in their power. How pure and lofty are the institutions upheld by such men! There is a woman in Washington, the proprietress of one of these houses, who boasts that "it would be impossible to carry on the Government without her aid."

During the war, Washington was literally overrun

with such houses. Says Colonel Baker, in his *History of the Secret Service:*

"The horses of staff officers, the ambulance, and orderlies, could be seen during the night, and after the sun had risen, even, waiting before the kennels of vice, for those who were within them.

"The scenes which transpired at the midnight hour, in these dens of corruption, beggar language.

"At an hour appointed, and with a concerted plan, similar in all its details to that which was sprung upon the gamblers, with my force I made a raid upon the disreputable houses.

"The moment came, the signal was given, doors were opened, the windows raised, and a scene of confusion and comico-tragic nature followed, which must have been witnessed to have been appreciated. Faces quite covered to avoid recognition, gas turned off, and a general stampede of gentlemen sporting martial emblems, were some of the incidents attending the onset upon the intrenchments of vice in the midnight quiet of the nation's capital. Between sixty and seventy officers and men were arrested and locked up in the guard-house, for reflection upon their suddenly interrupted debauchery."

Besides these better-class houses, there are a number of a character ranging from a bagnio to a dance-house, which are viler, more utterly wretched and horrible than any similar dens in any city of the country.

ASSIGNATION HOUSES

as such, are not common in the city. There is in fact

very little need of them, as several of the lower class hotels are used for the purpose. One or two of these houses are so well known that no virtuous woman ever dreams of crossing their thresholds, and to be seen in one of them is considered good proof of immorality. The boarding-houses of the city are known to be put to such uses. Women living in them, form intrigues with men also boarding in the house, or with strangers, and receive their visits in their own rooms. If the affair is conducted quietly, and no remarks are made by the other boarders, the proprietor of the house passes it over in silence. The hotels are used in the same way. The proprietors are men of philosophy, and as long as their guests conduct their meetings with a proper degree of secresy, say nothing, but upon the first breath of scandal, or the least impropriety in public, out the offenders go—to repeat the affair at some other house.

It would be idle to enter more into the details of this subject. There is but one system upon which vice of this kind is carried on, the world over, and we have no desire to dwell upon it longer.

XXXIII.

THE ARSENAL.

THE Washington Arsenal of the United States stands at the extreme southern end of the city, on Greenleaf's Point, at the mouth of the Eastern branch of the Potomac. It commands a fine view of Washington, Georgetown, Alexandria, the Potomac River, and the Virginia shore, and as the channels of both rivers lie close to the shore, possesses every facility for shipping and receiving military stores.

The buildings and grounds are quite extensive, the establishment constituting one of the principal arsenals of Construction in the United States. The workshops are large, and are provided with improved machinery of all kinds for manufacturing ordnance stores and equipments, large quantities of which are prepared and kept here for distribution among the various posts of the army.

The Model-Office contains an interesting collection of models or patterns of the various weapons used in our own service, and in the armies of many European nations.

The *Gun-lot* contains a fine array of heavy ordnance and balls for the armaments of forts and land batteries; and in front of the old Arsenal Square are many trophies won from the enemies of the Republic in battle.

The Arsenal is interesting not only because of the work done there, but because it contains

THE GRAVE OF JOHN WILKES BOOTH.

"In order to establish the identity of the body of the assassin beyond all question," says Colonel Baker, in his *History of the Secret Service*, "the Secretary of War directed me to summon a number of witnesses residing in the city of Washington, who had previously known the murderer. Some two years previous to the assassination of the President, Booth had had a *tumor* or *carbuncle* cut from his neck by a surgeon. On inquiry, I ascertained that Dr. May, a well-known and very skilful surgeon of twenty-five years' practice in Washington, had performed the operation.

"Accordingly, I called on Dr. May, who, before seeing the body, minutely described the exact locality of the tumor, the nature and date of the operation, &c. After being sworn, he pointed to the scar on the neck, which was then plainly visible. *Five* other witnesses were examined, all of whom had known the assassin intimately for years. The various newspaper accounts referring to the mutilation of Booth's body are equally absurd. Surgeon-General Barnes, U. S. A., was on board the gunboat where the post-mortem examination was held, with his assistants. General Barnes cut from Booth's neck about two inches of the *spinal* column through which the ball had passed; this piece of bone, which is now on exhibition in the Government Medical Museum in Washington, is the only relic of the assassin's body above ground, and this is the only mutilation of the remains that ever occurred. Immediately after the conclusion of the examination, the Secretary of War gave orders as to the disposition of the body, which had become very offensive, owing to the condition in which it had remained after death; the leg, broken in jumping from the box to the stage, was much discolored and swollen, the blood from the wound having saturated his underclothing. With the assistance of Lieut. L. B. Baker, I took the body from the gunboat direct to the old Penitentiary adjoining the Arsenal grounds. The building had not been used as a prison for some years previously. The Ordnance Department had filled the ground-floor cells with fixed ammunition—one of the largest of these cells was selected as the burial-place of Booth—the ammunition was removed, a large flat stone lifted from its place, and a rude grave dug; the body was dropped in, the grave filled up, the stone replaced, and there rests to this hour all that remained of John Wilkes Booth."

THE OLD PENITENTIARY

was situated in the Arsenal Grounds, and for some years has been used as a storehouse for ordnance materials. It is now being demolished, and in its place will be erected the new quarters for the officers and men on duty at the Arsenal.

It was in this building that the trials of the Assassination Conspirators took place, and in the yard, which was formerly enclosed with a high brick wall, Mrs. Surratt, Atzeroth, Harold, and Payne were hanged on the 9th of July, 1865, for complicity in the murder of President Lincoln, and for the attempt upon the life of Secretary Seward.

These dark and terrible memories will long make the spot an object of interest to the curious—an interest which will probably increase rather than diminish with the lapse of time.

XXXIV.

THE WASHINGTON MONUMENT.

WHEN the War of the Revolution closed in the triumph of the States, it was proposed to erect a bronze statue of GEORGE WASHINGTON, as a memorial of the great services he had rendered the country. Congress authorized the American Minister to France to order it, but a lack of funds prevented the execution of the scheme. In 1799, Congress passed joint resolutions ordering that a marble monument to Washington "be erected by the United States," and in 1800 the House of Representatives appropriated one hundred thousand dollars for the purpose of "creating a mausoleum." Again, in 1801, the House passed a bill appropriating two hundred thousand dollars for this purpose, but it was so late in the season, that the amendments which were tacked on to the bill in the Senate did not receive the concurrence of the House. The subject was then permitted to remain unnoticed until 1816, when it was revived by Mr. Huger, of South Carolina; but the resolutions introduced by him were indefinitely postponed.

In the same year the State of Virginia made an effort to secure the remains of Washington for burial at Richmond, but the request of the Legislature was refused by Bushrod Washington. In February, 1832

NATIONAL WASHINGTON MONUMENT.

the two Houses of Congress passed a joint resolution asking that the remains of Washington and his wife might be deposited in the Capitol. The State of Virginia, however, unwilling to lose the precious trust confided to it, interposed, and requested the proprietor of Mount Vernon "not to consent to the removal of the remains of General Washington." Mr. John A. Washington, the owner of the estate, complied with the wishes of Virginia, and declined to grant the request of Congress.

This matter being definitelv settled, it was proposed to build a monument, and in 1833 the first determined effort to erect a National Washington Monument was begun. The "Washington Monument Society" was established, with Chief Justice Marshall as its President. The organization went to work with energy, and at length succeeded in inaugurating the measure. On the 4th of July, 1848, the corner-stone of the present structure was laid, with appropriate ceremonies, in the presence of the President and Vice-President of the United States, and both Houses of Congress, together with a vast concourse of persons. The address was delivered by the Hon. Robert C. Winthrop, of Boston, then Speaker of the House of Representatives.

"The stone, weighing twelve tons, had been prepared with a cavity lined with zinc, into which the inscription plate was placed, together with about one hundred other articles, consisting of books, portraits, maps, newspapers, coins and medals, Masonic records, and the design of the monument. The Grand Master wore the apron and used the gavel with which Washington laid the corner-stone of the Capitol. The inscription upon the plate was as follows:

'4TH JULY, 1776,

'DECLARATION OF INDEPENDENCE OF THE UNITED STATES OF AMERICA.

'4TH JULY, 1848,

'THIS CORNER-STONE LAID, OF A MONUMENT, BY THE PEOPLE OF THE UNITED STATES, TO GEORGE WASHINGTON.'

"The names of the officers of the society were also inscribed on the plate. The ceremony of the day was closed by a brilliant display of fire-works in the evening.

"The foundation of the monument is solid rock. The base of the shaft is 81 feet square, and the shaft is to rise to the height of 600 feet, and to be encircled by a grand colonnade or pantheon 250 feet in diameter and 100 feet high; over the portico of which is a colossal statue of Washington, 30 feet high, in a chariot drawn by six horses, driven by Victory, all of colossal proportions. The colonnade is to consist of 30 columns, 12 feet in diameter and 45 feet high, surrounded by an entablature of 20 feet, and a balustrade 15 feet in height. The entablature will be decorated with the arms of the States, enclosed in wreaths of bronze. The portico consists of a projection supported by four columns, and is reached by a grand flight of marble steps. Over the centre of the portico will be emblazoned the arms of the United States. The interior, or rotunda, will be ornamented with statues of the signers of the Declaration of Independence, set in niches in the surrounding wall, and upon the wall, above the niches, will be represented, in basso-relievo, the principal battles of the Revolution. Conspicuous in front of the entrance of the rotunda, will stand a statue of Washington. Within the stylobate, or base of the monument, will be a labyrinth of apartments arranged in a most intricate manner.

"The material of which the facing of the monument is constructed, is what is known as Symington's large crystal marble, procured from the vicinity of Baltimore. The body of the wall is of blue gneiss. The interior lining is to be decorateed with blocks presented by the different States and foreign nations, societies and city corporations, ornamented with coats-of-arms and appropriate inscriptions, and so disposed in the wall as to be visible in ascending the shaft of the monument. The ascent will be by a spiral iron staircase, lighted with gas—the only openings, except the doors below, being star-shaped windows near the top. It is proposed to close the apex with a cone of glass. Besides the staircase, the ascent will be made by means of machinery up the centre of the shaft. The present height of the structure is 184 feet."

The monument stands immediately on the shore of the Potomac, directly west of the Capitol and south of the White House. It is surrounded by a lot of thirty acres, which will be enclosed and handsomely ornamented when the monument is finished.

The area is called Monument Square, and is situated at the intersection of Louisiana and Virginia Avenues, upon the Mall.

The whole original estimated cost of the monument was one million one hundred and twenty-two thousand dollars. Up to the present time, two hundred and thirty thousand dollars have been expended on the unfinished structure. The Society have the sum of ten thousand dollars invested in Government bonds. They use the interest of this, or so much of it as is necessary, to defray the expense of guarding and protecting the work.

It is the intention of the Society to make an energetic effort, during the present year, to raise the means necessary to carry on the work. We trust the movement will be successful. It has long been a matter of reproach to us that we have no *national* memorial to the Father of his Country. Maryland has a beautiful column surmounted by his statue, and the Capital of Virginia contains the masterpieces of American art devoted to the same purpose; but throughout this broad land we have nothing intended to perpetuate the memory of Washington that can be called *national.* Worse than this, our people have looked with coldness and neglect upon the only effort to erect such a memorial, and in the midst of all our wealth and prosperity it has been found impossible to raise the sum of one million of dollars necessary to complete it.

There never has been a time when this amount could be raised so easily. The country is full of money, and millions are yearly expended in extravagance and folly. A little more genuine patriotism would relieve the nation from the ridiculous position in which this unfinished structure places it.

XXXV.

GENERAL GRANT.

Few persons visit Washington without trying to obtain a sight of General Grant, for no man is so thoroughly looked up to and reverenced by the people of the Union at large, as the great Conqueror of the Rebellion. The General, however, has his hands full with his official duties, and has but little time to devote to "lion hunters." Consequently it is difficult for any one to obtain an interview with him during his office hours, unless he has some legitimate business to transact with him; and, fortunately for him, the most ardent sight-seer has the decency not to intrude upon him in the privacy of his own home.

The majority of the visitors to the Capital, therefore, being unable to behold the General himself, are forced to content themselves with seeing

HIS RESIDENCE,

which is situated on I Street, near New Jersey Avenue. Strangers can best find it by starting from the Baltimore dépôt, which is on New Jersey Avenue, and going *from* the Capitol. A walk of five or ten minutes will enable them to reach I Street. Just on the brow of the hill, to your left as you go up the Avenue, are three large houses of Baltimore pressed brick, with freestone trimmings. They constitute the famous "Douglas Row," so called in consequence of having been erected by the late Senator Douglas, who resided in the central mansion, which is now the property of one of the churches of the city, and used as a school. Ex-Mayor Wallach resides in the house at the corner of New Jersey Avenue, and the mansion at the other end of the row is that of General Grant. It was purchased and presented to him by a number of prominent citizens, just after the close of the war.

It is located in a very handsome part of the city, and upon high ground, which affords an abundance of pure air. There is a large yard at the side, tastefully laid off, and the street is better graded and paved than most of the Washington thoroughfares. In front, the gigantic Capitol looms up grand and white in the distance, and far beyond it the blue waters of the Potomac glitter in the sunlight.

The house is double, with a wide hall running from the front entrance to the rear, with two large rooms on each side. Through the open window you catch a glimpse of a large library on the left of the hall, handsomely fitted up, with its walls lined with well-filled book-cases. There is an air of elegant repose about the building especially pleasing, and you go away feeling that you have seen not only one of the most noted places in the city, but also one of the most thoroughly comfortable residences in the country.

It is said that the General, in deference to the wishes of his wife, intends remaining at his residence after his inauguration, and using the White House only for the discharge of his official duties, and for ceremonies of State—a sensible resolution, and one which we hope will be carried out.

HIS HEADQUARTERS.

The official duties of his present position are discharged by the General at the "Headquarters of the Army," which, as we have said, are located on 17th Street West, nearly opposite the War Department. The reception-room of this building is a small, square parlor to the left of the street entrance. It is thronged with visitors daily. Some of them have business with the General; others come for office; others, again, to bore him with well-meant but very officious advice; and others, still, merely to pay their respects and offer their congratulations. The General receives them courteously, and dismisses them at the earliest possible moment. Many try to sound him as to his future plans, or his views upon public affairs, but he puts them off blandly, and keeps his own counsel. The newspaper men try his patience sorely, but he is polite to them also, and listens to them in a courteous silence, neither assenting nor dissenting, until, in perfect despair, they, too, take their departure.

When all are gone, and the receptions for the day are over, the General resumes

HIS CIGAR,

which he has laid aside during the interviews, with a feeling of deep relief. That cigar cf his, like Napoleon's gray overcoat, and Frederick the Great's cane, has passed into history, and has become almost a part of the man. It has aided the General to baffle many a well-laid plan to force him to commit himself by some hasty or ill-advised speech, and was no doubt of great assistance to him in his studies of the plans of his campaigns during the war. And when he goes into the White House, it will cheer him amidst the trials of his new position, and still enable him to accomplish that most difficult of all human feats—to "hold his tongue" when it is not necessary to use it

XXXVI.

THE GOVERNMENT PRINTING-OFFICE.

The printing-office of the Government is located a little to the left of General Grant's residence, and near the intersection of New Jersey and Massachusetts Avenues. It was built by Cornelius Wendell, and was purchased from him, with all its contents, by the Government, in 1860, for the sum of $135,000. It is in charge of Mr. John D. Defrees, the Superintendent of Public Printing.

The following description of the office and its workings is most interesting:

"If you stand on Capitol Hill, at the top of the high flight of stairs leading into the Senate, and look straight north, you will see the Government Printing-Office. It is in dreary contrast to the pure whiteness of the Capitol. A long rectangle of sooty brick, domineered by a scorched cupola, from whose apparent ashes rises the Phœnix of a gilt eagle. This eagle, troubled by the proximate confusion of Irish shanties and building lots, is less busied with his destiny than with the points of the compass, which he holds transfixed in his talons, and by these you perceive that just to the north is the Catholic church of St. Aloysius, noisy with a chime of bells, while the settled quarter of the city lies west of and behind the printing-office.

"Making a straight way from Capitol Hill across Tiber Creek, which you will cross by stepping-stones deposited in its basin, and taking a foot-path across lots where geese and pigs browse upon plentiful barrenness, you will reach the printing-house in ten or fifteen minutes, and hear the hum of its machinery while you take in *coup d'œil.*

"The near exterior view is no better than the remote one. A huge factory of red brick, about three hundred and fifty feet long, with the gables and one side facing separate streets, and the other side fenced up to enclose boiler houses, paper storehouses, wagon-sheds, waste-paper barracks, and an accessory wing for stereotyping, and for a machine-shop—this is all that a passing pedestrian knows of the Government Printing-Office.

"INSIDE.

"Entering by a door in the long exterior side of the rectangle, we ascend a few steps and emerge into a great composing-room, taking up the full length of the building, and here, between two winks, we may see five hundred men setting type at the case. At the end of the room nearest us is the office of the printer and his clerks, and in the small private office in the corner we find Mr. Defrees busily engaged.

"He is a plainly-dressed, quiet-mannered man, a printer by trade, not above forty-five years old, smooth-faced, gray-eyed, with a business-look about him, and he is an Indianian, long publisher of the Indianapolis *Journal*. By birth he is a Kentuckian, of the State which produced Blair and Rives, the pioneers of political printing in Washington.

"The salary of Mr. Defrees is $3,583. He is allowed four clerks and a messenger, and he must superintend the entire business of the office, while all contracts for paper, &c., are made by a committee of the Senate and the House. The public printing-office is therefore relieved from all the imputations of corruption which used to attach to it, and the character of the printer himself has never suffered imputation. He is one of the most modest and attentive officials of the Government, bright in public affairs, and in business a man of parts and powers. It is among the wise contingencies that he may become a member of the Cabinet of General Grant.

"Permission being promptly accorded to look at the printing-office, we first traverse this immense composing-room. It is amply and equally lighted, and in perfect silence the work goes on. At one corner is the corps of proof-readers; at the further end are the stereotypers, living in a great furnace-like room. Down-stairs, in the press-room, likewise the whole length of the building, some forty Adams' presses standing in rows, and to every press a pair of girls for feeders. At the bottom of the room is the mighty Bullock press.

"THE BULLOCK PRESS.

"Do you know what the Bullock press is? It is

the press that is going to weed out Hoe, most probably, within five years. It is the invention of a Philadelphia machinist named Bullock, who was caught in the shafts of his machinery, and immolated upon his own offspring. It is a press which, unwinding paper from an endless roll, carries it over and under a large rotary cylinder, and prints both sides of a sheet at the rate of sixty-three double impressions a minute. Less than every second it releases forty book pages. Without the jangle and crash of the Hoe press, without a squad of men to man successive stories, and heavy and dripping impressions lying in delay to be turned over, and fed to the press again, it requires but three men to manage it; its sound is a cheerful and energetic click, short, sharp, decisive, and pleasing; it takes but little comparative space, and its operations are performed with such ease, that the eye incredulously sees the swift effectiveness of its work. The six-cylinder Hoe press always looked to me, in motion, like a crew of airy firemen on ladders, saving goods from second and third-story windows. It begins work with extraordinary pretension, starts with the dignity of a provincial stage-coach, ships out poor, little thin sheets of paper with the noise of a thunder cloud, and half the miracle of its performance is forgotten in the miracle of its bluster.

"The Bullock press looks like a black draught horse, hitched to a roll of white paper, and walking up a tread-mill. Over its back, one glistening roller turns, under its hams another flies like a polished muscle, and beneath the fore-paws of the pony, the printed sheets drop like the flash of a pacer's shoes. The widow and family of Bullock are proprietors in part of this press, which is being manufactured by a company, of which Wendell, ex-printer, is a member, and Knapp, a rich Washingtonian, is president. The New York *Herald* took out a Hoe press some weeks ago and put up a Bullock. Col. Hoe threatened to bring suit against the Bullock people, but did not do it. His own patent has expired, and Congress refused to renew it. Hoe is a man of versatile and prolific talent, and nobody will probably attempt to compete with him in making his presses.

"SOME FIGURES.

"The great Bullock press costs $25,490. In one year new type added cost $18,804; printing-ink, $19,717; coal, 700 tons; new machinery, $5,000.

"In the bindery, 400,000 Russian leather skins were used, 760 packs of gold leaf (costing nearly $7,000), nearly $5,000 worth of twine, and as much of glue. Paper for post-office blanks alone cost $48,000. The binding of books consumed $73,000, and binding materials $113,000. Engraving and lithographing cost $111,000.

"These figures show an activity and outlay such as is witnessed in no single printing-office in the world.

"The paper that runs this huge printing-office comes from various manufacturers, and is not ordered by the Congressional printer, but by a joint committee of Congress. It is ordered in reams of 500 sheets, and sometimes paid for by the pound. In the latter case, from twenty to thirty cents is commonly paid, and, by the ream, the prices vary from $8.50 to $13. Three thousand reams came from Baltimore, 19,000 reams, and also 20,000 pounds came from Manchester, Conn., 4,000 from Lancaster, Pa., 1,000 from Philadelphia, exclusive of 168,000 pounds, and 20,000 reams came from New York. The manufacturers furnishing the bulk of the paper were Jessup, Keeney, Magarge, Warren, and Daer. The cost of all this paper was $635,000, considerably past half a million, yet this was less than the sum paid for five preceding years, the cost of the paper being, in 1865, more than a million and a quarter of dollars, and averaging, for five years, about $820,000. At the end of this economical year, about $228,000 worth of paper remained in storage. Government never insures its property, and this immense amount of inflammable matter is stored in sheds adjacent to the printing-office and guarded by watchmen. Little do the workers at the paper-mills on the running waters of the Wissahickon and the Croton, know of the processes through which their pulp will go, and of the intelligences it will carry to far frontiers, to the cabinets of foxy foreign diplomats, to the libraries of the world.

"The printing for the Executive Department of the Government costs nearly as much money as the total work done for Congress. The Executive Departments, with the courts, required, in 1867, about $757,000 worth of printing, while the House of Representatives ran up a bill of $455,000, and the Senate,

$186,000. In addition to this, acts of Congress warranted about $233,000 additional of work done for miscellaneous objects. Mr. Seward is a dainty hand with the types, and will have no bindings but the best. His bill was about $32,000 last year. The Supreme Court and its satellite courts take less than half as much, or nearly $15,000. The Congressional printer himself has a little bill of $700, but the Attorney-General is most modest of all, not reaching the figure of $600, nor does the new Department of Education consume more. The Agricultural Department, with its huge reports, passes $35,000. The monstrous appetite of the Treasury leads every thing, with nearly $300,000, and the War Department follows it with $148,000. Next come the Post Office, Navy, and Interior Departments, ranging from $78,000 to $52,000.

" GOVERNMENT LITERATURE.

"Now let us see what kind of documents the Government is printing. Last year 156 separate books and documents were turned out of this office, a variety of work which was not probably equalled by the Harpers, Appletons, Lippincotts, Fields, and Scribners together. The entire number of copies printed was not far from 900,000.

"Mr. Seward, with his usual luxuriousness, had an appendix to his diplomatic correspondence prepared, at a cost of $29,000. The book made 754 pages, and of 22,000 odd copies printed, the Secretary took 10,000 himself. The diplomatic correspondence in two volumes, attached to Johnson's messages for

1867, made also about 2,200 pages costing $35,000, and Mr. Seward privately "bagged 7,500 copies." Also, to continue with Mr. Seward, his annual international commercial report made 830 pages, and cost $10,000, and Mr. Seward took 950 copies.

"The largest documents were those of Mr. Seward's diffuseness, and also the following:

"Report on Southern railroads, 1,000 pages. Report on Delano and Morgan, 1,504 pages. (This Delano is an expensive dog—how much is Ben Eggleston to cost when he contests?) Report of Hogan, contesting Pile's seat, 632 pages. (Hogan is a literary chap, evidently.) Report of the Commissioner of Patents, 2,180 pages. Lanman's Dictionary of Congress, 610 pages. (This is more than all copies Congress unitedly owns of any dictionary of the English language.) A select committee report their views on the Indians to the tune of 544 pages. Smithsonian annual report, 472 pages. (This report is made up of interesting magazine articles, where all subjects are considered from cheese to asteroids). Confidential communications from the President, 872 pages. (A penny for this thought, and posterity will dispute the bill as excessive!) Three Army Registers, 1,404 pages. (Ben Wade's celebrated report on the conduct of the war—supplement to it, 1,269 pages.) Laws of the United States, 788 pages. Report of the Commissioner of the Land Office, in English, French, German, and Swedish, 346 pages. (This is the most practical and valuable report issued.) Agricultural report, 612 pages. (This is a very expensive book, printed to the amount of 166,000 copies, at a cost of $144,000. Something too much of this!) The biggest bills, besides the above, are for binding the *Congressional Globe*, $33,000. Ditto (bound more), $27,000. Patent Office report, $24,000. The message of Andrew Johnson, fricasseed and abridged, $39,000.

"Beside these books and many others, there is another little batch of books ordered for Mr. Seward, of his favorite diplomatic correspondence, of 10,050 copies. Also the Agricultural Department is a candidate for 100,000 more copies of its big report. The Patent Office people want to be in print 21,000 copies extra; and there is a tremendous book on the death of Mr. Lincoln, which is the most costly book, probably, ever issued in the United States. This most expensive book ever issued by a government, considering its cubic contents, and the extraordinary nature of its subject-matter, is the appendix to Mr. Seward's diplomatic correspondence, containing expressions of sympathy and condolence with the nation on the fate of Abraham Lincoln. The cost-price of producing the book will be $18,200, or more than $6 a copy, while the bindings on some special copies, ordered for the crowned heads, &c. abroad, will probably bring them up to $20 or $25 a copy. Seward's united works, correspondence and all, will make about twenty volumes, valuable, indeed, but the extra gilt might be delegated to the crowned heads to put to their library books."

XXXVII.

HOW THE PEOPLE'S MONEY IS SQUANDERED.

We have already referred to the extravagance of Congress, in making appropriations of the public funds. This is one way in which the people's money is squandered. But Congress is not alone guilty in this matter. There is a vast amount of extortion practiced upon the Government, with the complicity of its agents. The following will illustrate the manner in which this is done. We merely remark here that the Patent Office is not the only scene of such operations. It is believed that there is not a department of the Government, but is similarly afflicted to a greater or less extent.

THE PATENT OFFICE FRAUDS.

On the 4th of January, 1869, the following charges appeared in the Washington correspondence of the *New York Tribune:*

"During the latter portion of the last session of Congress, Mr. Ela, of the Printing Committee of the House, was charged with the investigation of charges of fraud against the persons holding the contracts for supplying the Interior Department with stationery. That investigation, in conjunction with one similar, made by the Retrenchment Committee, led to the introduction of a joint resolution annulling the contracts which were held by a firm doing business in this city Congress adjourned, however, without passing the resolution. Afterward, the Commissioner of Patents made complaint to the Secretary of the Interior, that the stationery and printing of his Bureau were of a very inferior quality, and not what he bargained for. The Secretary of the Interior ordered a Commission to examine into the complaints, and report to him. It is charged that the stationery contractors managed to have their friends appointed on the Commission, and a report sustaining them was, of course, made. Instead of finding any abuse in the quality of the supplies that were furnished, they asserted that the contractors ought to be paid for 300,000 sheets of bond paper, for which they never had a contract, and which the Acting Commissioner of Patents at that time never ordered. These contractors furnished 300,000 sheets last May, at eight cents a sheet, which the Committee on Printing ascertained could be furnished at about one cent and a half a sheet. At the rate it is now used, this was enough to last a dozen years. It would seem that a man fitted to examine a patent, ought to see an abuse in this, if he could not find any in their getting pay for $7,000 or $8,000 worth of goods in about one month, where the men, who kept an account of all received for more than three quarters of the time, didn't receive $500 worth, and nobody can find who got the rest. The report, made by the Printing Committee in July last, showed that a large sum had been paid for blank books, so large as to astonish the present Commissioner of Patents, and he set about to see who had received them. He found six index books had been charged at $25 apiece, and that six had been received not worth seventy-five cents apiece. He found forty-six caveat books charged at more than $40 apiece, when there couldn't be ten found in the Office, and they not worth half the price charged. He also discovered that the Patent Office was paying $40 per 1,000 for patent cards, worth about $5, and $22 for card tags, worth about $3, and that 150,000 had been paid for, of which only 50,000 could be accounted for as having been received. Brown manilla envelopes, the Committee found, were costing $48 per thousand, which, with the printing added, probably cost $1 a thousand, and while 140,000 were paid for, the Patent Office reported only 40,000 as having been received. They found, also, $140 a thousand were paid for patent heads, which are now costing but $25 per thousand. There were 28,000 charged and paid for, but not half the number could be accounted for as used. Notwithstanding all these abuses, Secretary Browning's Commission cleared the contractors of any frauds or irregularities, and ordered that they be paid an additional $24,000, for goods never ordered. This amount the Secretary of the Interior has ordered to be paid."

This article was followed the next day by another, giving still further particulars. Said the *Tribune:*

"The Commissioner of Patents having declined to pay the bills of the contractor for furnishing stationery and bond paper for the Patent Office, on the ground that there was fraud in the contract, the Secretary of the Interior appointed a Commission, composed of B. F. James, Norris Peters, and E. W. Griffin, principal examiners in the Patent Office, to inquire into the alleged fraud. The charge is made, that these Commissioners were in collusion with the contractors, and their report amounts to nothing. This the Commission deny. They say they investigated the matter thoroughly and impartially. In their report, they say the articles furnished were such as were specified in the contracts and schedules attached, and at the prices specified, or by a special or implied agreement, so far as the Patent Office is concerned, with the Commissioner of Patents, to furnish such unenumerated articles as were required, at prices paid and agreed to be paid by him. The terms and conditions of the contract proper, necessarily exclude any inquiry into its character, or of the prices stipulated to be paid, unless fraud is shown. And we are also of opinion that bills presented to the Patent Office, accepted and paid, are also an estoppel on the part of the Office as to the character of goods purchased and the prices paid therefor. Such purchases may be considered a matter of contract, particularly when the payment of the bills rendered are by means of a requisition upon the Treasury Department for the amount required, signed by the Commissioner of Patents and the Secretary of the Interior, making it *ipso facto* a contract with the Department proper, and becomes a subject of review only upon proof of fraud.

The unadjusted accounts of the contractor against the Patent Office on their bills rendered the 1st of September, amounting to about $5,000, and their claim for balance due on contract on bond paper, amounting to $24,000. The items comprising the first bill are proven to have been delivered by the contractors, by persons having cognizance of such matters. As regards the bond paper, the Commission set forth that there is no doubt that the Commissioner of Patents contracted with the contractor to purchase 600,000 sheets of bond paper, at eight cents per sheet. The Office received upon this contract 330,240 sheets, and the contractors admit they have on hand 270,000, which have been tendered to the Office and refused. The Commission recommend that the contractor deliver the additional 270,000, the balance of the 600,000 contract, and that the Patent Office should adjust and pay the bills above referred to. This is the defence of the Commission and the contractors, but the Commissioner of Patents and the Printing Committee of the House also made investigations of the charges, and they are of the opinion that the evidences of fraud having been practiced are flagrant and need further investigation. In connection with this matter comes the report, that President Johnson will remove Commissioner Foote within the next ten days and nominate a successor. Secretary Browning is said to be in favor of Foote's removal, and his friends are pressing the matter at the White House. The Printing Committee of Congress care nothing for Foote nor Browning, but wish merely to protect the Government."

WASTE IN THE GOVERNMENT.

Having presented some startling facts in relation to the extravagance of Congress, it may not be out of place to recur to the matter, and offer, for the consideration of the reader, some additional evidence upon the subject, which we take from the columns of the *Chicago Tribune*, one of the ablest Republican journals in the country. The assured position of the *Tribune*, as a Republican journal, affords incontestible proof that, in bringing forward these facts, it is influenced by no hostility to Congress, but is moved to such a course solely by its desire to see inaugurated an era of retrenchment and reform.

"The appropriations for the Senate for the next year are put down at $730,000, or, with seventy-two Senators, about $10,000 apiece. The Representatives require, meantime, $2,000,000. These appropriations can be largely reduced. A great burly fellow named Jones, is "Keeper of Senate Stationery," altogether a sinecure office, at a salary of $2,102. Every Senator has one and a fraction of a servant, there being about eighty retainers to the Senate, besides a promiscuous excess of runners, policemen, firemen, and altogether, about half a regiment of spongers—Jones being probably the idlest and fattest. The Congressional printer, forced to take a regiment of drones whom he does not want, expends, according to expectation, about $1,400,000, but in the end this and other estimates have to be pulled up by extra Congressional appropriations. The library of Congress demands about $50,000, $13,000 of which goes to buy books, and

$17,000, having nothing to do with the library, is appropriated to certain remote botanic gardens. The working expenses of the library, *per se*, are extremely cheap and diminished, and the appropriation to buy books is one of the most insufficient in the enumeration. Yet, for very shame's sake, Congress has tacked on to the library expenses the cost of raising bouquets for the parties of their households, too many of which get to the bosoms of cyprians to make them presentable in the lobbies of the Capitol. The most modest, the mightiest, and yet the mite-est appropriation is that for the library, an institution of which many Congressmen know nothing, but whose quiet treasures atone for much ignorance, illiteracy, and misinformation which one sees in the flanks of the Capital. Altogether, the two Houses of Congress demand for the coming year $5,300,000, according to their own estimate, rendered by the Secretary of the Treasury. This is about half the cost of the Capitol building, yet how small is it compared to the sums Congress throws away in corrupt enterprises of which we never hear twice. The Sutro tunnel, so near passing, would have cost, if I mistake not, $7,000,000 at a pop. Within a few days all the proposals will have been received from various parties for printing the debates of Congress. This is a big job, and all the jobbers, little and big, will endeavor to get in upon it. Now, it is plain that these debates can be printed at only two places in this district—at the *Globe* office, where they have been printed these many years, and which is provided with about $200,000 worth of presses and material, or at the Government printing-office, which is also adapted to do so large an amount of work. Besides these two offices, there are none in the District of Columbia which can get out the debates in newspaper shape every day, and be also at work upon the *Congressional Globe* for the bindery. If, therefore, Mr. John W. Forney, Mr. Frank Moore, or any body else, means to bid for this contract, let Congress look to it that the lucky contractor is not to get the money, and the work afterwards return to the Government printing-office for necessity's sake. This is the probability, that some speculator, without a cent in his pocket, may be, will bid for this contract, expecting to compel the proprietors of the *Globe* to let their office to him, or expecting, if he fail to get the *Globe* office, that Congress will afford him relief by opening the hospitality of the Government printing-office. In the latter case the work will be paid for twice over. Up to this time the Rives family has been a good servant of the Government. There has never been any issue about the *Globe's* reliability or integrity. My private belief is, that Government ought to print its own testaments, but it is sure that no new outsider can do any better. Once this contract was given to Gales & Seaton, and they came back upon the Government for relief to the tune of $100,000. The Postmaster of Washington tells me that the loss in money of his Post Office, which has to be made up by the Treasury, is $80,000 a year. He attributes this altogether to the franking privilege, which makes Washington Post Office a reservoir for tons of free matter, and amounts to a prohibition of stamp selling. If members of Congress were paid $500 a year in postage stamps, non-commutable, and the franking privilege abolished, the country would be the gainer. A number of clerks, a dollar's worth of parchment for each bill, a mile of circumlocution, and a chance for an incendiary at their place of storage, are involved in the antiquated and useless habit of transcribing all the bills passed by Congress. According to old English ceremony, there was a Master of the Rolls; therefore, we have rolls and their master, and the expense entailed in this ridiculous piece of parchment-reverence is an exceedingly large item. These parchment-bills are never called for, the laws being printed in official books, and from these books applied judiciously. The Master of Rolls is a functionary of the State Department, and, of course, he has nothing to do. Drop the parchment, the transcribing clerks, and save us some money! This I mean to harp upon."

XXXVIII.

THE FREEDMEN.

PREVIOUS to the war the institution of slavery existed in the District of Columbia, and the colored population consisted, in a great measure, of slaves. About the beginning of the second year of the late war, however, it became evident to all that it was the purpose of the General Government to receive and protect all slaves from the surrounding country who sought an asylum in the District. This conviction spread rapidly among the negroes in Maryland and Virginia, and they abandoned their masters and old homes, and came into Washington in great numbers —to such an extent, indeed, that it seemed the city would be overrun with them. "They came," says a recent writer, herself a former slave, "with a great hope in their hearts, and with all their worldly goods on their backs. Fresh from the bonds of slavery, fresh from the benighted regions of the plantation, they came to the Capital looking for liberty, and many of them not knowing it when they found it. Many good friends reached forth kind hands, but the North is not warm and impulsive. For one kind word spoken, two harsh ones were uttered; there was something repelling in the atmosphere, and the bright, joyous dreams of freedom to the slave faded—were sadly altered in the presence of that stern, practical mother, reality. Instead of flowery paths, days of perpetual sunshine, and bowers hanging with golden fruit, the road was rugged and full of thorns, the sunshine was eclipsed by shadows, and the mute appeals for help too often were answered by cold neglect. Poor, dusky children of slavery, men and women of my own race, the transition from slavery to freedom was too sudden for you!"

The change was indeed too sudden, and the poor creatures were utterly unprepared for it. Their life-long bondage had made them think freedom an existence in which no labor was necessary, and they came believing, and, in many instances, induced to believe, that the Government would undertake their entire support. They overcrowded the city to such an extent, and were so utterly helpless, that the authorities were compelled to establish camps or quarters for them. They flocked to these places, where they were enabled to live by means of rations issued to them by order of the War Department. They suffered fearfully during the war. Disease and death were busy amongst them, and so abject was their condition, that it must be confessed they were decidedly worse off as freedmen, than they had been as slaves. Diseases of various kinds, engendered by the filth in which they lived, carried off many of them. When the war closed, an effort was made to induce them to leave the city and go elsewhere, but they were slow to avail themselves of the opportunities held out to them. Since April, 1865, however, they have been gradually thinned out, but to-day the city is still over run with them.

As a class, their condition is very wretched, the majorty of them living in abject poverty. If they were willing to work, there is not employment enough for them in the District, but too many of them show no dispositon to earn a livelihood in any manner but by stealing. The majority live in the greatest squalor and filth, and are given to idleness, drunkenness, and immorality. Having seen much of the city before and since the war, the writer can testify that it is infinitely worse off for the presence of these people. It would be a blessing to the place, and a merciful kindness to the freedmen themselves, if the Government would forcibly break up their haunts, drive them out of the city, and scatter them through the country, for their present existence is a curse to them, both morally and physically. So far the Government has done nothing but encourage them in habits of idleness, lawlessness, and vice.

The colored people proper of the District, by which term we mean those who were born in it, or have lived in it many years, are very different from the refugee freedmen we have been describing. They are, as a class, intelligent, respectable, and industrious. Nearly all of them have some steady, honorable employment, at which they work faithfully. They hold themselves aloof from the freedmen in the camps or villages, and consider themselves vastly superior to them, and justly so. As a class, they have the good will and respect of their white neighbors, and are proving themselves worthy of it. Some of them are men of property and nearly all have a knowledge of reading and writing. They send their children to school, and exert themselves in every way to benefit their condition. They feel keenly the discredit which the refugee freedmen have brought upon their race, and are exceedingly anxious that they should leave the city.

The following account of an interview between the correspondent of a St. Louis journal and the butler of a high officer of the Government is interesting in this connection:

"I saw a venerable negro in his full harness yesterday, at the house of an official. He had waited upon no end of great people from the era of Monroe down. He knew me as a visitor merely, at the house of his 'boss.' The boss went out, temporarily.

"'Finn,' he said, 'get into a talk with Cassius. He's clever as you make 'em. Take him on the sober side.'

"'Come in, Cassius.'

"'Cassius, I would like to have a little private talk with you. Do you know my business?'

"'Yas, sah; you write for the papers and things.'

"'That's what's the matter! It is in your power, Cassius, to be of great service to your race and mine. You can do this by telling me the truth. I know that you are a shrewd man; you have saved some money; you have political frames of mind. All your life is not a monkey life, as most people believe. The problem of the black race which troubles us, even now that you are free, will trouble you and us much longer, unless we understand each other. You are a salaried liar, Cassius! You dodge and skulk for your master, swear he is not at home, keep away 'bores,' 'bag' cigars at his parties—I have watched you. You are a Washington servant—no worse than many grades of white politicians. It is a low life, Cassius.'

"'Mr. Finn,' said Cassius, 'you're severe.'

"'Am I right?'

"'You ben lookin' at me, sah.'

"'Now, come! What are you colored people up to?'

"'Mr. Finn,' said Cassius, 'de laws of human nature are juss de same. Skins may differ, as de poet says, but affection, or human nature, never waries. For de lass twenty years de cullud people of de Dee-streek have had ringleaders—intelligent men, who kep' 'em adwised. I was one of 'em. We chieftains could read, and we did read. We consulted. We found foce (force) was out ob de question. We so advised our people. But we saw that de Norf and Souf must go to war some day, and it was plain dat in some way we would get mixed up in de war. As to the end ob dat war, our hearts was troubled. We thought de Southern man would win. He was de fighting jackall.

"'It proved contrariwise. But it was so ordered dat de black man's help was necessary. Dat necessity, sar, saved us, brought us out, and we air now on our pins.

"'Mr. Finn, dere are mo' cullud people going to

school now in de Deestreek dan whites. In no cullud quarter or family is dere objection to schools. All is enthusiasm; de same cannot be said of Berks County, Pennsylwaney, and some oder white deestreeks. Dere never was a people dat hungered and fursted for education like de Amercan citizens of African descent.

"'Mr. Finn, we're savin' money. De money-puss controls. Dere are some tolabul rich cullud men in de Deestreek.

"'Sar, we know what is impossible. As to socially pushin' among white folks, it is not congenial to either color. As to marryin' into 'em, where is de use? A good mahogany face is, to my min', de color ob de gole-paved streets. We can't prevent licentiousness altogether. Neither can you. Nature draws de dividin' line between de colors. Sometimes a nasty imagination will cross it from boff-sides.

"'Lassly, sar, it wouldn't improve your idee ob my sagacity to say dat I took cigars and brandy from my boss. Consider, sar, dat I don't do it. But, if you want to pursue dese questions in social science furder, come to my house of a Sunday, and I will give you a cigar quite as good as de boss's, and perhaps, by accident, de identical brand! De Lord dat created men wid inalienable rights, give 'em, also, inalienable perquisites.'"

ARLINGTON VILLAGE,

situated on Arlington Heights, in Virginia, just opposite the city, is one of the various settlements established by the Government to relieve the Capital from being overflowed by the freedmen. It lies within the famous Arlington estate, formerly the property of the wife of Washington, and at the time of the breaking out of the war the home of General Robert E. Lee. In spite of this latter ownership, it is a pity the Government did not spare the place. It is so intimately connected with the memory of the illustrious Washington, that it should have been set apart and spared from the desecration and vandalism to which its various occupants, since 1861, have subjected it.

The village is in charge of the Freedmen's Bureau, and is in better condition than the majority of such establishments throughout the country, so that it cannot be justly regarded as a fair specimen of them. The officers of the Bureau have, frequently, hard work to keep the negroes in subjection, and to enforce their orders. Once or twice it has been necessary to summon the aid of the military. Yet the establishment has done little for the permanent good of the black man. It has but encouraged his habits of idleness and dependence, and it would seem far better to abandon it as soon as possible, and thus relieve the country of the heavy load of taxation which its support renders necessary.

XXXIX.

MUNICIPAL AFFAIRS.

THE city of Washington is governed, under the authority of a charter derived from Congress, by a Mayor and Common Council elected by the people. The former is chosen for a period of two years. The business of the municipal authorities is carried on at

THE CITY HALL,

which is situated on Judiciary Square. It faces the intersection of D Street North and Louisiana and Indiana Avenues, on the south, and is bounded on the north by H Street, on the east by Fourth Street West, and on the west by Fifth Street West. It was begun in 1820, and completed in 1850. It was originally proposed to build it from the proceeds of a lottery, but the cost of erecting it has been about equally divided between the city and the General Government. Congress showed a decided unwillingness to contribute any thing towards it, and even begrudged the sum necessary to make it habitable.

It is at present a plain, awkward building, situated in one of the handsomest parts of the city. It contains the office of the Mayor, the rooms used by the Board of Aldermen and City Council, the various local Courts of the District, and the Criminal and

Circuit Courts of the United States held in the District.

Immediately in front of the City Hall is a handsome pillar of white marble, on which stands a

STATUE OF LINCOLN,

cut out of the same material. The pillar is thirty-five feet high, and the statue is life-size. The whole structure cost $7,000, and was erected by the voluntary contributions of the citizens of Washington. It was executed by Mr. Lot Flannery, of Washington City, formerly a lieutenant in the United States Army. It was dedicated, with appropriate ceremonies, on the 15th of April, 1868, in the presence of the President of the United States, Members of Congress, the Executive Departments, the Diplomatic Corps, and a vast and brilliant concourse embracing many of the most distinguished personages in the land.

THE WASHINGTON CHURCHES.

Washington is well provided with religious edifices, one or two of which are very handsome and in a very flourishing condition. There are five Baptist churches; six Roman Catholic; seven Episcopal; two "Friends' Meeting Houses;" one Jews' synagogue; three Lutheran churches; ten Methodist Episcopal; two Methodist Protestant; one New Jerusalem; seven Presbyterian; one Reformed German; one Unitarian; two colored Baptist; one colored Presbyterian; and seven colored Methodist churches in the city, making a total of fifty-six religious edifices completed and in use. There are several others in process of erection.

Trinity church (Episcopal), at the corner of Third Street West and C Street North, is perhaps the most fashionable and the wealthiest. St. John's (Episcopal), a plain little structure just opposite the White House, is noted as having been the place of worship sought by a large number of the Presidents.

ART GALLERIES.

There are several fine collections of works of art in the city, prominent among which is that of Mr. W. W. Corcoran, a wealthy banker, residing in perhaps the most magnificent house in Washington, just across the park from the White House. He is the owner of Powers' "Greek Slave," Leutze's "Milton at the Organ," and some of the finest works of American artists, of whom he has been a munificent patron. A year or two before the war, he erected a handsome "gallery of art" on Pennsylvania Avenue, just opposite the War Department, which is now occupied by the Quartermaster-General's Department of the Army.

Mr. J. C. Maguire and Mr. Jauvier also have excellent collections.

There are no public galleries, however, the paintings and statuary in the Government buildings being the only national works of art in the city.

THE MARKETS

are dirty and filthy in appearance, consisting of long low sheds, in which the various articles of food are exhibited for sale during the early part of the day. The supply of provisions is bountiful, and the vegetables and fruits are of the best quality. The season is earlier than that of the markets of most of our large cities, and those who are able to afford it, have here an opportunity of enjoying the first and best fruits of the ground.

The meats come, as a general rule, from the highlands of Virginia and Maryland, and are of an excellent quality. Venison, wild turkeys, ortolon, reed-birds, and canvas-back ducks are the principal articles of game to be found, and are seen here in perfection; while the shad and other fish, oysters and crabs of the Potomac, will compare favorably with those of any part of the world. And yet, with all this abundance of "good things," the hotels and boarding-houses set but indifferent tables.

THE PUBLIC SCHOOLS

are, as yet, in their infancy. There are five large "public schools," as they are called, which correspond to the "high schools" of most other cities, and a number of primary schools. The system is still incomplete, and capable of great expansion and reform. Of late years it has received more attention from the city authorities and the people, and there is now a fair prospect that the system will soon be placed upon a basis which will enable it to meet the wants of all classes of the community.

There are many private schools, some of which are excellent, and the city also contains several male and female boarding-schools.

Columbia College, the *National Medical College*, and *Gonzaga College* (a Roman Catholic institution), rank high amongst the educational establishments of the land. The first has sent forth some of the brightest names that have ever graced the annals of American law, theology, and science.

THE POTOMAC WATER WORKS,

by means of which the cities of Washington and Georgetown are supplied with fresh water, constitute one of the most wonderful and gigantic monuments of modern skill. They were constructed by the United States Engineer Corps, under the authority of the General Government, at a cost of nearly $4,000,000—a small sum, however, in comparison with the advantages which a steady supply of fresh water has brought to the Capital.

There is a Distributing Reservoir on Lee's Hill, in Georgetown, for the purpose of supplying that city with water.

The following description of the works is taken from *Bohn's Handbook of Washington:*

"The Aqueduct is a conduit of masonry, circular in form, and nine feet in internal diameter.

"It is built of stone or bricks set in hydraulic cement or water-lime, which in time becomes as hard as the brick itself.

"The whole length of the work, from the Great Falls of the Potomac to the Distributing Reservoir above Georgetown, is twelve and a half miles.

"The capacity of the work is to supply 67,596,400 gallons of water every twenty-four hours.

"New York has a supply of about 30,000,000 gallons.

"The greater part of the work is under ground; many hills have been tunnelled; many ravines crossed by embankments with culverts for the passage of the streams beneath the Aqueduct; but it is only at a few bridges that the Aqueduct itself can be seen, as all else is carefully covered with earth to protect it from frost or from decay, and the Aqueduct looks like an abandoned railway route from which the rails have been removed.

"The first structure to be seen in connection with the Aqueduct, is the bridge by which the water-pipes are carried over Rock Creek, which separates the cities of Washington and Georgetown.

"This is an arch of 200 feet clear span, composed of two immense cast-iron pipes, four feet in internal diameter, which, in the form of an arch springing from massive abutments of sandstone, support a horizontal roadway, and at the same time convey the water of the Aqueduct across the stream.

"Passing through Georgetown, and following the road along the bank of the canal, we find, just above the city, another bridge, in which, by a similar cast-iron arch of 120 feet span, the pipes cross the basin known as College branch, from the college upon the hill above it.

"About one mile above Georgetown, upon the brow of the table-land overlooking the Valley of the

Potomac, and at an elevation of 145 feet above tide, we find the Distributing Reservoir, an oblong sheet of water containing about forty acres.

"It is nearly a mile long, and a quarter of a mile in width.

"Here the Aqueduct proper of masonry ends; below this point, the water being conveyed in cast-iron pipes to send through the cities.

"The embankment of the Aqueduct forms a level road, and a pleasant drive through the beautiful scenery of the Potomac Valley.

"Two miles from the Distributing Reservoir we reach the Receiving Reservoir, in which the water, retained by an immense embankment sixty-five feet in height and several hundred feet in length, spreads out among the hills in an irregular shape, resembling a mountain lake.

"Its extreme length is about seven eighths of a mile. Its surface contains fifty-two acres, and its extreme depth is forty feet.

"Here are stored up, above the level to which the water could be drawn down in case of accident, or while clearing out the Aqueduct from the falls, 100,000,000 gallons of water.

"The two Reservoirs would supply, in case of any such emergency, or the interruption of the Aqueduct by a hostile force, 200,000,000 gallons of water.

"The gate-houses, which regulate the flow and supply of water here and at the other Reservoir, are built in a massive and durable style, as though intended to last for ages.

"The height of the water in this Reservoir is regulated by a waste-channel, excavated through the solid rock to a great depth. The materials taken from this excavation were used in the construction of the embankment which retains the water and forms the lake or Reservoir.

"The Aqueduct enters this Reservoir by a tunnel 800 feet in length through solid rock."

"Passing over the Reservoir, we find again the level road on top of the Aqueduct, which winds through a bold country for two miles further to the Cabin John Bridge.

"This is a stupendous arch of granite, spanning a ravine by a single leap of 220 feet. The depth of the ravine below the top of the bridge is 101 feet.

"This is the largest masonry arch in the world. The famous Grosvenor Bridge of Chester, in Great Britain, being of twenty feet less span.

"The width of the bridge is only twenty feet; its thickness at top 14 feet 6 inches; its extreme length 482 feet.

"The conduit, or water channel through it, is nine feet in diameter, lined with bricks and asphaltum.

"The whole of the masonry is laid in hydraulic cement.

"The country grows wilder as we proceed, and about $1\frac{1}{8}$ miles above Cabin John Bridge the Aqueduct crosses the Mountain Spring Brook by a graceful elliptical arch of masonry of seventy-five feet span.

"At the end of this bridge it plunges into the

mountain, and in the space of half a mile passes through two tunnels.

"The two bridges above this point are small; but there are many tunnels, and the scenery is very wild and beautiful.

"At the Great Falls, sixteen miles from the President's House, a dam of stone crosses the river, and a massive construction in cut stone guards the head of the Aqueduct, which here admits the water to its channel, passing under the Chesapeake and Ohio Canal.

"A gate-house contains the gates and valves by which the water is regulated in its flow towards the city.

"The first turf of this work was dug by President Pierce, on the 8th November, 1853, in presence of members of the Cabinet, of Congress, and the municipal authorities of the District cities.

"Appropriations were not given with regularity, and the work did not therefore proceed with the speed desired by the engineers. But, on the 3d of January, 1859, the day before the Senate occupied its new Chamber for the first time, the water brought from the Receiving Reservoir burst from the fountain at the foot of the Capitol, and rose with a jet of ninety-nine feet in height."

PUBLIC GROUNDS.

When the city was originally laid off, the Government reserved a considerable portion for parks and public grounds. The principal of these are the *Capitol Park*, *The Mall*, the square in front of the President's House, which is ornamented with a bronze statue of Jefferson, Lafayette Square immediately opposite, and the circles and triangles at the intersection of the various Avenues.

Lafayette Square contains the famous Jackson Statue, by Clark Mills. It is a bronze equestrian statue, and was executed at a cost of $50,000. It is composed of the cannon taken by General Jackson in his battles with the English forces during the second war with Great Britain.

At the junction of Pennsylvania and New Hampshire Avenues, and 23d Street West and K Street North, there is a large circle formed by the intersection of those thoroughfares. It is ornamented by an equestrian statue of Washington, also by Clark Mills. It is colossal in size, and is one of the finest works of its kind in existence. It is mounted on a handsome pedestal ornamented with scenes from the life of Washington.

THE PRESS.

The principal newspapers of Washington are the *National Intelligencer*, the *Chronicle*, the *Express*, and the *Star*. They are all dailies, and are respectable journals. The city has no first-class newspaper, such as the Capital of a great nation should have, and its press is so entirely local in its character as to be utterly devoid of interest to any but residents of the city. The *National Intelligencer* and the *Chronicle* are the principal journals, but would be regarded as belonging to the "second class" in any of the great cities of the Union.

XL.

IMPOSTORS.

Persons visiting Washington on business, are very frequently the dupes of impostors, with which the city abounds. These scoundrels represent themselves as Members of Congress, or as belonging to one of the important branches of the Government, and offer their services to facilitate your business in any way that lies in their power, for which they ask a sum which varies with the nature of the business, or of the service they propose to render. Such men are simply impostors, who are constantly on the watch for strangers, out of whose simplicity and ignorance of public affairs they expect to reap a rich harvest. It is best to decline all offers of assistance in Washington, whether gratuitous or for a stated compensation, unless the party making the offer is known to you to be a man of integrity, and capable of carrying out his promises. There are a plenty of men of character in the city who make it their calling to act as a medium between strangers and the various departments in the arrangement of business affairs between them. Such men are always easy to find, and a man who is fleeced by *Bogus Congressmen* and other impostors, has only his own stupidity to blame.

Men are not the only persons thus engaged. A

number of women, some of whom are beautiful, accomplished, and attractive, exert themselves to decoy strangers into trusting them. They offer to gain access to the President, the Secretaries, the heads of Bureaus, and other officials, at times when men are denied, and generally charge high for their services. What especial influence they may possess with members of the Government they refuse to explain, but not unfrequently induce men to pay them for services which they never render, or which, if rendered, accomplish nothing.

By placing their business in the hands of a competent, and known professional man, and turning a deaf ear to all impostors and adventurers, both male and female, strangers will always have justice done them, and save themselves from extortion and robbery.

www.ingramcontent.com/pod-product-compliance
Lightning Source LLC
LaVergne TN
LVHW021258110826
845150LV00003B/417

* 9 7 8 1 4 2 5 5 6 0 5 5 3 *